Fundamentals of
FINGERPRINT ANALYSIS

Fundamentals of
FINGERPRINT ANALYSIS

Hillary Moses Daluz

CRC Press
Taylor & Francis Group
Boca Raton London New York

CRC Press is an imprint of the
Taylor & Francis Group, an **informa** business

CRC Press
Taylor & Francis Group
6000 Broken Sound Parkway NW, Suite 300
Boca Raton, FL 33487-2742

© 2015 by Taylor & Francis Group, LLC
CRC Press is an imprint of Taylor & Francis Group, an Informa business

No claim to original U.S. Government works

Printed and bound in India by Replika Press Pvt. Ltd.

Printed on acid-free paper
Version Date: 20141030

International Standard Book Number-13: 978-1-4665-9797-6 (Hardback)

Library of Congress Cataloging-in-Publication Data

Daluz, Hillary Moses.
    Fundamentals of fingerprint analysis / Hillary Moses Daluz.
        pages cm
    Includes bibliographical references and index.
    ISBN 978-1-4665-9797-6 (hardback)
    1. Fingerprints. 2. Fingerprints--Identification. 3. Forensic sciences. 4. Criminal investigation. I. Title.

HV6074.D353 22014
363.25'8--dc23   2014027811

Visit the Taylor & Francis Web site at
http://www.taylorandfrancis.com

and the CRC Press Web site at
http://www.crcpress.com

This work is dedicated to
My father and mentor
Kenneth R. Moses

Contents

Section II
FINGERPRINT PROCESSING

Section III
FINGERPRINT ANALYSIS

14   Documentation   197

15   Crime Scene Processing   219

Preface

Due to the "*CSI* effect," interest in the forensic subdisciplines has burgeoned. Consequently, hundreds of forensic science programs have arisen in universities around the world over the past decade. While dozens of professional fingerprint texts are available, few, if any, are intended for students. *Fundamentals of Fingerprint Analysis* incorporates not only professional topics and technologies, but also the background of and basic science behind these subjects. A majority of forensic subdisciplines utilize some form of fingerprint analysis. Understanding the fundamentals of fingerprint analysis prepares the student for a career in the forensic sciences.

Wherever possible, the most current research and advances in the science of fingerprint analysis are presented. This text is, therefore, also applicable to criminal justice professionals, attorneys, and laypersons that want to learn more about forensics.

The laboratory manual entitled *Fingerprint Analysis Laboratory Workbook* is intended to accompany and enhance the topics addressed in the textbook. The book chapters align with the laboratory exercises. The laboratory exercises, introductory material, and post-lab questions give students hands-on experience and supplemental information. Hands-on exercises enhance comprehension and are enjoyable.

Acknowledgments

I would like to thank my husband, Norberto, for his unwavering support and encouragement. This book was written during a 6000-mile move, a new job, a change of duty station, our first home purchase, our wedding, and a promotion. Thank you for making me smile during a hectic year. Thank you to my mother for her tireless editing, suggestions, and support. Despite being 3000 miles away, you are always by my side.

Thank you to my proofreaders: Robert Ramotowski, Robert Gaensslen, Mike Stapleton, Mark Hawthorne, Wilson Sullivan, David Burow, Kathy and Peter Higgins, Kasey Wertheim, Kimberlee Sue Moran, Helen Gourley, Malory Green, and David Haymer.

I acknowledge the students, faculty, and staff of Chaminade University of Honolulu for inspiring this project and contributing to its success. I especially want to thank my graduate students, without whom many of the figures in this text would not have been possible: Malory Green, Christopher Inoue, Donna Hellmann, Kristin Harrison, Alicia Villegas, and Chelsea Knudson.

I thank the colleagues who have mentored, educated, and inspired me, especially John Thornton, my mentor, and the members of the California State Division of the International Association for Identification who nurtured my career from the beginning.

Finally, I acknowledge expeditionary forensic scientists working in battlefields around the world: my colleagues and friends who willingly put themselves at risk to combat terrorism and make the world a safer place to live.

Author

Hillary Moses Daluz is a senior latent print technician with American Systems analyzing evidence from improvised explosive devices at a forensics laboratory in the Washington, DC area. Daluz has worked in a diversity of forensics positions including a police identification specialist with the City of Hayward Police Department in California and forensic specialist with Forensic Identification Services. After earning her Master of Science in forensic science from the University of California, Davis, she deployed to the Joint Expeditionary Forensic Facility at Camp Victory in Baghdad, Iraq, as a latent print examiner. After returning stateside, she became a member of the faculty in the Forensic Sciences program at Chaminade University of Honolulu. Hillary Daluz is a member of the International Association for Identification, the Chesapeake Bay Division of the International Association for Identification, the California State Division of the International Association for Identification, and the California Association of Criminalists.

Introduction to Fingerprints

I

Introduction

1

Let no one despise the ridges on account of their smallness, for they are in some respects the most important of all anthropological data. We shall see that they form patterns considerable in size and curious variety in shape, which are little worlds in themselves.

Sir Francis Galton[1]

Key Terms

- Friction ridges
- Friction
- Forensic
- Evidence linkage triangle
- Testimonial evidence
- Physical evidence
- Integrity
- Pattern types
- Minutiae
- Class characteristics
- Individualizing characteristics
- Bifurcation
- Short ridge
- Ending ridge
- Dot
- Identification
- Individualization
- Exclusion
- Inconclusive

Learning Objectives

- Define the key terms.
- Understand the goal of forensic science.
- Identify the three facets of forensic investigations.
- Describe how professional and personal integrity are critical to the forensic scientist.
- Understand class and individual characteristics.
- Name the fingerprint pattern types and minutiae.
- Explain the two premises of fingerprint identification.

1.1   Evolutionary Development of Friction Ridges

Fingerprints, as well as palm prints and footprints, are made up of *friction ridges*. The Scientific Working Group on Friction Ridge Analysis, Study and Technology (SWGFAST) defines a friction ridge as "a raised portion of the epidermis on the palmar or plantar skin, consisting of one or more connected ridge units."[2] The word "palmer" refers to the hand: the palm of the hand, finger joints, and fingertips. The word "plantar" refers to the bottom of the foot and the toes. Friction ridges are minute, raised areas of skin similar in contour to mountain ranges. Just as mountains are pushed up through the earth's crust to the surface, so too are friction ridges pushed up through the layers of the epidermis to the skin's surface. Though friction ridges all appear to be of the same width and height, they are extremely variable. It is not easy to see these variations with the naked eye.

Why do humans and primates have friction ridge skin on hands and feet? The answer is *friction*. Friction is the measure of resistance when the surfaces of two objects are pressed together, or when two objects move against each other. An example is the friction of automobile tires. When the break is applied with force, the rubber of the tires may leave skid marks on the road. Another example of friction is the action of scraping a wooden surface with sandpaper. The rougher the surface, the more friction is created between two objects.

The friction ridges on the hands come into contact with objects constantly. We use our hands to grip objects throughout our daily lives. We turn doorknobs, drink from glasses, type on keyboards, drive vehicles, and write with pens. Our friction ridges allow us to perform all of these tasks. If we did not have friction ridges on our fingers, we could not easily grip a smooth drinking glass or a cell phone. Friction ridges create a rough, textured surface that provides resistance between our hands and anything we touch (Figure 1.1).

Friction ridges formed over thousands of years of evolutionary development. They are found not only on human hands and feet but also on the hands and feet of other primates (Figure 1.2). They are also found on the prehensile tails of primates (Figure 1.3). This fact was addressed in a thesis written by Johannes Purkinje, a Czech scientist who contributed extensively not only to the science of fingerprint analysis but also to physics and

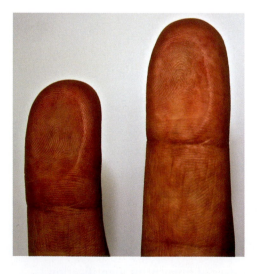

Figure 1.1 Friction ridges against a glass surface.

Figure 1.2 Chimpanzee fingerprints.

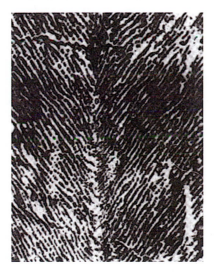

Figure 1.3 Friction ridges on the prehensile tail of a monkey (1829).

physiology.[3] His 1823 thesis entitled *Commentatio de examine physiologico organi visus et systematis cutanei*, or *A physiological examination of the visual organ and of the cutaneous system*, describes not only the presence of friction ridges in primates but also the presence of distinctive pattern types.[4]

1.2   Introduction to Forensic Science

Friction ridge development may have arisen due to thousands of years of evolutionary development, but it has another use in modern science, specifically forensic science. The word *forensic* comes from the Latin word *forensis*, which means "of the forum." In ancient Rome, the forum, or marketplace, was the center of civic life. Civil and criminal cases were heard in public before an assemblage at the forum where each side would give an oration

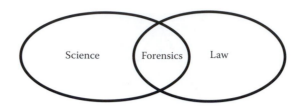

Figure 1.4 Forensic science is the intersection between science and legal matters.

to explain their complaint. The forum was essentially a court, though not in the sense we would think of a courtroom today.

Today, forensic science refers to any science applied to legal matters (Figure 1.4). There are many subdisciplines of forensic science, but all apply the topic to matters of law. For example, forensic anthropology is the study of decomposed or skeletonized remains as it applies to matters of the law. Forensic entomology is the study of arthropods—insects and spiders—as they apply to legal matters. "Legal matters" refer to crimes or prospective crimes as well as civil disputes.

No matter what subdiscipline you intend to practice, legal matters are decided in a court of law. Courtroom testimony is a critical final step in the analysis of forensic evidence, whether that evidence is bones, insects, or fingerprints. During this process, the forensic scientist explains what was done during the forensic investigation. Explaining the science behind the forensic analysis to a jury is often the most challenging part of the testimonial process. The forensic scientist may also be asked to recount the history, theory, and research and investigative methods of their science.

1.3   Fingerprints as Forensic Evidence

Fingerprint analysis is one of the most common and historically consistent subdisciplines of the forensic sciences. For over 100 years, fingerprints have been used to identify individuals. Fingerprints are taken from suspected criminals who have been arrested and compared to prior arrest records. Fingerprints are developed at crime scenes and in laboratories using fingerprint powders and chemical processing methods. They have been used to solve countless crimes over the course of history. Every day, thousands of fingerprint examiners all over the world make fingerprint identifications.

There are three major facets of forensic science: one, to demonstrate whether or not a crime has been committed; two, to identify the individuals involved and how those individuals are associated with other individuals and with the crime scene; and three, to reconstruct the crime scene and the sequence of events that occurred. Fingerprints may be used throughout these processes to provide investigative leads. Figure 1.5 illustrates the *evidence linkage triangle*, a common pictorial representation of the link between the crime scene, victim, and suspect (Figure 1.5). There may be more than one suspect, victim, or even crime scene. Fingerprints can link a victim to a crime scene, a suspect to a crime scene, and/or a suspect to a victim.

Fingerprints are collected from items of evidence to provide investigative leads. But they are also evidence in themselves. Gardner defines evidence as "anything that tends

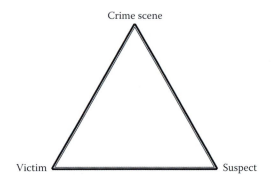

Figure 1.5 The evidence linkage triangle demonstrates the link between the crime scene, victim, and suspect.

to prove or disprove a fact in contention."[4] There are two types of evidence: testimonial and physical. *Testimonial evidence* refers to verbal accounts such as eyewitness statements or transcripts of interviews. This type of evidence is subjective, meaning it is subject to either intentional or unintentional biases of the individual. *Physical evidence* includes both physical evidentiary items (weapons, bloody clothing, etc.) and forensic evidence such as fingerprints, trace evidence, and DNA.

A scientist must be unbiased at all times. The key to an impartial forensic examination is *integrity*: recognizing that everyone has inherent biases and consciously pushing those biases aside. Integrity is defined by the *Merriam-Webster* dictionary as "firm adherence to a code of especially moral or artistic values."[5] It also relates the word integrity to "completeness," "soundness," and "incorruptibility."[5] In the discipline of forensic sciences, your personal and professional integrity must be compatible and irrefutable.

1.4   Fingerprint Analysis

Fingerprint evidence is valuable because fingerprints are unique. No two fingerprints are alike. Thus, fingerprint examiners can trace a fingerprint back to its source. Fingerprint comparison is the process of comparing two friction ridge impressions to determine if they came from the same source (i.e., did the same person make both impressions). Fingerprint examiners compare unknown fingerprints from crime scenes or items of evidence to known fingerprints and make a determination as to the source of the prints.

There are two types of structural characteristics of fingerprints that allow fingerprint examiners to compare fingerprints and make identifications: *pattern types* and *minutiae*. Pattern types—arches, loops, and whorls—are not unique to the individual. They are *class characteristics*. Class characteristics are those features that place an individual or object in a group or subcategory. Minutiae (pronounced mi-noo-sha) are *individualizing characteristics*. Individualizing characteristics are those features that are unique to one particular person or thing. Fingerprint examiners analyze both the class characteristics and individualizing characteristics of fingerprints in order to reach a conclusion.

Class and individual characteristics are used to describe many forensic evidentiary items such as shoeprints, tire tracks, biological evidence, and firearms evidence. Examples of class and individual characteristics are observable everywhere. For example, a suitcase may demonstrate both class and individualizing characteristics. The class characteristics include the following features: size, shape, presence or absence of wheels, color, fabric, number of zippered pockets, and number of zippers. Imagine your suitcase is a red, nylon carry-on suitcase with three zippered pockets and wheels. You check your bag with the airline and expect to identify it when you reach your destination and it is returned to you. If there are 300 suitcases on a revolving luggage carousel, you will look for the class characteristics of your own suitcase to determine which belongs to you. Each class characteristic narrows down the possible suitcases that match yours. Perhaps you will first look for suitcases that are red and then examine the size of each suitcase, then perhaps the presence or absence of wheels.

But what if there is another suitcase that looks just like yours? What individualizing characteristics can you use to distinguish your suitcase from its apparent twin? Unique characteristics accumulate on physical items with use. A suitcase might have a tear in the fabric, a dent, a loose wheel, or a missing zipper. Those are individualizing characteristics that may help you identify your suitcase. You may have placed individual characteristics on your bag intentionally by attaching a ribbon to the handle or a luggage tag with your name and contact information. The human brain identifies an object or person in a natural progression from recognizing class characteristics to confirmation by individualizing characteristics. You may not be able to read your luggage tag while your suitcase is coming around the conveyer belt, but you can certainly observe the sizes, colors, and styles of the suitcases as they approach to narrow down the possibilities. When the bag gets close enough for a more rigorous examination of its individualizing characteristics, you can then conclusively determine which bag is yours.

Fingerprint pattern types are class characteristics and are therefore used to narrow down the potential field of candidates who may be the source of the fingerprint in question, just like the color and size of a suitcase narrow down the possibility that suitcase belongs to you. There are three categories of fingerprint patterns: arch, loop, and whorl (Figure 1.6). There are eight subpattern types within those categories: ulnar loop, radial loop, plain whorl, double-loop whorl, central pocket loop whorl, accidental, plain arch, and tented arch (Figure 1.7). Other class characteristics of fingerprints include the presence of creases and scars, the ridge count of a loop, and the whorl tracing of a whorl pattern. These characteristics will be discussed in detail in Chapter 4 of this book.

In order to reach a conclusion, the fingerprint examiner must also analyze the minutiae: the individualizing characteristics in a fingerprint. The word "minutiae" refers to small details. The friction ridges that make up a fingerprint pattern are not continuous,

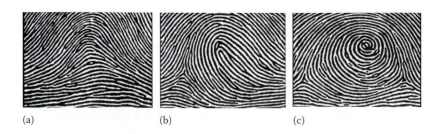

(a)   (b)   (c)

Figure 1.6 The three basic fingerprint pattern types: (a) arches, (b) loops, and (c) whorls.

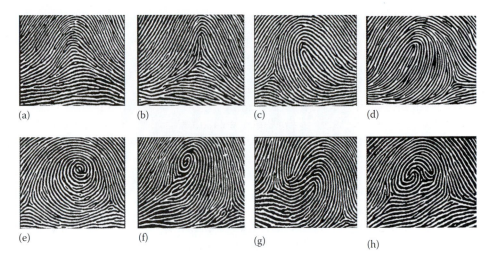

Figure 1.7 The eight fingerprint subpattern types: (a) plain arch, (b) tented arch, (c) right-slanted loop, (d) left-slanted loop, (e) plain whorl, (f) central pocket loop whorl, (g) double-loop whorl, and (h) accidental whorl.

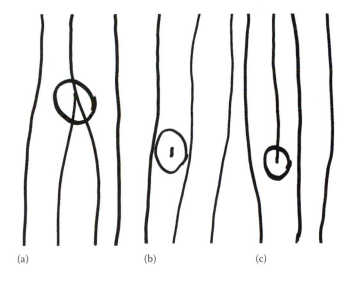

Figure 1.8 A line drawing of a (a) bifurcation, (b) dot, and (c) ending ridge.

as they may appear at first glance. There are three types of fingerprint minutiae: bifurcations, ridge endings, and dots (Figure 1.8). A *bifurcation* occurs when one friction ridge splits into two friction ridges like a fork in a road. A friction ridge may come to an abrupt end, forming an *ending ridge*. A friction ridge may be short, rather than continuous, with an ending ridge on each end. This is known as a *short ridge*. The third type of minutiae is the *dot*, which appears—true to its name—as a dot between two friction ridges. It is the shortest possible ridge (Figure 1.9). Minutiae are best observed under magnification. The standard fingerprint magnifier has 3× to 5× magnification, which allows us to compare the minutiae between unknown and known fingerprints (Figure 1.10).

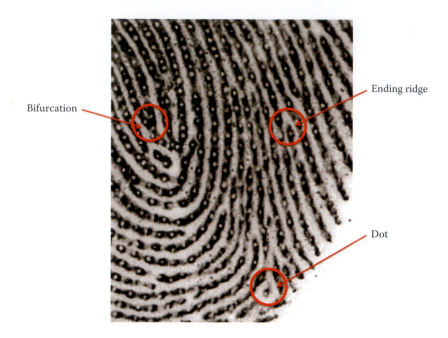

Bifurcation

Ending ridge

Dot

Figure 1.9 A bifurcation, dot, and ending ridge in a magnified portion of a fingerprint.

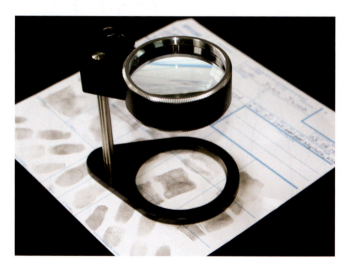

Figure 1.10 A fingerprint magnifier, also known as a loupe.

There are three possible conclusions to a fingerprint comparison: identification, exclusion, or inconclusive. Do the fingerprints match? We call this a positive *identification*, or *individualization*. This means the fingerprint originated from one source: one individual and no one else (Figure 1.11). The terms "individualization" and "identification" are synonymous, according to the SWGFAST.[6] An *exclusion* occurs when the same corresponding areas of two fingerprints are incompatible. An *inconclusive* result is reached when a fingerprint can neither be conclusively identified nor eliminated. Fingerprint comparisons will be discussed in detail in Chapter 16 of this text.

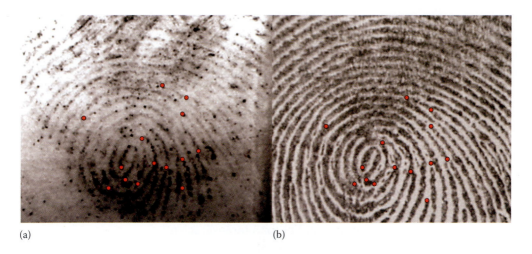

(a)   (b)

Figure 1.11 A fingerprint that has been identified to a suspect. (a) a latent fingerprint from a crime scene, (b) the left thumbprint of the suspect.

1.5 Uniqueness and Permanence

Two main premises form the basis for the science of fingerprint identification:

1. Fingerprints are unique.
2. Fingerprints are permanent.

Uniqueness means that there are likely no two people in the world with the same fingerprints. Even identical twins, with identical DNA, have different fingerprints. We know fingerprints are unique because of the inherent randomness of nature. Throughout the history of fingerprint identification, it has been widely accepted that no two people have the exact same fingerprints. Permanence means your fingerprints do not change throughout your lifetime. They form in utero from the deepest layer of the epidermis and do not change as you age.

This text explores the uniqueness and permanence of fingerprints in many contexts. It will first address the background, theory, and history of the science of fingerprint identification; followed by a discussion of the development, visualization, and documentation of latent fingerprints from evidence and crime scenes; and finally fingerprint comparisons and courtroom testimony.

1.6 Chapter Summary

Fingerprints are patterns made by friction ridges, which are raised portions of the epidermis found on the hands and feet. Friction ridges are the result of evolutionary development. They create a rough surface that allows humans to grip objects. Forensic science refers to any science applied to legal matters. Forensic scientists testify to their conclusions and opinions in a court of law. Fingerprints have been used as forensic evidence for over 100 years. Unknown fingerprints from crime scenes and evidentiary items are compared with the fingerprints of known individuals. A fingerprint comparison results in one of three conclusions: identification, exclusion, or inconclusive. Fingerprints are valuable forensic evidence because they are unique and permanent.

Review Questions

1. What are friction ridges?
2. Why do we have friction ridges on our hands and feet?
3. Define "forensic science."
4. What are the three facets of forensic science investigations?
5. Why is integrity an important quality for a forensic scientist?
6. What are the eight types of fingerprint patterns?
7. What are the three types of minutiae?
8. What class characteristics do we see in fingerprint impressions?
9. What individualizing characteristics do we see in fingerprint impressions?
10. What are the three possible conclusions of a fingerprint comparison?
11. What are the two premises of fingerprint identification?

References

1. Galton, F. 1892. *Finger Prints*. London, U.K.: MacMillan.
2. The Scientific Working Group on Friction Ridge Analysis, Study and Technology. 2012. Document #19, Standard terminology of friction ridge examination (latent/tenprint), Ver. 4.0. http://www.swgfast.org/documents/terminology/121124_Standard-Terminology_4.0.pdf (accessed February 16, 2013).
3. Cummins, H. and Kennedy, R. 1940. Purkinje's observations (1823) on finger prints and other skin features. *J. Crim. Law Crim. (1931–1951)* 31(3): 343–356.
4. Gardner, R. 2012. *Practical Crime Scene Processing and Investigation*. 2nd edn. Boca Raton, FL: Taylor & Francis.
5. *The Merriam-Webster Unabridged Dictionary*. 2013. Merriam-Webster, Inc. http://www.merriam-webster.com.
6. The Scientific Working Group on Friction Ridge Analysis, Study and Technology (SWGFAST). 2012. Document #103, Individualization/identification—Position statement (latent/tenprint), Ver. 1.0. http://www.swgfast.org/Comments-Positions/130106-Individualization-ID-Position-Statement.pdf (accessed February 16, 2013).

History

2

Key Terms

- Certification
- Anthropometry
- Classification
- Bertillonage
- Dactyloscopy
- Automated Fingerprint Identification System (AFIS)

Learning Objectives

- Define the key terms.
- Understand why it is important to know about history.
- Know the key historical figures and their contributions to fingerprint analysis.
- Compare and contrast anthropometry with fingerprint identification.
- Understand the concept of fingerprint classification.

2.1   Why Study History?

Why is a basic working knowledge of history important for the fingerprint examiner? Regardless of which type of forensic science one chooses to practice, it is important to know the major players and events that formed the subdiscipline. Knowing where we came from gives us a better understanding of where we are now as scientists and also where the science is headed. What are the future capabilities of the science? What type of research is necessary to advance the science? If you are studying to become a forensic scientist, you are the future of the science. The most effective scientist has a solid grasp of the history and development of the science.

Most fingerprint *certification* tests require knowledge of the history of fingerprint identification. A certification test is a voluntary exam that tests your general knowledge, professional capabilities, and competency. The certification examinations test not only your skill level but also your background knowledge about the science, including its history. The International Association for Identification conducts certification exams for many forensic disciplines.[1]

Finally, a working knowledge of history is important because you may be asked questions about historical figures and events when testifying in a court of law. All forensic scientists are expected to testify in court. You may be asked any number of questions regarding a forensic investigation, not just what you did and how you did it, but what is the history behind the science. Are there any historical court cases, events, or figures that influenced the examinations? A strong working knowledge of the science goes a long way to establishing credibility in a court of law.

2.2 Ancient History

There is plenty of evidence that ancient hominids had friction ridges on their hands and feet just as modern man and primates do. Unintentional fingerprint impressions have been recorded on ancient pottery and bricks. The earliest instances of friction ridge impressions on pottery were unearthed in China. These fragments were dated to approximately 4000 BCE.[2,3] Archaeologists speculate whether the impressions on the earthenware were tool-marks, decorative, intentional, or unintentional.

Exactly when the concept of using fingerprints for identification purposes was developed is unknown. Archaeologists have recorded instances of Middle Eastern potters "signing" their work with fingerprints impressed into the clay, though these fingerprints may have been merely identifying marks rather than impressions linked to a specific individual.[3] The noted archaeologist William Frederic Bade purportedly said, "I do not for a moment believe that the potters were aware that their fingerprints had the distinctiveness which is now recognized in the fingerprint system. It is the place and the arrangement of the impressions which served as distinguishing marks to them."[4] Any symbol or mark would have served the same purpose.[4] Paleolithic bricks also display impressed fingerprint patterns. These impressions were likely "toolmarks" that had a practical use: to provide a rough surface so mortar material would better adhere to bricks. Paleolithic stones were carved with geometric shapes resembling fingerprint patterns, though there is also debate as to whether the patterns were intentionally formed to mimic fingerprints (Figure 2.1).

Figure 2.1 A Scottish carved stone ball known as a "petrosphere" is carved with patterns resembling fingerprint patterns. (Retrieved from the website of the Ancient Wisdom Foundation, http://www.ancient-wisdom.co.uk/stoneballs.htm, accessed on January 7, 2014.)

Figure 2.2 Clay sealing from the archaeological site of Ur (2600–2350 BCE). (Photo courtesy of Kimberlee Sue Moran, Director, The Center for Forensic Science Research and Education.)

Impressed fingerprints have been found on clay sealings from ancient Mesopotamian archaeological sites dating around 2600–2350 BCE (Figure 2.2).[5] In ancient Babylonia, fingerprints were impressed into clay tablet contracts from 1913 to 1855 BCE.[2] Fingerprints were used as identifying marks in ancient China during the Qin and Han dynasties as early as 246 BCE.[6] Before the advent of paper, fingerprints were impressed into clay seals that bound important documents.[6] These were the ancient version of the wax seals seen in the western world hundreds of years later. In addition to a monogram or identifying mark or symbol, the Chinese used a fingerprint on the opposing side of the clay seal to further verify the author's identity and deter anyone from breaking the seal to read the contents of the document.[6] There are also examples of documents authored by the nobility in India that were validated by fingerprints.[2,3]

Chinese dynastic history is filled with examples of fingerprints used as personal marks long before European historical fingerprint records. Besides the clay seals used during the Qin dynasty, bamboo slips (a writing medium) have also been uncovered that record how fingerprints were used in burglary crime scene investigations.[6] Throughout the Han dynasty and Six Dynasties period (206 BCE to 589 CE), the availability of paper and silk writing materials provided a new substrate for recording fingerprints.[6] Anthropometric records, records measuring the shape or dimensions of the finger or hand, were commonplace.[6] Throughout the remaining history of dynastic rule, anthropometric records and deliberately recorded friction ridges were used on the following official documents: army rosters, IOUs, engagements and divorces, deeds for lands and homes, and records of indenture.[6] Fingerprints were also used as evidence in criminal and civil disputes, including recording confessions.[6]

2.3 Fingerprint Science: Seventeenth–Nineteenth Centuries

The seventeenth and eighteenth centuries gave birth to the scientific revolution, a period of history characterized by major scientific breakthroughs that opened up the floodgates of scientific advancement. This was the era of Copernicus, Sir Isaac Newton, and

Galileo Galilei. Newton's laws of motion and the concept of heliocentricity—the idea that the earth and other planets revolve around the sun—were being accepted as mainstream. Mathematics, chemistry, and astronomy were nascent and emerging fields in the western world.

Nehemiah Grew, the "father of plant physiology," performed the first scientific analysis of friction ridges using the newly invented microscope.[2,3,7,9] He described terminology related to friction ridge patterns and structures.[3,9] He also described the physiological aspects of sweat pores and the placement of creases. The following is an excerpt from Grew's 1684 publication, *The Description and Use of the Pores in the Skin of the Hands and Feet*:

> *For if any one will but take the pains, with an indifferent Glass, to survey the Palm of his Hand very well washed with a Ball; he may perceive… innumerable little Ridges, of equal bigness and distance, and everywhere running parallel with one another. And especially, upon the end and first Joynts of the Fingers and Thumb, upon the top of the Ball, and near the root of the Thumb a little above the Wrist. In all which places they are regularly disposed into Spherical Triangles and Ellipticks.[7]*

Within this treatise, Grew not only describes but also illustrates fingerprint structures (Figure 2.3).[7] Marcello Malpighi, a contemporary of Nehemiah Grew, also published his microscopic observations of friction ridges. He was the first scientist to describe the function and evolutionary importance of friction ridges.[2]

The nineteenth century was an era of exploration and scientific curiosity. Scientists were going out into the world, making observations, and applying the scientific methodology formulated in the previous century. There was a burgeoning interest in nature and how things work. Today, scientists are specialists with narrow research concentrations, whereas in the nineteenth century, scientists were generalists who studied entire disciplines. It was common for a "naturalist" to study medicine, evolution, and the structure and function of animal and plant species. Another scientist might study astronomy, geology, and physics.

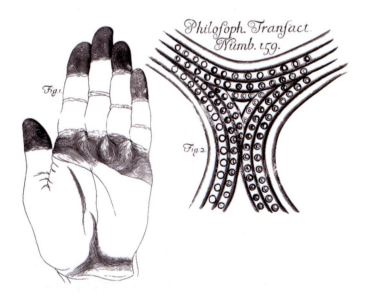

Figure 2.3 Nehemiah Grew's illustrations of friction ridges and pores. (Reprinted from Grew, N., *Philos. Trans. R. Soc. Lond*, 14: 566. With permission.)

Figure 2.4 Charles Darwin.

As we became more scientifically advanced as a society, scientists became more specialized. We see that today in the field of forensic sciences. The discipline has grown from a general forensics discipline into many subdisciplines, such as fingerprint examination, serology, DNA analysis, drug chemistry, firearms and toolmarks, and toxicology.

Major scientific theories originated in the 1800s. The noted naturalist Charles Darwin traveled the Galapagos Islands on the *HMS Beagle*, making observations that eventually led to his evolutionary theory of natural selection (Figure 2.4). Darwin was influenced by other great scientific minds of the century such as Charles Lyell, a geologist whose theory of "uniformitarianism" asserted that the earth was formed, and continues to be formed, by slow-moving processes.[6] Charles Lyell's publication *Principles of Geology* was as influential in its time as Charles Darwin's *On the Origin of Species*, which was published in 1859 (Figure 2.5).[8]

Art also played an important role in the advancement of scientific knowledge through observation. Centuries earlier, Leonardo da Vinci famously sketched and diagramed the human form as well as other scientific phenomena and feats of engineering. Prior to the advent of the camera, scientific observations were recorded in line drawings with minute attention to detail. We see this in the work of Johannes Purkinje whose line drawings of friction ridge patterns are exceptionally detailed (Figure 2.6).[9] We also see examples of biological art in the work of Thomas Bewick, a British naturalist, botanist, and author.[9] Bewick made wooden engravings of his own fingerprints in great detail. The wooden engravings were used as stamps, which he used in conjunction with his signature.[9] This demonstrates a knowledge and careful observation of friction ridge structures.

The science of fingerprint analysis began to take shape in the mid-1800s in the colonies of the British Empire, specifically, in India. British administrators, doctors, scientists, and representatives went to India to perform various administrative and governance functions. Sir William Herschel was an administrator for the East India Company in the province of Bengal (Figure 2.7).[9] As a magistrate and collector, he was in charge of the courts, prison, deed registrations, and pension payments.[2,9] In India, fingerprints and handprints had been used to authenticate and sign documents for hundreds of years. Herschel continued with this practice as contracts with handprints held greater significance than those with

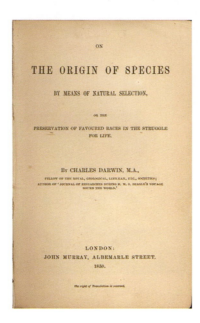

Figure 2.5 *On the Origin of Species* was Charles Darwin's definitive work on his studies of ecology and evolution.

Figure 2.6 Johannes Evangelista Purkinje.

signatures alone. As a result, he became the first British man to acknowledge the individualizing power of fingerprints.[3] Though Herschel has been credited as the first European to recognize the uniqueness of fingerprints, it was JCA Mayer of Germany who published a statement in 1788 stating, "Although the arrangement of skin ridges is never duplicated in two persons, nevertheless the similarities are closer among some individuals. In others the differences are marked, yet in spite of their peculiarities of arrangement all have a certain likeness."[3] Later in life, Herschel experimented with the concept of permanence by fingerprinting himself over a period of 50 years.[2]

Figure 2.7 Sir William J. Herschel.

Figure 2.8 Dr. Henry Faulds.

Dr. Henry Faulds is another important figure in the history of fingerprint analysis (Figure 2.8). Faulds was a medical missionary to India and Japan who studied fingerprint structures extensively. He was the first European to publish an article stating that visible fingerprints, such as bloody, greasy, or sooty fingerprints, may be useful for solving crimes.[9] This article entitled "On the Skin-Furrows of the Hand" was published in *Nature* in 1880.[10] Faulds wrote a letter to Charles Darwin to share his observations, and Darwin referred him to his cousin, Sir Francis Galton.[9]

A contemporary of Herschel and Faulds, Galton wrote the first book on fingerprints in 1892 entitled *Finger Prints*.[11] His research was based on the research of his contemporaries, as well as the historical use of fingerprints by Asian cultures. Galton described fingerprints as unique and permanent, the premises we rely on today. He also described the minute structures within patterns called minutiae, or Galton details, which are the identifying features used in fingerprint comparisons.

2.4   Criminal Records and Classification

Alphonse Bertillon, a French scientist, is credited with devising the first anthropometric method of criminal identification and classification.[3] *Anthropometry* is the measurement of biological characteristics. *Classification* is a method of organizing criminal records so they may be relocated in order to compare them with new arrests. Criminals were initially identified through extensive, if primitive, photographic records. The records were called rogues' galleries. A recidivist could give a police officer a fake name, but a photograph, now known as a "mug shot," could identify the criminal's true identity. However, it is fairly simple to change one's appearance with a simple haircut or adjustment in facial hair or clothing.

Bertillon's method of classification was based on anthropometry, or anatomical measurements, which he called *Bertillonage*. The justification for this method of identification is based on the randomness of physiological variation. Bertillon devised a system of classification of criminals based on physiological measurements that were recorded on a card bordering a mug shot (Figure 2.9).

While Bertillon's assumptions were theoretically sound based on the concept of natural variation, there were several problems with this form of classification. One hindrance was the need for specialized equipment and measuring tools. Many of these items were cumbersome. The process was also time consuming, requiring very specific measurements. Another flaw of Bertillonage is that it does not take into consideration the proportions between height and limb length. Also, criminals did not always cooperate with their captors and would not remain still long enough for an accurate battery of measurements to be taken and recorded (Figure 2.10).

At that time, there was much debate about whether a Bertillonage card or fingerprint card should be the preferred criminal record. There is a story circulated in newspapers about two men who were arrested and booked at Leavenworth Penitentiary.[12] One of these men was William West, and the other was named Will West. William West was arrested in 1901. Will West was arrested in 1903. When Will West's anthropometric measurements were taken, the records clerk searched the files and matched his anatomical dimensions with William West's previous Bertillonage record. When confronted with this, Will West asserted that he had never been arrested before and that the record the clerk found did not belong to him. They were, in fact, two different men, similar in appearance, with similar anthropometric measurements (Figure 2.11). In this case, fingerprints easily distinguished these two men (Figure 2.12). This event, whether or not it is based in fact, occurred right around the time Leavenworth Penitentiary abandoned Bertillonage and began to routinely fingerprint all incoming inmates. Since fingerprints were considered a superior form of identification, they replaced Bertillonage not only in the United States but also throughout the world.

The population explosion of the industrial revolution led to a dramatic increase in criminal activity. By the late 1800s, it became clear that a *classification* system was needed to organize the large volume of fingerprint records so they might be easily filed and searched. Two men are credited with devising the two most enduring systems of fingerprint classification: Juan Vucetich and Sir Edward Henry.

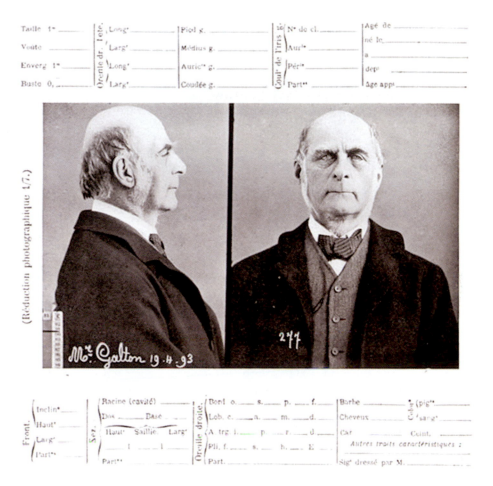

Figure 2.9 Sir Francis Galton's Bertillonage card was recorded when Galton paid a visit to Alphonse Bertillon's laboratory in 1893.

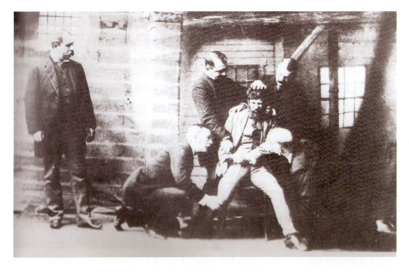

Figure 2.10 An uncooperative suspect is restrained for the purpose of taking anthropometric measurements.

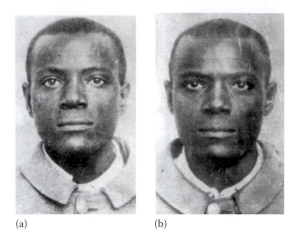

(a)   (b)

Figure 2.11 (a) Will West and (b) William West.

Figure 2.12 The fingerprints of Will West and William West.

Juan Vucetich was a Croatian immigrant to Argentina who became a statistician at the Buenos Aires Police Department (Figure 2.13).[2] Vucetich rose to become the head of the Identification Bureau.[2] In 1891, he read Galton's research and realized the superiority of fingerprints to Bertillonage.[2] Vucetich developed the first classification system still in use today in mostly Spanish-speaking countries. This system, which he called *dactyloscopy*, resulted in his 1904 publication, *Dactiloscopia Comparada*.[13] Vucetich classified fingerprint cards by assigning letters and numbers to pattern types found on each finger, starting with the thumb. The alphanumerical designation of the right hand is located in the numerator; the alphanumerical designation of the left hand is located in the denominator. Thus, the first system of classification was devised.[3]

Juan Vucetich was instrumental in solving one of the first murders using fingerprint evidence from a crime scene. Two children were found murdered in Buenos Aires in 1892.[2] The children's mother, Francisca Rojas, accused a man named Velasquez of the crime. She claimed he was a jilted lover.[2] Rojas was in love with another man. When Inspector Alvalez, an investigator who was trained by Vucetich, examined the crime scene, he found a bloody thumbprint on the door.[2] After comparing and matching Rojas' fingerprints with the bloody fingerprint found on the door, he confronted her, and she confessed to killing her own children.[2] While the bloody thumbprint did not in itself prove Rojas committed murder, it did compel her confession. In 1894, Mark Twain

Figure 2.13 Juan Vucetich.

introduced the use of fingerprints as evidence to popular culture in a novel entitled *Pudd'nhead Wilson*.[2] In the plot of this story, the principal forensic evidence of a murder is a bloody fingerprint.

Several British fingerprint pioneers worked on classification systems around this time, including Sir Edward Henry, Sir Francis Galton, and Sir William Herschel. Sir Edward Henry, the inspector general of police in Bengal, India, is credited with developing the classification system used throughout the English-speaking world for the next 100 years. The classification system was the result of collaboration between Henry, an Indian police officer and mathematician named Khan Bahadur Azizul Haque, an Indian police officer named Rai Bahadur Hem Chandra Bose, and Sir Francis Galton.[14] Similar to the Vucetich system, pattern types are given specific designations and the formula is represented in fraction form. The even-numbered finger designations are located in the numerator, and the odd-numbered finger designations are located in the denominator. Unlike the Vucetich classification system, the fingers are assigned numbers, starting with the right thumb. The various classification systems will be covered in more depth in Chapter 4.

The beginning of the twentieth century marked the beginning of fingerprints as the primary means of identifying criminals throughout the world. The classification systems devised by Henry and colleagues, as well as Juan Vucetich, allowed a substantial volume of fingerprint cards to be efficiently organized, filed, and retrieved. The first fingerprint bureau was established at Scotland Yard in London, England, in 1901 (Figure 2.14).

2.5 The Twentieth Century

Fingerprinting was introduced to North America in 1903 when the New York State Prison System began routinely fingerprinting inmates.[2] In 1904, the New York State, in partnership with Scotland Yard, presented a display about criminal fingerprinting at the World's Fair in St. Louis, Missouri (Figure 2.15).[2] They shared their knowledge with police officers from

Figure 2.14 A photograph of Scotland Yard (ca. 1800s).

Figure 2.15 A photograph of the St. Louis World's Fair (ca. 1904).

across the country as well as Canada.[2] Throughout the 1900s, the science of fingerprint identification was described and refined, and new methodologies were developed. The first professional fingerprint organization was formed in Oakland, California, in 1915 and was named
the International Association for Criminal Identification.[14] This is the oldest active international forensic association, which has since been renamed the International Association
for Identification (Figure 2.16). In 1924, J. Edgar Hoover established the Federal Bureau of
Investigation (FBI)'s Identification Division, followed by the FBI Laboratory in 1932.[2]

   By the mid-1900s, the volume of criminal arrest records began to overwhelm the classification methods used to organize and store them. The consistency of population growth,

Figure 2.16 The logo of the International Association for Identification. (Reprinted from the International Association for Identification.)

and subsequent increase in crime and arrest rates, necessitated a new method of storing, sorting, and searching criminal fingerprint records. Throughout the 1960s and 1970s, the newly invented computer was considered a likely apparatus for digitizing and searching large volumes of data such as fingerprint records.[15] This goal was realized in the early 1980s when the *Automated Fingerprint Identification System (AFIS)* known colloquially as the "fingerprint computer" was developed, utilized, and disseminated in Europe, Asia, and North America.[3,15]

Today, scientific and technological advancements continue to shape the field of fingerprint analysis. Advancements in chemistry have provided countless chemical reagents for developing and visualizing latent, or invisible, fingerprints from crime scenes. Advancements in technology continue to make fingerprint computers smaller, faster, cheaper, and more accurate. Scientific progress is not made in a vacuum. It is built on the shoulders of those who came before us and consequently improved our own understanding through their work and scientific ingenuity. We continue to learn from our history as we reach into the future.

2.6   I Had a Case: Applying Fingerprint Technology to Archaeological Research

Forensic archaeologist Kimberlee Sue Moran (founder of Forensic Outreach) describes her research in traditional archaeology matching fingerprints on clay sealings using AFIS technology:

Cylinder seals and sealings are a ubiquitous feature of Mesopotamian archaeology. Seals are used on jar stoppers, bullae, mud brick, on lumps of clay around string attached to bags, boxes, baskets, on storeroom doors, and later on tablets and envelopes. As with other sealing practices in other ancient cultures, the act of sealing an object with clay and rolling one's personal cylinder seal across it was a means of verifying the activity or transaction and providing proof that tampering was absent. However, little is known about the individuals actually responsible for the act of sealing, record keeping and other administrative duties. Sealing took place for hundreds of years before seals began to be inscribed with names or rank.

In the act of holding, molding, and sealing, the surfaces of the hand inevitably come into contact with the pliable clay leaving behind friction ridge detail. As the clay dries, the mark hardens and is preserved for millennia. Through the investigation of fingerprint remains some of the following questions may be addressed:

1. Who has touched this object? When did they live?
2. Can we deduce their employment, position, and/or status in society?
3. Was a particular cylinder seal used by an individual or a group?
4. Did an individual use one seal or multiple? Did it matter which seal was used for what?

While the most desirable outcome is to "match" fingerprints found on multiple objects, both positive and negative results have ramifications, either confirming or negating archaeological theories on the use of sealing and on the individual active within the community and society at large.

A pilot study was conducted to determine whether it was possible to recover enough objects with friction ridge detail and whether the detail was sufficient for comparison. [Four hundred forty] sealings from the [archaeological] site of Ur (2600–2350 BC) were chosen for this study. Roughly a third of these sealings had some friction ridge detail present, and 90% of those had enough detail to make them worth photographing.

[One hundred five] digital images of friction ridge detail were entered into a local [AFIS database]. Two sets of potential matches were achieved. Two sealings – U13666 and U13875– were returned by the software as possible matches (Figure 2.17). U13666 appears to come from a door sealing. It is unclear what type of sealing U13875 is. The second set of positive results includes U14177, a sealing from what appears to be a jar with an impression containing animal designs, and a leaf-shaped seal containing a stylized design (U12778) (Figure 2.18). U12778 has multiple palmar impressions. The jar seal also seems to match another set of palmar detail, this time on a random lump of clay containing an incised star design. Having the

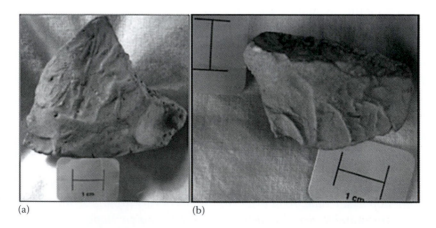

(a)   (b)

Figure 2.17 Clay sealings U13666 (a) and U13875 (b) from the archaeological site of Ur (2600–2350 BCE). (Photo courtesy of Kimberlee Sue Moran, Director, The Center for Forensic Science Research and Education.)

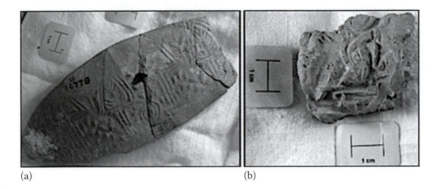

(a)   (b)

Figure 2.18 Clay sealings U14177 (a) and U12778 (b) from the archaeological site of Ur (2600–2350 BCE). (Photo courtesy of Kimberlee Sue Moran, Director, The Center for Forensic Science Research and Education.)

same individual appear on three very different objects was surprising in light of our current theories of administrative functions within this society. Do archaeologists need to re-examine their views?

The case study described above was the first one of its kind to utilize computerized comparison techniques and to demonstrate that fingerprints are more than just a curiosity; they are artifacts in their own right, and as such, they can influence our interpretation of and inspire new questions about the object on which they are found. By using technology to match fingerprints between objects, new avenues of research and interpretation are created.

2.7   Chapter Summary

Knowing the history of fingerprint analysis gives us a better understanding of how the science evolved and where it is progressing in the future. Knowledge of the history of the science is also required for certification tests and courtroom testimony. Examples of ancient fingerprint patterns can be seen impressed into pottery and bricks. Fingerprints were used to represent personal identity in ancient China and India. Important modern European and American historical figures were Sir William Herschel, JCA Mayer, Dr. Henry Faulds, Sir Francis Galton, Alphonse Bertillon, Juan Vucetich, and Sir Edward Henry.

Anthropometry, or Bertillonage, was the first scientific form of criminal identification. Anthropometry was an identification record based on anatomical measurements of the individual. Fingerprints replaced anthropometry due to their superior individualizing power. Several classification methods were developed to categorize, store, and search for fingerprint records. The AFIS largely replaced these manual classification methods.

Review Questions

1. Why is it important to know the history of your science?
2. Which civilization was the first to recognize the individualizing power of fingerprints?
3. How did the invention of the microscope benefit the advancement of the science of fingerprint analysis?

4. How did Sir William Herschel contribute to the field of fingerprint analysis?
5. Which historical figure first published the concept that fingerprints are unique and may be useful for solving crimes?
6. Who wrote the first book on fingerprints in 1892?
7. What is fingerprint classification?
8. Why was Bertillonage an inferior method of criminal identification to fingerprinting?
9. Who is responsible for developing the fingerprint classification system used primarily in English-speaking countries?
10. What contributions did Juan Vucetich make to the science of fingerprint analysis?
11. What is AFIS?

References

1. The International Association for Identification. 2013. IAI forensic certifications. http://www.theiai.org/certifications (accessed February 16, 2013).
2. Barnes, J. 2011. History. In The Scientific Working Group on Friction Ridge Analysis, Study and Technology (SWGFAST) et al. *The Fingerprint Sourcebook*. U.S. Department of Justice, Office of Justice Programs. Washington, DC: National Institute of Justice.
3. Ashbaugh, D. 1999. *Quantitative-Qualitative Friction Ridge Analysis: An Introduction to Basic and Advanced Ridgeology*. Boca Raton, FL: Taylor & Francis.
4. Cummins, H. 1941. Ancient fingerprints in clay. *J. Crim. Law Crim.* 32(4): 468–481.
5. Astrom, P. and Sjoquist, K. 1991. *Knossos: Keepers and Kneaders*. Gothenburg, Sweden: Astrom.
6. Xiang-Xin, Z. and Chun-Ge, L. 1998. The historical application of hand prints in Chinese litigation. *J. Forensic Identif.* 38(6): 277–284.
7. Grew, N. 1684. The description and use of the pores in the skin of the hands and feet. *Philos. Trans. R. Soc. Lond.* 14: 566–567.
8. Desmond, A. and Moore, J. 1994. *Darwin: The Life of a Tormented Evolutionist*. New York: W.W. Norton & Company.
9. Berry, J. and Stoney, D. 2001. History and development of fingerprinting. In Lee, H. and Gaensslen, R.E. (eds.), *Advances in Fingerprint Technology*, 2nd edn. Boca Raton, FL: Taylor & Francis.
10. Faulds, H. 1880. On the skin—Furrows of the hand. *Nature.* 22: 605.
11. Galton, F. 1892. *Finger Prints*. London, U.K.: MacMillan.
12. Olsen, R. 1995. A fingerprint fable: The Will and William West case. *The Print.* 11(1): 8–10.
13. Vucetich, J. 1904. Dactiloscopia Comparada, el Nuevo Sistemica Argentino: Trabajo hecho expresamene para el 2. Congreso medico latino-americano. Establecimiento tipografico. Buenos Aires, Argentina: J. Peuser.
14. The International Association for Identification. 2012. IAI history. http://www.theiai.org/history (accessed February 16, 2013).
15. Moses, K. 2011. Automated Fingerprint Identification System (AFIS). In The Scientific Working Group on Friction Ridge Analysis, Study and Technology (SWGFAST) et al. *The Fingerprint Sourcebook*. U.S. Department of Justice, Office of Justice Programs. Washington, DC: National Institute of Justice.
16. Ancient Wisdom Foundation. 2012. The Scottish Stone Balls. http://www.ancient-wisdom.co.uk/stoneballs.htm (accessed on July 1, 2014).
17. Grew, N. 1684. The description and use of the pores in the skin of the hands and feet. *Philos. Trans. R. Soc. Lond.* 14: 566.

Physiology and Embryology

3

> One who undertakes an intensive study of dermatoglyphics finds himself led into fascinating excursions throughout the realm of… "the natural history of man."
>
> **Harold Cummins**[1]

Key Terms

- Embryology
- Morphogenesis
- Stem cells
- Differentiation
- Gene expression
- Genome
- Epigenetics
- Basal layer
- Mitosis
- Volar pads
- Primary and secondary ridges
- Furrows
- Friction ridge units
- Uniqueness and permanence

Learning Objectives

- Define the key terms.
- Describe permanence and uniqueness in the context of embryological and physiological development.
- Describe cell differentiation.
- List the epigenetic factors influencing fingerprint development.
- Explain how friction ridges and minutiae are formed in utero.

3.1   Biological Uniqueness

Fingerprints are unique. There are likely no two fingerprints alike anywhere in the world. How do we know that fingerprints are unique? There is no way to compare every fingerprint in the world to every other fingerprint in the world. You may have heard the adage "nature never repeats itself." If you understand natural variation, and the concept that no two things in nature are exactly alike, you begin to appreciate the potency of fingerprint evidence. No two ears of corn have the same pattern of kernels. No two zebras have the same pattern of stripes. No two cheetahs have the same pattern of spots. And no two fingerprints have identical configurations of minutiae.

Minute differences between similar biological entities are due to the complex biochemical processes that create every cell of every organism. Natural variation is observable when viewed on a microscopic scale. Two objects that look alike to the naked eye may look very different under a microscope. Cummins and Midlo state, "Corresponding parts of the same species may seem to present little or no difference if the inspection is merely casual. But many unlikenesses become apparent if the objects are examined closely, and the number of differences increases as attention is directed to more and more minute characteristics."[1] In a letter to the editor of the *Journal of Forensic Science*, John Thornton wrote about this assumption of uniqueness as "The Snowflake Paradigm," since it is commonly believed that no two snowflakes are the same.[2] He further describes this uniqueness premise as it relates to fingerprint analysis:

> *The assumption of absolute uniqueness on the part of all tangible objects is a doctrine that has pervaded the interpretation of physical evidence. The doctrine generally takes one of two forms. The first is the metaphysical argument advanced by a number of classical philosophers (Heraclitus, Parmenides, Zeno and Plato), and further developed in the 17th century by Leibniz. This argument states that an object can be identical only to itself.*
>
> *The second form of the uniqueness argument is the one invoked for forensic science purposes. It too is generally accepted as true, but since it has an empirical component it is probably not susceptible of direct testing. This form of argument is frequently voiced as "Nature never repeats itself," and is attributed to the Belgian statistician Quetelet. (As an aside, what Quetelet actually said was that "Nature exhibits an infinite variety of forms")....[2]*

It is one thing to simply state that no two snowflakes are alike and another thing to prove it. Since we could never compare every fingerprint to every other fingerprint in the world, just as we could never compare every snowflake, we must understand how they are formed to understand the concept of biological uniqueness.

In order to appreciate the inherent biological differences that make fingerprints unique, we must first begin with a discussion about how fingerprints are generated. Human embryological development is a complex process that starts with the joining of two cells, the sperm and the egg. *Embryology*, or *developmental biology*, is the study of the development of an organism from the egg stage through birth. Three fundamental aspects of developmental biology are cell growth (how cells grow and divide), cell differentiation (what kind of cells they will become), and morphogenesis (what structures the cells will form).[3]

After the fertilization of the egg by the sperm, the process of cell growth through mitosis, or cell division, begins (Figure 3.1). Initially, all cells look alike. These cells are called

Figure 3.1 Mitosis is the process in which one cell replicates its DNA and splits into two cells.

stem cells. As development continues to the embryonic stage, cells begin to differentiate. They change from stem cells into specialized cells. The word *differentiation* means "to become different." Differentiation occurs when a cell is given a biochemical signal that controls what type of cell it will become. A stem cell might become an epithelial cell, which can then differentiate further into one of many different types of skin cells. A stem cell may differentiate into a liver cell, a red blood cell, or a kidney cell.

Cell signaling molecules and complex biochemical processes are the result of *gene expression*. Even though every nucleated cell in your body contains your entire *genome*, or genetic code, only a small part of that genetic code is expressed, or used. Some genes are turned on; some are turned off. Many different processes control the turning on and off of genes regulating the development and differentiation of each cell in the human body. But the environment also plays a part in cell differentiation in ways that the field of *epigenetics* is elucidating. Epigenetics is the study of things that control gene expression outside the genetic code itself.[3] Epigenetic factors influencing friction ridge growth may include the mother's nutrition, disease, environmental factors, or the position and environment of the fetus in the uterus.

Considering there are 20,000–30,000 genes in the human genome and that many factors control how each of those genes is expressed, it is easy to see how nature could never repeat itself.[4] There are simply too many factors controlling the various aspects of biological development for any two organisms to develop the exact same way.

Biological development is a unique, randomized, natural process. This is the basis of the premise that no two fingerprints are exactly alike, and therefore every fingerprint is unique. This process, as it applies to fingerprints, will be discussed in detail. To understand these processes, we must first discuss the physiology of friction ridge skin.

3.2   Layers of the Skin

An understanding of the uniqueness of fingerprints begins with an understanding of the physiology of human skin and the developmental processes that created it. Human skin is not one homogenous layer of tissue. It is a complex of many layers, each with distinct functions and morphologies. The skin is the largest organ of the human body, with important jobs including homeostasis (regulation of body temperature), water retention, synthesis of vitamin D, protection from the elements, and sensation (the sense of touch).[5] Skin also has an excretory function.[5] Water and waste products from inside the body are collected by the sweat glands and excreted through the sweat pores on the surface of the skin (Figure 3.2).

The skin is made up of three main layers: the epidermis, the dermis, and a layer of subcutaneous fatty tissue known as the hypodermis.[5] The epidermis is the top section of skin stratified into five layers: the stratum corneum, the stratum lucidum, the stratum granulosum, the stratum spinosum, and the stratum basale (Figure 3.3).[5] The stratum corneum, otherwise known as the "horny layer," is the top layer of the skin. This is the layer we can see. This durable outer "shell" is composed of keratinocytes, a type of skin cell filled with fibrous protein bundles called *keratin*.[5,6] Most of the cells of the epidermis are keratinocytes.

The deepest layer of the epidermis, the stratum basale, is also known as the *basal layer*. The basal layer is a single layer of epithelial cells responsible for generating the cells that

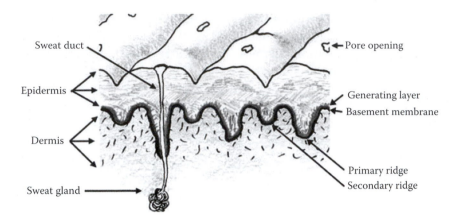

Figure 3.2 A cross section of friction ridge skin. (Reprinted from Wertheim, K. and Maceo, A., *J. Forensic Identif.*, 52(1), 37, 2002. With permission.)

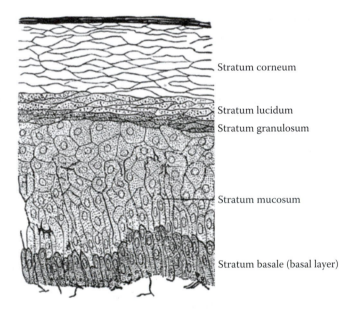

Figure 3.3 The five layers of the epidermis: stratum corneum, stratum lucidum, stratum granulosum, stratum spinosum, and stratum basale. (From Lewis, W.H., *Gray's Anatomy*, 20th edn., 1918.)

will become friction ridges. The basal layer is constantly generating new cells that migrate through the layers of the epidermis to the surface of the finger. Cells are generated through the process of *mitosis*, the splitting of one cell into two individual cells. As the basal cells divide, they push up through several layers of skin (Figure 3.4).[5] Throughout this process, adjacent cells are bound to each other via adhesion proteins known as *desmosomes*.[1,5,6] When the skin cell reaches the surface, it is shed and replaced by the cell beneath it. This process of cellular generation, migration, and shedding is a continuous cycle.

Below the epidermis is a deeper layer of skin tissue known as the dermis. The basement membrane zone (also called the dermal–epidermal junction) attaches the dermis to the epidermis.[5–7] This zone is composed of fibers from the basal cells reaching into the dermis,

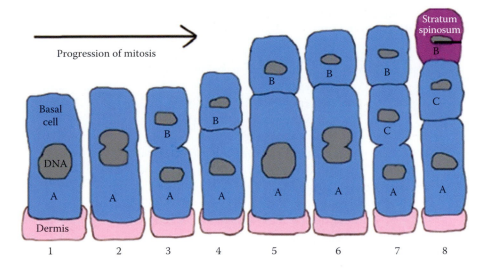

Figure 3.4 Basal cells (A) undergo mitosis. The resultant daughter cells (B and C) are pushed up through the layers of the skin. (Reprinted from Maceo, A., Anatomy and physiology of adult friction ridge skin, in *The Fingerprint Sourcebook*, National Institute of Justice, Washington, DC, 2011, pp. 2–7.)

as well as fibers from the dermis reaching toward the basal layer.[5] Just like the roots of plants, the fibers anchor the layers together. The dermis is a thick, elastic layer that contains the sweat glands, blood vessels, and nerve endings.

Dermal papillae, structures found in the upper layer of the dermis, are peg-like projections pushing up toward the epidermis.[5,8–10] The dermal papillae create a greater surface area for the transfer of nutrients from capillaries to both the dermis and epidermis. All of these structures develop while the fetus is growing in utero.

3.3 Embryological Development of Friction Ridges

Friction ridge skin forms in the fetus within the first two trimesters of human development. The sequence of the stages of development is set, but the duration of each stage varies by individual (Table 3.1). These processes may overlap, creating even more variation. Fetuses grow and develop at different rates, just like how teenagers going through the developmental process of puberty will grow and develop at different rates. However, each individual cell, structure, and organism experiences *differential growth*. Differential growth is "a difference in the size or rate of growth of dissimilar organisms, tissues or structures."[11]

Cell differentiation leads to differential growth, which results in *morphogenesis*. The word morphogenesis comes from the Latin words *morpho*, meaning shape, and *genesis*, to come into being. In this case, morphogenesis refers to the origin of biological shape or form. This process starts with the development of the fetal hand around 6 weeks after the egg is fertilized.[1,8] Between 6 and 7 weeks gestation, the paddle-like hand of the fetus begins to resemble a hand with fingers.[1,8] The webbing initially seen between the "fingers" begins to dissipate.[8]

Around this time, swellings called *volar pads* grow on the fingertips and palmar areas of the developing hand (Figure 3.5).[8–10,12] In most mammals, such as dogs and cats, volar

Table 3.1   Embryological Development of Friction Ridges over Time

Weeks	Developmental Processes
6–7	Webbing between cartilaginous "fingers" begins to dissipate.
	Volar pads appear.
7–10	Volar pads grow.
	Volar pads vary in position, size, and shape.
10–15	Volar pad regression begins.
	Epidermal ridge cells begin to replicate in basal layer.
	Primary ridges form.
	Sweat glands form.
15–17	Secondary ridge formation initiates.
	The top layer of the epidermis (stratum corneum) forms.
17–25	Secondary ridges form between all primary ridges.
	Ridges are apparent on skin surface.
	Dermal papillae form.
	Friction ridges have adult morphology.

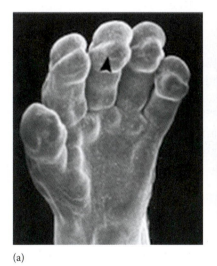 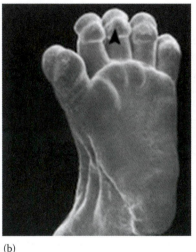

(a)   (b)

Figure 3.5 Scanning electron micrographs of the human embryonic hand (a) and foot (b) at the end of the second month of development. The volar pads are indicated with black arrows. (Reprinted from Carlson, B.M., *Human Embryology and Developmental Biology*, Elsevier, Oxford, U.K., 2011, p. 152.)

pads are present throughout adulthood. You can see these volar pads in many nonprimate mammals. They are the soft swellings on the bottoms of an animal's paws (Figure 3.6). Since most mammals do not use hands to grasp and manipulate objects, friction ridges do not form. The volar pads serve as padding for walking on all fours.

Volar pads continue to grow between 6 and 10 weeks of human fetal development.[1,8–10,12,13] They start to vary in position, size, and shape. Around the 10th or 11th week, the volar pads begin to recede or deflate (Figure 3.7).[8–10] This initiates the development of primary friction ridges in what Alfred Hale of Tulane University called "localized increases

Figure 3.6 Volar pads on an adult cat.

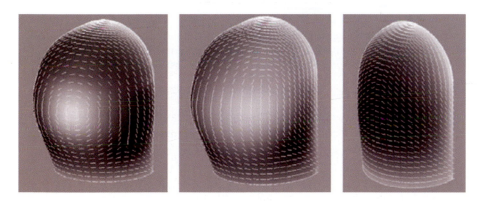

Figure 3.7 Volar pad recession. (Reprinted from Kucken, M. and Newell, A.C., *J. Theor. Biol.*, 235(1), 79, 2005. With permission.)

in basal cell activity."[14] During the process of volar pad recession and friction ridge development, the epidermal layers begin to form and thicken. Around weeks 14 and 15, sweat glands form and coil up deep within the deeper layers of the dermis, the thicker layer of tissue below the epidermis.[8,9] The sweat glands are connected to the surface where they will expel sweat through pores spaced along the fingerprint ridges.

The cells that will form the primary ridges, those that we can easily see on our fingers and palms, start to differentiate in the deepest layer of the epidermis, the basal layer.[8–10,14] This is where the initial formation of friction ridges takes place. Dr. William Babler, a well-known researcher in the field of prenatal friction ridge development, refers to these developing epidermal ridge cell areas as "localized cell proliferations" that start in the center of the regressing volar pad.[9] Ridges begin to form in different areas of the receding volar pad and spread out to eventually join and form the patterns and minute details we see on our fingers.

Friction ridge formation is affected by the growth stresses of the changing skin surface. As volar pads recede, and the skin stretches and compresses. Friction ridges develop at

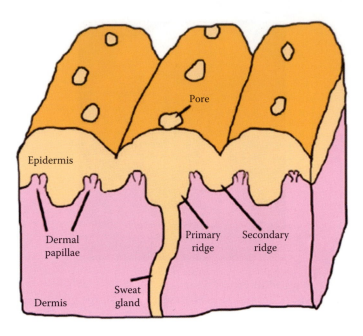

Figure 3.8 Schematic cross section of friction ridge skin showing the primary and secondary ridges and dermal papillae. (Reprinted from Maceo, A., Anatomy and physiology of adult friction ridge skin, in *The Fingerprint Sourcebook*, National Institute of Justice, Washington, DC, 2011, pp. 2–5.)

right angles to the plane of growth stresses and compression forces in the receding volar pad.[7–9,14] Primary ridges will continue to form and push up through the epidermal layers to the surface until around week seventeen of prenatal development.[8,12]

Between weeks 15 and 17, secondary ridges begin to form.[7–9,12,13] Secondary ridges are minute ridges that form in the furrows, or valleys, between primary friction ridges. They are found between every primary ridge deep in the epidermis, but contain no sweat glands (Figure 3.8). Secondary ridge formation signals the end of primary ridge formation. Friction ridges do not develop only on the fingers, but also spread out across the surface of the palm, finger joints, feet, and toes, though the friction ridges on the feet lag behind those on the hand by about 1 week.

Dermal papillae also form around this stage of development between the primary and secondary ridge structures.[8,14] Hale writes, "The dermal papillae are shaped through pressures and growth stresses exerted by an epidermis which is increasing in area as well as thickness."[14] At around 19 or 20 weeks, primary ridges are completed and can be seen on the surface of the skin.[8,9] By week 25, friction ridge formation is complete.[8–12,14] The permanent patterns of these mature friction ridges are the fingerprints the fetus will have throughout its adult life.

3.4 Embryological Development of Minutiae

Friction ridges are composed of hundreds of *friction ridge units* each fused to its neighbor to form a generally continuous structure. Ridge units are the building blocks of friction ridges. Each ridge unit is comprised of one sweat gland and corresponding sweat pore. There are

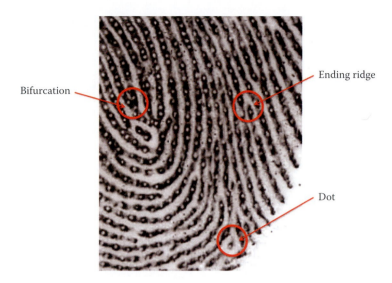

Figure 3.9 An enlargement of a fingerprint with visible minutiae: ending ridges, bifurcations, and dots.

many factors that influence the development of each friction ridge unit. The fusion of various friction ridge units results in a diversity of primary ridge structures and morphology. The width of each ridge unit is variable, resulting in friction ridges that are not smooth, but contoured, similar to mountain ranges. There is variation in the widths of ridge units, the depth of ridge penetration into the dermis, the alignment of the units, and the spacing between the ridges.[8,9] The placement, shape, and size of the pore on each ridge unit are also unique.

Fingerprint patterns form as a result of volar pad morphology. However, fingerprint pattern types are not unique structures. The uniqueness is demonstrated in the details in the small areas of the pattern: the types and locations of minutiae. You will recall that there are three types of minutiae: bifurcations, ending ridges, and dots (Figure 3.9). Minutiae form as a result of the proliferation of primary ridges and growth forces as the surface of the finger changes in dimension and size during fetal development. Dr. William Babler states, "Minutiae reflect the formation of new ridges subsequent to the period of initial ridge formation."[9] As the hand grows, the increase in surface area allows the friction ridges to spread out, creating more room for new primary friction ridges to develop between their predecessors. Ridges continue to form in the open spaces until the process of primary ridge formation ends (Figure 3.10).

As friction ridges develop, they do not always form a continuous curve. Growth stresses create ridge path deviations that result in *bifurcations*. Alfred Hale examines the development of bifurcations in his 1951 publication, *The Morphogenesis of Volar Skin in the Human Fetus*.[14] He states that bifurcations "arise out of the lateral swellings described on the primary ridge" and further asserts that growth forces stretching the epidermis pull new ridge units away from the primary ridge, thus creating a forking or bifurcating ridge.[14] Thus, a bifurcation is a splitting apart of one primary ridge rather than the fusion of two separate primary ridges.

Ending ridges form as a result of the timing and rate of primary ridge proliferation. As the finger grows and spaces open up between primary ridges, new primary ridges form in the open space. They will continue to extend as friction ridge units fuse and lengthen the

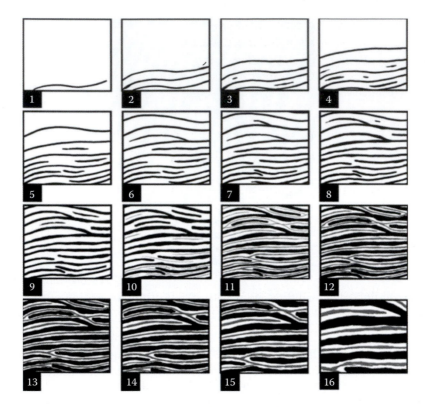

Figure 3.10 Line drawings representing the formation of minutiae as friction ridges develop in utero. The black lines represent friction ridges. The gray lines represent secondary ridges. (Reprinted from Wertheim, K. and Maceo, A., *J. Forensic Identif.*, 52(1), 51, 2002. With permission.)

developing ridge. Eventually, around the fifteenth to seventeenth week of fetal development, the process of primary ridge proliferation stops. This terminates the extension process, and developing ridges come to an abrupt halt. This creates an ending ridge. If a new ridge began elongating just before primary ridge formation was terminated, it will not have had time to lengthen. This creates a *short ridge*. Short ridges can vary in length but may be as short as one friction ridge unit in length. These are frequently referred to as *dots*. Thus, ending ridges and short ridges are the result of the same process. When the proliferation of primary ridges stops, the ridge elongation stops.

Thus, as Hale states, "the minutiae are the products of the interaction between stress and the ability of ridges to multiply, as well as the chronology of their origin."[14] Without random variability in friction ridge development and minutiae formation, fingerprints would not be unique. The uniqueness premise of fingerprint analysis is the result of the properties and mechanisms of differential growth. The following are factors that contribute to the development of volar pads, ridge units, and minutiae and thus to the uniqueness of fingerprints:[7–9,14]

- Genetics
- Epigenetic factors (nutrition, position, environment, etc.)
- Growth stresses due to differential growth
- Volar pad topography (thickness, height, width, and contour)

- Compression due to volar pad recession
- Metacarpal bone formation and morphology
- Timing and rate of ridge maturation
- Vessel–nerve pairs in the dermal papillae

3.5 Permanence

The second premise that forms the basis for the science of fingerprint identification is the idea that fingerprints are permanent. If fingerprint patterns changed throughout one's life, they would not be useful for identification. As is discussed earlier, the basal layer is the generating layer for the friction ridge patterns seen on the surface. The basal layer can be thought of as the blueprint for the building of friction ridges. The blueprint never changes. It is set for life. Every cell in the basal layer generates identical daughter cells through the process of mitosis.

It is possible for changes to occur in isolated portions of the friction ridge pattern if the basal layer is cut, burned, or mutilated. When this occurs, a *scar* is formed (Figure 3.11). The dermis and the layers of the epidermis will be repaired, but the blueprint is damaged. Flattened keratinocytes will migrate upward, forming non-ridged areas of skin within the friction ridge pattern.[5] These permanent scars are also useful in the initial stages of the fingerprint comparison process, since they may be unique in shape and size. Regardless of whether the structures of the epidermis are friction ridges or scars, they are persistent throughout an individual's life. The science of fingerprint analysis is dependent on uniqueness and permanence.

3.6 Chapter Summary

Friction ridge skin forms between the 6th and 25th week of fetal development. Three aspects of developmental biology—or embryology—that contribute to this process

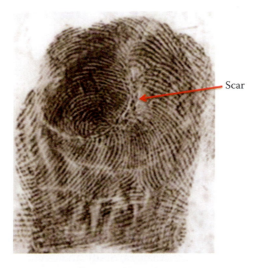

Figure 3.11 A photograph of an inked fingerprint with a visible scar through the core of the pattern.

are cell growth, cell differentiation, and morphogenesis. Friction ridges are formed in the basal layer of the epidermis as the volar pads recede. As the cells are generated, they divide through a process called mitosis. The cells are then pushed up through the various epidermal layers to the surface, where they are shed and replaced by the cells beneath them.

There are many factors of friction ridge development that contribute to their uniqueness. These factors include genetics, epigenetic factors (nutrition, position of the fetus, environment, etc.), growth stresses, volar pad topography (thickness, height, width, and contour), compression due to volar pad regression, bone formation and morphology, the timing and rate of ridge maturation, and the presence of vessel–nerve pairs in the dermal papillae. Many of these processes also contribute to the formation and locations of minutiae. The basal layer forms the blueprint for the generation of friction ridges, which accounts for the permanence of friction ridge patterns.

Review Questions

1. How do we know that no two fingerprints are alike?
2. What is cell differentiation?
3. What is epigenetics, and what does it have to do with fingerprint development?
4. Which layer of the skin is responsible for friction ridge generation?
5. How are friction ridge cells formed?
6. What is the function of the dermal papillae and where are they located?
7. What are volar pads?
8. At which week of fetal development is friction ridge formation usually complete?
9. What factors contribute to the uniqueness of fingerprints?
10. How are bifurcations formed?
11. Which types of minutiae are formed due to the cessation of primary friction ridge formation?
12. What is a scar, and how does it form?

References

1. Cummins, H. and Midlo, C. 1976. *Finger Prints, Palms and Soles—An Introduction to Dermatoglyphics*. South Berlin, MA: Research Publishing Co.
2. Thornton, J. 1986. The snowflake paradigm. Letter to the editor. *J. Forensic Sci.* 31(2): 399–401.
3. Muller, W. 1996. *Developmental Biology*. New York: Springer.
4. Claverie, J. 2001. What if there are only 30,000 human genes? *Science.* 291(5507): 1255–1257.
5. Maceo, A. 2011. Anatomy and physiology of adult friction ridge skin. In The Scientific Working Group on Friction Ridge Analysis, Study and Technology (SWGFAST) et al. *The Fingerprint Sourcebook*. Washington, DC: National Institute of Justice, U.S. Department of Justice, Office of Justice Programs.
6. Maceo, A. 2004. Permanence and Ageing. CLPEX message board. http://www.clpex.com.
7. Mulvihill, J. and Smith, D. 1969. The genesis of dermatoglyphics. *J. Pediatr.* 75(4): 579–589.
8. Wertheim, K. 2011. Embryology and morphology of friction ridge skin. In The Scientific Working Group on Friction Ridge Analysis, Study and Technology (SWGFAST) et al. *The Fingerprint Sourcebook*. Washington, DC: National Institute of Justice, U.S. Department of Justice, Office of Justice Programs.

9. Babler, W. 1991. Embryologic development of epidermal ridges and their configurations. *Birth Defects Orig.* 27(2): 95–112.
10. Cummins, H. 1946. Dermatoglyphics: Significant patternings of the body surface. *Yale J. Biol. Med.* 18: 551–565.
11. *Mosby's Medical Dictionary*, 8th edn. 2009. Differential growth. http://medical-dictionary. thefreedictionary.com/differential+growth (accessed February 13, 2013).
12. Babler, W. 1979. Quantitative differences in morphogenesis of human epidermal ridges. *Birth Defects-Orig.* 15(6): 199–208.
13. Babler, W. 1987. Prenatal development of dermatoglyphic patterns: Associations with epidermal ridge, volar pad and bone morphology. *Coll. Anthropol.* 11(2): 297–304.
14. Hale, A. 1951. Morphogenesis of volar skin in the human fetus. PhD dissertation, Department of Anatomy of the Graduate School of Tulane University, New Orleans, LA.
15. Wertheim, K. and Maceo, A. 2002. The critical stage of friction ridge pattern formation. *J. Forensic Identif.* 52(1): 37.
16. Lewis, W.H. 1918. *Gray's Anatomy.* 20th edn. PA: Lea & Febiger.
17. Maceo, A. 2011. Anatomy and physiology of adult friction ridge skin. In *The Fingerprint Sourcebook*, The Scientific Working Group on Friction Ridge Analysis, Study and Technology (SWGFAST) et al. U.S. Department of Justice, Office of Justice Programs. Washington, DC: National Institute of Justice, pp. 2–7.
18. Carlson, B.M. 2011. *Human Embryology and Developmental Biology.* Oxford, U.K.: Elsevier, p. 152.
19. Kucken, M. and Newell, A.C. 2005. Fingerprint formation. *J. Theor. Biol.* 235(1): 79.
20. Maceo, A. 2011. Anatomy and physiology of adult friction ridge skin. In *The Fingerprint Sourcebook*, The Scientific Working Group on Friction Ridge Analysis, Study and Technology (SWGFAST) et al. U.S. Department of Justice, Office of Justice Programs. Washington, DC: National Institute of Justice, pp. 2–5.
21. Wertheim, K. and Maceo, A. 2002. The critical stage of friction ridge pattern formation. *J. Forensic Identif.* 52(1): 51.

Fingerprint Patterns and Classification

4

Key Terms

- Arch
- Loop
- Whorl
- Minutiae
- Ridge flow
- Core
- Delta
- Recurve
- Radial loops
- Ulnar loops
- Ridge count
- Typelines
- Plain whorls
- Double-loop whorls
- Central pocket loop whorl
- Accidental whorl
- Whorl tracing
- Plain arches
- Tented arches
- Upthrust
- Classification
- Automated Fingerprint Identification System (AFIS)
- The Henry Classification System
- Tenprint card
- National Crime Information Center (NCIC)

Learning Objectives

- Define the key terms.
- Describe the characteristics of arches, loops, and whorls.
- Understand the purpose of fingerprint classification.
- Calculate the primary Henry classification from a tenprint card.
- Describe NCIC classification codes and their uses.

4.1 Fingerprint Patterns

As friction ridges spread out across the surface of the developing fingers, they form one of three patterns: an *arch*, a *loop*, or a *whorl* (Figure 4.1). Each pattern type can be broken down into several subpatterns, which will be discussed in detail later in this chapter. The pattern formed is dependent on the dimensions of the volar pad, its size, shape, and position on the finger.[1] Pattern type is a function of the volar pad's 3D regression combined with the proliferation of friction ridges. As early as 1924, it was hypothesized that volar pad height and symmetry influence pattern formation.[2] "High," symmetrical volar pads form whorls. Asymmetrical volar pads form loops. And "low" volar pads form arches.

While the minute details, or *minutiae*, within your fingerprint are unique to you, there is evidence to suggest your fingerprint pattern is inherited. As with eye color or hair color, your fingerprint patterns may appear similar to those of your mother or father. Besides genetic factors, environmental factors also play a role in inheritance. It is more likely you inherited your parents' volar pad formations and rate of friction ridge development than the actual patterns themselves. The patterns we see on our fingerprints display what we will call *ridge flow*, which is an illustrative method of describing how the friction ridges form patterns.

Most fingerprint pattern types have one or more of the following features formed as a result of ridge flow: the *core* and *delta*. The core of a fingerprint, like the core of an apple, is the center of the pattern (Figure 4.2). It is the focal point around which the ridges flow. The second feature of most fingerprints is the delta (Figure 4.3). A delta is an area of friction ridge skin where ridge paths flowing in three different directions create a triangular pattern. These patterns appear similar to lake or river deltas: areas where the flow diverges.

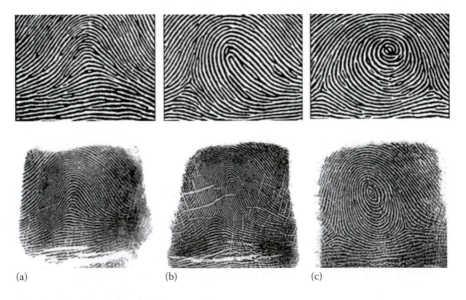

(a)   (b)   (c)

Figure 4.1 The three basic fingerprint pattern types: (a) arches, (b) loops, and (c) whorls.

Figure 4.2 The core of a loop pattern.

Figure 4.3 The delta of a loop pattern.

4.2 Loops

The loop pattern is the most common fingerprint pattern found in the population. Approximately 60%–70% of fingerprints in the population are loops. Loops are patterns in which the ridges enter on one side of the finger, make a U-turn around a core, and exit out the same side of the finger. Figure 4.4 illustrates a variety of fingerprints with loop patterns (Figure 4.4). If you think of the loop as a physical structure, you can imagine that water poured into the core will flow out only at one side of the print. A loop must also have at least one intervening, looping ridge between the delta and the core. This looping ridge is known as a *recurve*, which is another word to describe a ridge that makes a U-turn.

Figure 4.4 Various loop fingerprint patterns.

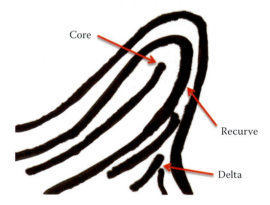

Figure 4.5 The three requirements of a loop pattern are a sufficient recurve, one delta, and a ridge count across a looping ridge.

The Federal Bureau of Investigation (FBI)'s "Fingerprint Training Manual" defines the loop pattern: "A loop is that type of pattern in which one or more ridges enter upon either side, recurve, touch or pass an imaginary line between delta and core and pass out or tend to pass out upon the same side the ridges entered."[3] Thus, the three requirements for a loop pattern are (Figure 4.5)

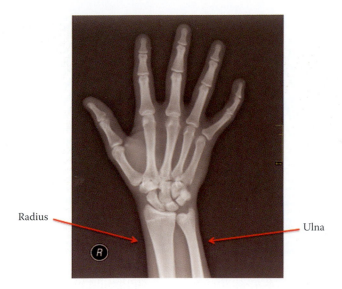

Figure 4.6 The bones of the forearm: radius and ulna.

1. A sufficient recurve
2. One delta
3. A ridge count across a looping ridge (discussed in detail below)

There are two subcategories of loops: radial loops and ulnar loops. Radial and ulnar refer to the bones of the forearm, the radius and ulna, as is shown in Figure 4.6. *Radial loops* are loops that are slanted toward the radius, the inner bone of the forearm. These loops flow toward the thumb. *Ulnar loops* are loops that are slanted toward the ulna, the outer bone of the forearm. The ulna is the bone associated with the elbow. These fingerprints flow toward the little finger of the hand.

When latent, or unknown, fingerprints are collected from crime scenes or from items of evidence, we may not be able to tell whether a finger on the right hand or the left hand made the loop pattern. In this case, we may refer to these loops as either right-slanted loops (also referred to as "right loops") or left-slanted loops (also referred to as "left loops").[4] It is interesting to note that most loops on the index, middle, ring, and little fingers are ulnar loops. If radial loops are encountered, they are most often found on index fingers of both hands.

Loops are further characterized by their *ridge count*. Ridge count refers to the number of friction ridges that cross an imaginary line between the core and delta (Figure 4.7). Ridge count, similar to pattern-type formation, is the result of volar pad morphology and the rate of embryological development. If friction ridges spread across the surface of the volar pad at a faster rate, the volar pad will have less time to recede, which allows for more ridges to cover a larger area of volar skin.[5] If the rate of friction ridge development is slower, the volar pad has more time to recede before the friction ridges proliferate, and the ridge count may be lower.[5]

The FBI's *Fingerprint Training Manual* describes how to "count" ridges.[3] The counting begins at the delta. But where do we start counting if the delta is not a defined point within the pattern? Deltas are not often well-defined triangles, but are instead ambiguous

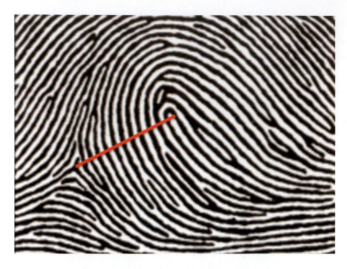

Figure 4.7 A loop pattern with a ridge count of 12.

areas of ridge flow. The FBI manual defines a delta as "that point on a ridge at or nearest to the point of divergence of two typelines, and located at or directly in front of the point of divergence."[3] In order to find the point of origin at which to start counting, you must find the *typelines*.

Typelines are the two friction ridges, either continuous or broken, that diverge from the delta in opposite directions and surround the main pattern[3] (Figure 4.8). If the ridge forming the typeline is broken, the typeline continues with the neighboring ridge away from the core.[3] The midpoint of the delta is located where the two typelines divide, or immediately in front of that point (nearest to the core).[3]

The ridge count proceeds to the core. The core of the print may be an obvious point at the center of the patterns, or it might be more ambiguous. If the innermost ridge is a loop,

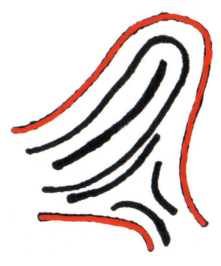

Figure 4.8 A line drawing of a loop pattern. The red lines demonstrate the typelines of this particular fingerprint.

you should count to a point just past the center of the print. Once you have found the delta and the core, you can count the intervening ridges. This is the ridge count used to characterize a loop pattern.

4.3   Whorls

The second most populous fingerprint pattern type is the whorl, which is found in approximately 30%–35% of fingerprints in the population. A whorl is a circular pattern. Most friction ridges in these patterns make complete circuits around a central core. Whorl patterns must have at least two deltas and a sufficient recurve in front of each delta.[3] There are four subcategories of whorls: plain whorls, double-loop whorls, central pocket loop whorls, and accidentals.

Plain whorls are the most common type of whorl. Some plain whorls resemble targets. The core is well defined at the "bull's-eye" of the target. Some resemble elongated, concentric ellipses. A requirement for a plain whorl is that an imaginary line drawn from delta to delta must cut through at least one recurving ridge (Figure 4.9). This distinguishes plain whorls from central pocket loop whorls, which will be discussed later.

Double-loop whorls are technically whorl patterns, since they have two deltas, but they consist of two distinct loops curved around each other like a yin-yang symbol, as is illustrated in Figure 4.10. These two intertwined loops have two distinct shoulders (Figure 4.10). Double-loop whorls are most commonly found in the thumbs.

A *central pocket loop whorl* resembles a small whorl pattern trapped within a loop. There are, however, two deltas associated with this pattern, which is what makes it a whorl. It can be difficult to distinguish a central pocket loop whorl from a plain whorl. The difference is that in a central pocket loop whorl, an imaginary line drawn from delta to delta does not cut through a recurving ridge (Figure 4.11).

An *accidental whorl*, otherwise known as an *accidental*, is any combination of two distinct pattern types. The accidental fits none of the definitions given earlier. This is the only

Figure 4.9 A plain whorl. A line from delta to delta cuts through several recurving ridges, as shown.

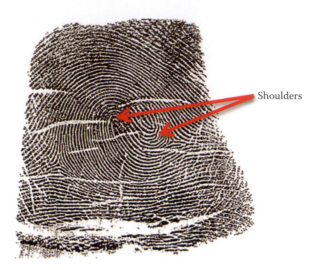

Figure 4.10 A double-loop whorl with two distinct shoulders.

Figure 4.11 A central pocket loop whorl. A line from delta to delta does not cut through a recurving ridge.

pattern type in which you will see more than two deltas.[3] Most often, this pattern displays some combination of a loop and a whorl (Figure 4.12).

Whorls are further characterized by the proximity of their left and right deltas. This categorization is called *whorl tracing*, or following a friction ridge path from the left delta to a place opposite the right delta. As you follow along the ridge, it may bifurcate (fork) or end. If either of these occurs, you can either follow the lower ridge of the bifurcation or drop down to the ridge below an ending ridge and continue tracing all the way to the right-hand delta. You can then count the ridges between the tracing ridge and the delta.

Through the process of tracing, whorls can be classified as *inner* (I), *meet* (M), or *outer* (O) (Figure 4.13). The FBI "Fingerprint Training Manual" describes this process as follows:[3]

Figure 4.12 An accidental whorl pattern.

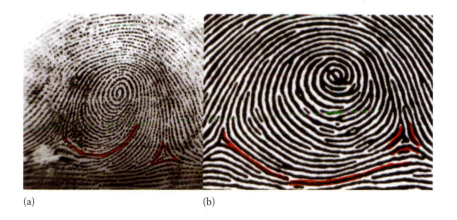

(a)   (b)

Figure 4.13 Whorls demonstrating (a) inner and (b) outer tracing.

- If there are three or more ridges inside the right delta, the tracing is an—I—*inner*.
- If there are three or more ridges outside the right delta, the tracing is an—O—*outer*.
- If there are one or two ridges either inside or outside the right delta, or if the tracing stops on the right delta itself, the tracing is an—M—*meeting*.

Tracing for whorls, like ridge counting for loops, becomes important when you consider the classification formulas discussed below.

4.4 Arches

Arches are the least common fingerprint pattern. They are found in approximately 5% of fingerprints in the general population. A fingerprint arch is similar to an architectural arch, or a wave. The friction ridges enter one side of the fingerprint, make a rise in the center,

Figure 4.14 A plain arch.

and exit out the other side of the print. There are no deltas in an arch pattern. The core is indistinct in most arches. There are two types of arches: plain arches and tented arches.

Plain arches are characterized by a smooth arching pattern with all of the friction ridges rising and falling relatively uniformly through the pattern (Figure 4.14). It cannot have any looping ridges, recurves, or ridges angular to the wave pattern.[3]

Tented arches are arch patterns that contain one or more ridges at an angle to the flow of the arch, often perpendicular to the ridges at the base of the print. Another way to describe the tented arch is "a type of pattern which possesses either an angle, an upthrust or two of the three basic characteristics of the loop."[3] An *upthrust* is a vertical or angular protrusion in the center of the print that ends abruptly (Figure 4.15). A tented arch is also characterized as any pattern possessing two of the three requirements for a loop. Thus, it appears to be a loop, but it lacks either a delta or a recurve or ridge count. For example, a fingerprint may possess a recurve and a delta, but no intervening ridge between the delta

Figure 4.15 A tented arch with an upthrust.

Figure 4.16 A tented arch with the appearance of a loop.

and core, as illustrated in Figure 4.16. This pattern, which at first glance resembles a loop, is a tented arch.

Knowledge of pattern types, cores, deltas, ridge counting, and whorl tracing is important when you consider the classification schemes discussed below. It is important to be able to distinguish a loop from a tented arch, or a tented arch from a plain arch. While the following classification systems are quickly being replaced by digital computer files, you should be able to analyze a fingerprint pattern without the assistance of a computer.

4.5 Fingerprint Classification

Classification is the process of coding and organizing large amounts of information or items into manageable, related subcategories or classes. A library classifies books both by organizing them by genre and author and by assigning alphanumerical designations according to the Dewey Decimal System. The number and letter combination on the spine of the book allows us to quickly and easily find one book in a library of thousands. Similarly, taxonomy is a method of classifying living organisms. They are sorted into the following categories, by increasing selectivity: kingdom, phylum, class, order, family, genus, and species. An example of the taxonomic designation of the common house cat would be as follows: kingdom Animalia, phylum Chordata, class Mammalia, order Carnivora, family Felidae, genus *Felis*, and species *catus*.

Fingerprint classification is the process of organizing large volumes of fingerprint cards into smaller groups based on fingerprint patterns, ridge counts, and whorl tracings. When an individual is arrested, it is important to search the files for a duplicate of that fingerprint record to verify a recidivist's (repeat offender's) identity. In the mid-1800s, prior to the advent of fingerprint records, individuals were photographed for rogues' galleries, which were collections of mug shots. Bertillonage was another classification system based on anthropometric measurements, but it fell out of favor by the turn of the twentieth century. Many individuals give false names when arrested, or change their appearance, so the fingerprint record becomes the only reliable verification of their identity.

Fingerprints were historically stored in filing cabinets according to their alphanumeric classification designations. When an individual was arrested and fingerprinted, the fingerprint card was classified and the filing cabinets searched according to that classification label. In some agencies, they are still entered and searched by hand. The advent of the *Automated Fingerprint Identification System (AFIS)*, commonly known as the fingerprint computer, has mostly negated the need for manual classification and filing of hard copies of fingerprint records. Fingerprints are now recorded on a scanner (a "livescan" device) attached to a computer. They are stored digitally, just like digital photographs. However, similar to learning about the history of fingerprints, knowledge of historical classification systems gives us a better understanding of pattern types and the analysis of friction ridge impressions. Many employers, as well as fingerprint certification tests, require a working knowledge of the basic classification schemes addressed in the following.

4.6   Henry Classification

Sir Edward Henry, Azizul Haque, and Chandra Bose developed the *Henry Classification System* in 1897.[6] The Henry system became the most widely used classification system in English-speaking countries. Juan Vucetich also developed a classification system used in Spanish-speaking countries. Prior to the advent of both the Vucetich and Henry systems, Bertillon, Purkinje, Galton, and Faulds also worked on fingerprint classifications systems.[7] Classification systems have been modified and applied in countries such as Hungary, Portugal, Prague, Germany, Japan, Spain, Holland, Italy, Russia, Mexico, Egypt, Norway, Cuba, Chile, and France.[6]

Most of these systems involve analyzing the pattern types of the fingers and assigning alphanumeric designations to each finger. In both the Henry and Vucetich systems, the resulting classification resembles a fraction, with a numerator above a classification line and a denominator below the classification line. There may be several sets of letters (both upper and lower case) and numbers both above and below the classification line.

There are six components, or parts, to the Henry Classification System: the *primary, secondary, subsecondary, major, final,* and *key.* This text will focus on examples of primary classification. Primary classification assigns numerical value to only the whorl patterns present in the fingerprint record. It is written as a fraction, but unlike a fraction, it is never reduced. One number will appear in the numerator, and one number will appear in the denominator. The fraction line is known as the classification line.

Each finger is numbered from 1 to 10, starting with the right thumb as finger number one, proceeding through the right index, right middle, right ring, and right little fingers. The left thumb is finger number six, followed by the left index, left middle, left ring, and left little fingers. The fingerprint card, also known as a *tenprint card*, is numbered 1–10 (Figure 4.17). The fingers are each assigned a point value if a whorl is found on that finger. The point values decrease by half as you proceed through the remaining eight fingers (Table 4.1). For example, if there is a whorl located on the number one finger (the right thumb), it is assigned a value of 16. If there is a whorl located on the number eight finger (the left middle finger), it is assigned a value of two.

The numerator is the sum of the point values for the *even* numbered fingers plus one. The denominator is the sum of the point values for the *odd* numbered fingers plus one.

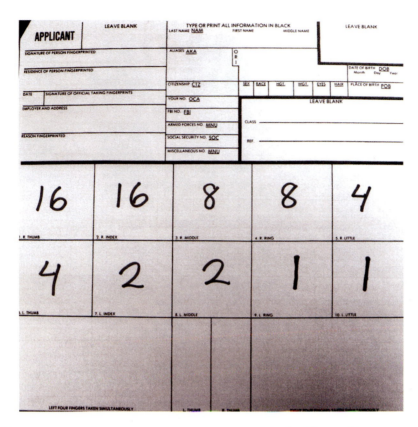

Figure 4.17 The point values assigned to each finger using the Henry Classification System.

Table 4.1 Finger Numbers and Point Values of Whorls in the Henry Classification System

Finger	Finger Number	Point Value of a Whorl
Right thumb	1	16
Right index	2	16
Right middle	3	8
Right ring	4	8
Right little	5	4
Left thumb	6	4
Left index	7	2
Left middle	8	2
Left ring	9	1
Left little	10	1

The number one is added to both the top and bottom values in order to avoid a fraction that reads 0/0. Therefore, if there are no whorls present in any of the 10 fingers, the primary classification is 1/1 rather than 0/0. If every finger on the tenprint card is a whorl pattern, the primary classification is 32/32. There are, in fact, 1024 possible variants of the primary classification component of the formula. Figure 4.18 is an example of how to find the primary classification from a tenprint card (Figure 4.18).

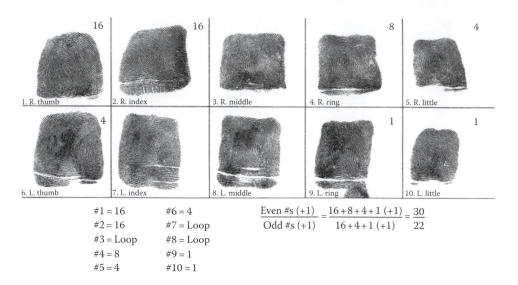

#1 = 16   #6 = 4

#2 = 16   #7 = Loop

#3 = Loop   #8 = Loop

#4 = 8   #9 = 1

#5 = 4   #10 = 1

$$\frac{\text{Even \#s}\ (+1)}{\text{Odd \#s}\ (+1)} = \frac{16+8+4+1\ (+1)}{16+4+1\ (+1)} = \frac{30}{22}$$

Figure 4.18 An example of primary Henry classification.

4.7 NCIC Classification

The *National Crime Information Center (NCIC)*, a division of the FBI's Criminal Justice Information Services (CJIS), is a national repository of computerized criminal justice information. It was created in 1965 during the J. Edgar Hoover era and has since been expanded and upgraded to its current incarnation, NCIC 2000, which launched in 1999.[8,9] NCIC is accessible by criminal justice agencies in all 50 states, Washington, DC, Puerto Rico, Guam, the US Virgin Islands, and Canada.[10] It includes 21 databases that include such information as criminal records, missing persons, the sex offender registry, stolen property records, fugitive records, orders of protection, and suspected terrorist activity.[10] As of 2011, the FBI reported 11.7 million active records.[10] The goal of NCIC is to provide an investigative tool not only to identify property but also to protect law enforcement personnel and the public from individuals who may be dangerous.

NCIC also includes fingerprint classification information. It is important to understand NCIC classification in order to decipher these codes if you work in any capacity within the criminal justice system. The NCIC fingerprint classification system applies a 2-letter code to each pattern type. The 2-letter codes for each of the 10 fingers are combined to form a 20-character classification. Each fingerprint's code is listed in sequence, from the number 1 finger (right thumb) to the number 10 finger (left little finger). Ridge counts of loops and whorl tracings are also included in the coding system to further classify pattern types. Table 4.2 lists the NCIC classification codes.

If an individual has plain whorls with a meet tracing on fingers 2–10 and a double-loop whorl with an outer tracing on finger number one, the NCIC classification would read as follows:

dOPMPMPMPM
PMPMPMPMPM

Table 4.2   NCIC Classification Codes

Pattern Type	NCIC Code
Ulnar loop ridge count	01–49
Radial loop ridge count +50	51–99
Plain arch	AA
Tented arch	TT
Plain whorl, inner tracing	PI
Plain whorl, outer tracing	PO
Plain whorl, meet tracing	PM
Double-loop whorl, inner tracing	dI
Double-loop whorl, outer tracing	dO
Double-loop whorl, meet tracing	dM
Central pocket loop whorl, inner tracing	CI
Central pocket loop whorl, outer tracing	CO
Central pocket loop whorl, meet tracing	CM
Accidental, inner tracing	XI
Accidental, outer tracing	XO
Accidental, meet tracing	XM
Mutilated or extensively scarred	SR
Amputation	XX

The NCIC classification of an individual with plain whorls (outer tracing) on his or her thumbs and plain arches on his or her remaining fingers would be

POAAAAAAAA
POAAAAAAAA

NCIC is unique in that it does not include the actual fingerprint images. It only includes the classification described previously. A working knowledge of NCIC fingerprint classification codes can give you a wealth of information regarding the fingerprint patterns of the individual queried in an NCIC search, including a tentative identification of a person of interest, such as a suspect or a missing person.

4.8   Chapter Summary

There are three basic fingerprint pattern types: loops, whorls, and arches. Loops are the most common pattern type in the general population. A loop is a pattern in which friction ridges enter on one side of the finger, make a U-turn around a core, and flow out the same side of the finger. There are two types of loops: ulnar loops and radial loops. Loops can be further characterized by a ridge count from the delta to the core. Whorls are patterns in which the ridges make a complete circuit. They are the second most populous fingerprint patterns in the population. Whorls have at least two deltas and can be further characterized by whorl tracing. There are four subcategories of whorls: plain whorls, double-loop whorls, central pocket loop whorls, and accidentals. Arches are the least common fingerprint pattern type. They are patterns in which the ridges enter on one side of the finger, make a rise or wave in the center, and flow out the other side. There are two types of arches: plain arches and tented arches.

Classification systems categorize fingerprint records according to the pattern types found on the fingers. The Henry classification uses alphanumeric designations for fingerprint pattern types and lists them above and below a classification line. NCIC classification is a system that applies a two-letter code to each fingerprint pattern type.

Review Questions

1. List the three basic fingerprint pattern types in order from least common to most common.
2. How many deltas are most often observed in the following pattern types?
   Arch
   Loop
   Whorl
3. What are the three requirements of a loop pattern?
4. What are the four subcategories of whorls?
5. How do you "trace" a whorl, and what are the three possible types of whorl tracings?
6. What makes a tented arch different from a plain arch?
7. What is the primary Henry classification of an individual with whorls on his right and left thumbs and index fingers?
8. What is the primary Henry classification for an individual with the following NCIC classification code:

   dM7017AA12
   dM7219TT16

References

1. Babler, W. 1987. Prenatal development of dermatoglyphic patterns: Associations with epidermal ridge, volar pad and bone morphology. *Coll. Anthropol.* 11(2): 297–304.
2. Bonnevie, K. 1925. Studies on papillary patterns of human fingers. *J. Genet.* 15(1925): 1–104.
3. Federal Bureau of Investigation. 1987. *Fingerprint Training Manual.* Identification Division Technical Section., Washington, DC: U.S. Department of Justice.
4. Olsen, R. 1978. *Scott's Fingerprint Mechanics.* Springfield, IL: Charles C. Thomas.
5. Wertheim, K. 2011. Embryology and morphology of friction ridge skin. In *The Fingerprint Sourcebook.* The Scientific Working Group on Friction Ridge Analysis, Study and Technology (SWGFAST) et al., Washington, DC: National Institute of Justice, U.S. Department of Justice, Office of Justice Programs.
6. Barnes, J. 2011. History. In *The Fingerprint Sourcebook.* The Scientific Working Group on Friction Ridge Analysis, Study and Technology (SWGFAST) et al., Washington, DC: National Institute of Justice, U.S. Department of Justice, Office of Justice Programs.
7. Bridges, B. 1942. *Practical Fingerprinting.* New York: Funk & Wagnalls Company.
8. Walton, R. 2006. *Cold Case Homicides: Practical Investigative Techniques.* Boca Raton, FL: Taylor & Francis.

9. Hutchins, L. 2011. Systems of Friction Ridge Classification. In *The Fingerprint Sourcebook*. The Scientific Working Group on Friction Ridge Analysis, Study and Technology (SWGFAST) et al., Washington, DC: National Institute of Justice, U.S. Department of Justice, Office of Justice Programs.

10. Federal Bureau of Investigation. 2013. National Crime Information Center. Criminal Justice Information Services. http://www.fbi.gov/about-us/cjis/ncic/ncic (accessed February 16, 2013).

Known Fingerprints

5

Key Terms

- Exemplars
- Known prints
- Inked prints
- Record prints
- Standards
- Major case prints
- Tenprint cards
- Flats
- Slaps
- Plain impressions
- Writer's palm
- Hypothenar
- Handiprint System®
- Livescan
- Algorithm
- Rigor mortis
- Putrefaction
- Maceration
- Mummification
- Desiccated

Learning Objectives

- Define the key terms.
- Name the three methods of recording friction ridge skin.
- Understand the advantages and disadvantages of each process.
- Describe the various methods for recording known prints from decomposing skin.

5.1 Known Fingerprints

In order to analyze friction ridge skin, one must first record the pattern digitally or with fingerprint ink or powder. The resulting records are known as *exemplars* or *known prints*.

They are also known as *inked prints, record prints,* or *standards.*[1] Known fingerprints are recorded for four reasons:

1. To serve as an official record of a person's identity
2. To search for a match to a prior arrest record
3. To compare to unknown, or latent, fingerprints
4. To input into the Automated Fingerprint Identification System (AFIS) for subsequent searches

It is therefore important to take comprehensive records of the friction ridge skin in order to provide the best possible exemplars for identification purposes.

Records of the friction ridge skin on the fingers, finger joints, palms, and even feet and toes may be needed for identification. Records of fingers, palms, the writer's palm (side of the hand), and the joints, tips, and sides of fingers are known as *major case prints.* The three most common methods of recording friction ridges are inked impressions, powdered impressions, and digital scans.

5.2   Inked Fingerprint Records

The most common medium for recording friction ridge skin is ink. Inked fingerprints are recorded on *tenprint cards.* Tenprint cards are $8'' \times 8''$ printed white cards formatted to official government specifications. A tenprint card, such as the card pictured in Figure 5.1, contains demographic information along with the fingerprints of each of 10 fingers (Figure 5.1). Each finger is rolled in ink and subsequently rolled into the corresponding box on the tenprint card. The finger is rolled from "nail to nail" to capture the entire friction ridge surface. This means the finger must be rolled from one side of the finger (at the nail) all the way around to the other side of the nail (Figure 5.2). A fingerprint rolled from nail to nail should be roughly rectangular in shape (Figure 5.3).

The fingerprints should be rolled with the individual standing slightly back from the table with the arm bent at an approximate 90° angle. When the thumb is rolled, the subject's hand is rotated toward the body. When the fingers are rolled, the subject's hand is rotated away from the body. This allows the hand to be manipulated from the point of most to least resistance. The individual taking the fingerprints controls the subject's hand to ensure the most comprehensive fingerprint record is taken. If the subject attempts to assist by moving his own fingers, the prints will be smudged or incomplete.

The four fingers of the right hand and left hand are inked and recorded simultaneously at the bottom of the tenprint card along with impressions of the thumb. These impressions are known as the *flats, slaps,* or *plain impressions.* The flats of the four fingers together are placed in the section of the tenprint card labeled "four fingers taken simultaneously." The sections for the flats of the thumbs are labeled "R. thumb" and "L. thumb." It is important to record information here that may not be available in the previously mentioned rolled prints, such as the ridge detail in the fingertips. This is accomplished by lifting the thumb and fingers up to the tips when the flats are inked and recorded.

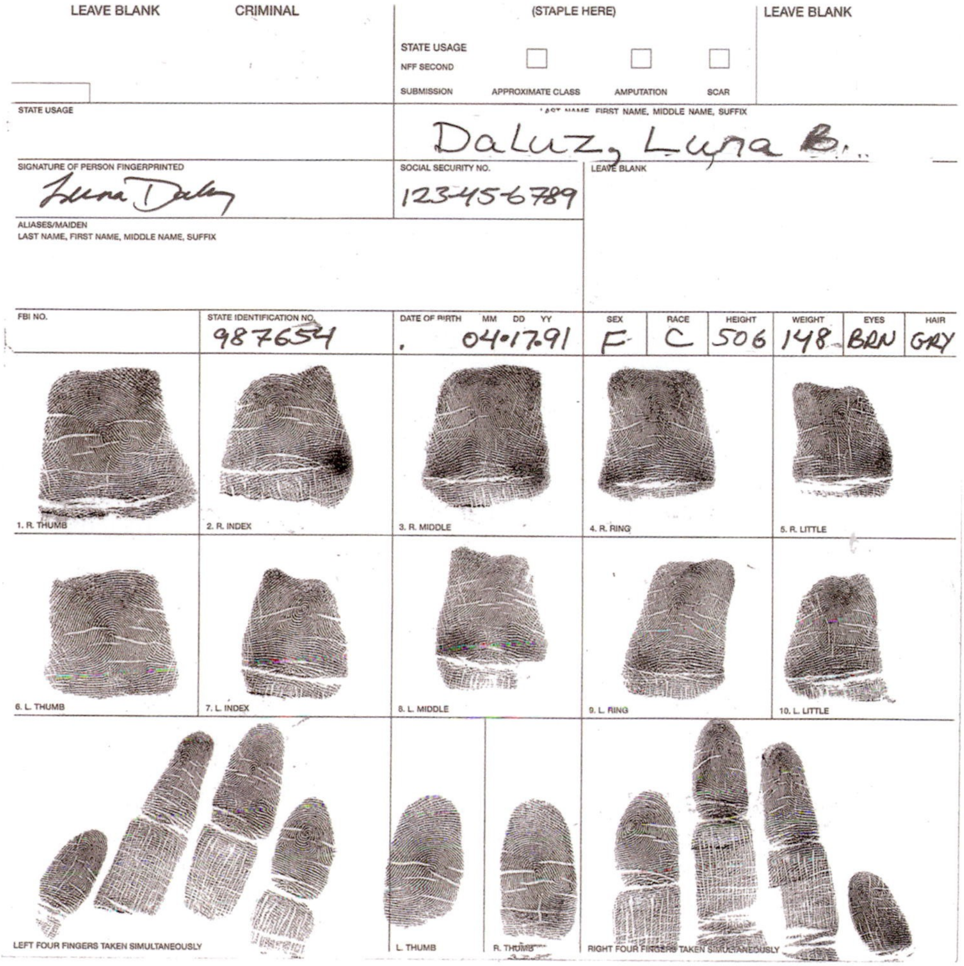

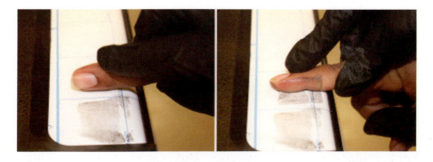

Figure 5.1 A tenprint card with demographic information.

Figure 5.2 Rolling a fingerprint in ink onto a tenprint card.

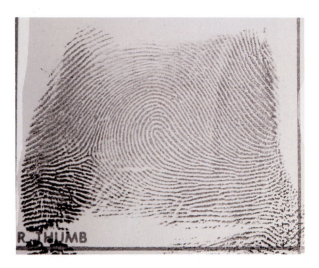

Figure 5.3 The rectangular shape of a comprehensive record of an inked fingerprint rolled from nail to nail.

Ink is the traditional medium for recording fingerprints, palm prints, and major case prints. The following materials are used for recording fingerprints using ink (Figure 5.4):

- Gloves
- Ink pad (or a light layer of ink rolled out onto a glass slab)
- Tenprint card
- Fingerprint card holder
- Re-tabs (correcting labels for if you make a mistake when rolling the fingerprints)
- Hand cleaner/wet wipes

Figure 5.4 Materials for recording known fingerprints in ink onto a tenprint card.

The process of collecting rolled fingerprint records in ink from a suspect is as follows:

1. Set up the card in the card holder so the first row of boxes is clearly visible and the card is secure (Figure 5.5).
2. Take control of the subject's right hand.
3. Roll a thin layer of ink onto the right thumb (Figure 5.6).
4. Roll the right thumb onto the corresponding box on the tenprint card with light, even pressure.
5. Repeat with the remaining fingers (Figure 5.7).
6. Record the flats by pressing the four fingers of the right hand lightly onto the ink pad and rolling the fingers upward to ink the tips of the fingers (Figure 5.8).

Figure 5.5 A tenprint card secured in a card holder.

Figure 5.6 Rolling a thin layer of ink onto a suspect's hand.

Figure 5.7 Rolling inked fingers onto a tenprint card.

Figure 5.8 Recording the four fingers of the hand simultaneously on a tenprint card.

7. Press the four fingers onto the flats section of the card with light pressure and roll the fingers upward to record the tips of the fingers (Figure 5.9).
8. Press the right thumb lightly to the ink pad and roll the thumb upward to ink the tip of the thumb.
9. Press the right thumb lightly to the area designated for the thumb flats and roll the thumb upward to record the ridge detail on the tip of the thumb (Figure 5.10).
10. Repeat this procedure for the left hand.

It may also be necessary to record the palm of the subject. The palm is coated with a light layer of ink and recorded on a white sheet of paper or a palm print card as shown in Figure 5.11. The *writer's palm*, the section of the meaty side of the hand that rests on a

Figure 5.9 Rolling the inked fingers upward to record the tips of the fingerprints on a tenprint card.

Figure 5.10 Recording the thumb on a tenprint card.

surface when one holds a pen or pencil, is also recorded. This area of the palm is known as the *hypothenar*.

5.3 Powdered Fingerprint Records

Fingerprint powder is also used as a medium to record friction ridges. This method is quick and easy and results in high-quality major case prints. Unlike fingerprints recorded

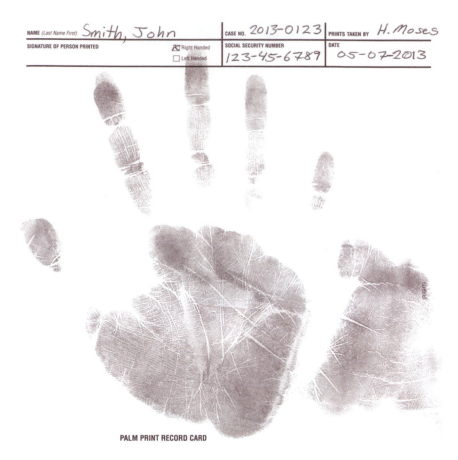

NAME *(Last Name First)* Smith, John | CASE NO. 2013-0123 | PRINTS TAKEN BY H. Moses

SIGNATURE OF PERSON PRINTED | ☒ Right Handed ☐ Left Handed | SOCIAL SECURITY NUMBER 123-45-6789 | DATE 05-07-2013

PALM PRINT RECORD CARD

Figure 5.11 The inked palm print and writer's palm of the right hand.

in ink, powdered friction ridges often display better detail including well-defined ridge shapes and pores. The hand is powdered and recorded on flexible, white adhesive sheets with clear acetate covers. These sheets, known as the *Handiprint System*®, are available from CSI Forensic Supply (formerly known as Kinderprint Co.).

The following materials are used for recording major case prints using fingerprint powder (Figure 5.12):

- Handiprint system
- Black fingerprint powder
- Fiberglass fingerprint brush

The process of collecting major case prints in powder from a subject is as follows:

1. Peel the backing off of the white adhesive sheet and place it on the table with the adhesive side up (Figure 5.13).
2. Lightly powder the subject's hand using a standard fingerprint brush and fingerprint powder (Figure 5.14).
3. Press the powdered hand to the adhesive sheet and turn the hand over (Figure 5.15).

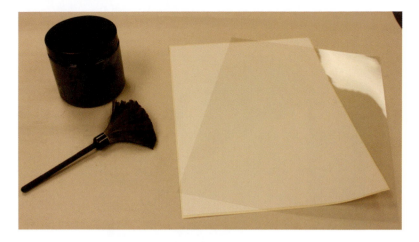

Figure 5.12 Supplies for recording major case prints using black fingerprint powder.

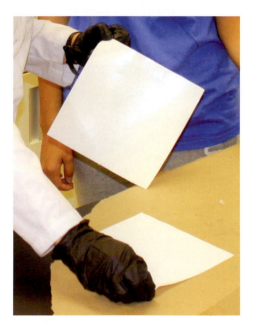

Figure 5.13 Preparing a white adhesive sheet to record major case prints.

4. Press the adhesive sheet to every section of the palm (including the hypothenar), finger joints, sides of finger joints, fingers, sides of fingers, and fingertips (Figure 5.16).
5. Pull the adhesive sheet from the subject's palm and place it adhesive side up on the table (Figure 5.17).
6. Carefully place the clear acetate cover over the powdered print on the adhesive sheet taking care to avoid trapping air bubbles (Figure 5.18).
7. Record the subject's demographic information on the back of the acetate sheet.

While this method is simple and results in high-quality major case prints, the resulting record is not in the official government format required for filing or for entry into an AFIS.

Figure 5.14 The subject's hand is sufficiently coated with powder.

Figure 5.15 The subject's hand is pressed to the white adhesive sheet.

For these purposes, a standard fingerprint or palm print card should be used. The powder method is often the best method for collecting exemplars to compare to unknown latent fingerprints from when additional friction ridge detail is needed. This method is also effective for collecting exemplars from deceased persons.

5.4   Digital Fingerprint Records

Fingerprints are also recorded on a *livescan* device, which scans and digitizes fingerprints similar to a document scanner (Figure 5.19). This method does not require ink, powder,

Figure 5.16 The adhesive sheet is pressed onto all surfaces of the hand.

Figure 5.17 The white adhesive sheet is peeled from the subject's hand.

or any other medium to capture the print. The livescan operator, the individual taking the fingerprints, rolls the individual's fingerprints onto a plastic or glass plate in a manner similar to rolling inked prints onto a tenprint card. The resulting digital fingerprint image resembles an inked impression on a tenprint card. The livescan acquires the image and the computer processes it using a computer *algorithm*: a set of procedures the computer follows to process data.

Figure 5.18 The clear acetate is mounted to the white adhesive sheet.

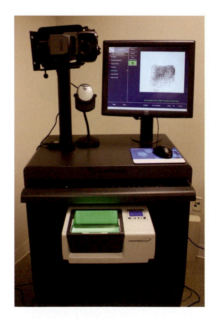

Figure 5.19 A livescan station with a camera, barcode scanner, computer monitor, keyboard, and glass plate for scanning fingerprints.

Livescan fingerprinting has several advantages over and is quickly replacing inked fingerprinting for the following reasons:

1. Livescan prints are digital and can be stored on computers rather than in large numbers of file cabinets required by manual tenprint cards.
2. Unlimited numbers of exact copies of the fingerprints can be reproduced on the computer printer.

3. Livescan prints can be instantly transmitted between agencies using computer networks.
4. Image quality is more uniform due to the quality control standards built into the livescan device.
5. Livescan devices directly connect to AFIS. This makes it possible to take a person's prints; search them automatically against local, state, and national records; and get results back, often in minutes.

5.5 Fingerprints from Deceased Individuals

It is often necessary to collect postmortem exemplars from deceased individuals for identification purposes. In the case of the recently dead, fingerprint acquisition is a simple process. Ink or powder may be used to record the fingerprints. For inked fingerprints, postmortem print kits are available. They include fingerprint strips and a postmortem record strip holder, often referred to as a "spoon" (Figure 5.20). This tool makes it easier to roll the fingerprints of the corpse laid out in a supine position. The Handiprint System® may also be used for recording postmortem friction ridge skin. The acetate sheet is cut into squares slightly larger than the finger to be recorded. Each finger is powdered, recorded, and documented individually (Figure 5.21).

There are several challenges to fingerprinting individuals who are in more advanced stages of decomposition. One challenge occurs when the subject is in *rigor mortis*. Rigor mortis is the stiffening of the body, which can occur 2–4 h after death and develops fully between 6 and 12 h postmortem (Figure 5.22).[2] Rigor mortis occurs when metabolism stops with the cessation of cellular respiration after death.[2] Without adenosine triphosphate (ATP), the energy source for the body, the muscles can no longer contract. The deceased subject's hands may be completely stiff and inflexible. In this case, the rigor

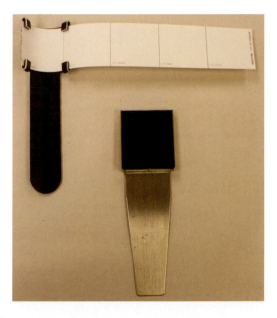

Figure 5.20 Materials for inking fingerprints of deceased individuals.

Figure 5.21 Powdered fingerprint from a deceased individual.

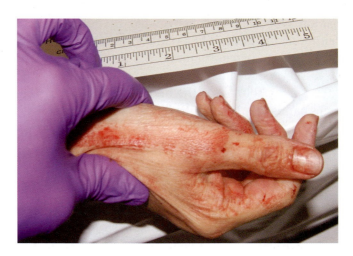

Figure 5.22 The fingers of this decedent are curled and stiffened by rigor mortis.

can be "broken" forcibly at each finger joint. The fingers are then printed using ink or powder.

Decomposing friction ridge skin undergoing putrefaction, maceration, or mummification presents a more challenging scenario. *Putrefaction* is the breakdown of the cells of the human body after death by bacteria and fungi. *Maceration* occurs when skin is submerged in water and the tissues become swollen.[1] Friction ridge skin may loosen from the dermal layer.[1] *Mummification* occurs when the skin is dehydrated. The friction ridge skin is dried, leathery, and shriveled.

Figure 5.23 Burned and putrefied friction ridge skin.

Putrefied friction ridge skin is fragile (Figure 5.23). It may be moist and peeling off in layers. Prior to attempting to ink or powder the finger, the area must be cleaned and dried. At this point, it may be possible to ink the finger and collect useable fingerprints. If the skin is separating from the dermis, the recorder may choose to remove the skin and roll it with his gloved finger. This must be done with great care since the decomposing skin is fragile and tears easily. If the skin is too badly decomposed for these techniques, the fingers can be soaked in a 10% solution of formaldehyde.[1] Formaldehyde solution firms up the putrefied skin, after which it may be recorded with ink or powder.

Macerated skin may be swollen and wrinkled. It may be possible to clean, dry, and record the fingerprints in the usual manner using powder or ink. If the skin is too wrinkled, it may be stretched slightly in order to record more ridge detail. Another option for dealing with wrinkled skin is to inject glycerin or a product known as "tissue builder" under the skin.[1] This procedure puffs up the finger thus eliminating the wrinkles. The liquid may leak, so it is recommended to tie a string or secure a rubber band just above the injection site.[1] If the skin is loosened from the dermis, it may be recorded similar to the putrefied skin by removing it and placing it on the recorder's gloved hand for rolling with ink.

Mummified skin, also referred to as *desiccated* skin, must be rehydrated prior to recording with ink or powder (Figure 5.24). The fingers can be severed from the hand and soaked in a 1%–3% solution of sodium hydroxide or potassium hydroxide for 24–48 h.[1] If the skin is peeling, the outer layers can be removed gently under warm running water with a soft-bristled toothbrush.[1] If the skin is stiff, the fingers may be soaked for a further 24–48 h in a solution of one tablespoon of dishwashing liquid in water.[1] When the skin is rehydrated, it is recorded using ink or powder.

Decomposed skin may also be recorded using white silicone casting material. Fingerprint powder is applied to the clean, dry finger. The silicone casting material is mixed according to the manufacturer's directions and applied to the finger. When it hardens, it can be gently peeled off the finger surface (Figure 5.25). Regardless of the method utilized, great care should be exercised when working with fragile skin.

Figure 5.24 Mummified skin during the rehydration process.

Figure 5.25 Silicone casting material with a black powdered fingerprint.

5.6   Chapter Summary

Known fingerprints—also referred to as exemplars, inked prints, record prints, or standards—are recorded for three reasons: to search for a match to a prior arrest record, to compare to unknown fingerprints from crime scenes or evidentiary items, or to input into the AFIS for subsequent searches. Exemplars may be recorded in ink, powder, or via livescan, a digital scanner. Exemplars are collected from deceased individuals to determine absolute identity. Friction ridge skin in advanced stages of decay requires special handling. Mummified skin should be rehydrated, decomposed skin firmed, and loose, peeling skin gently removed prior to inking or powder printing the finger.

Review Questions

1. What are the three reasons for recording exemplar fingerprints?
2. What are major case prints?
3. Why is it important to roll fingerprints from "nail to nail"?
4. What details may be seen when exemplars are recorded with powder rather than with ink?
5. What is livescan?
6. What are some of the advantages of livescan over inked methods?
7. How are deceased individuals in rigor mortis fingerprinted?
8. How is putrefied friction skin recorded?
9. How is mummified friction ridge skin recorded?

References

1. Cutro, B. 2011. Recording living and postmortem friction ridge exemplars. In *The Fingerprint Sourcebook*. The Scientific Working Group on Friction Ridge Analysis, Study and Technology (SWGFAST) et al. Washington, DC: National Institute of Justice, U.S. Department of Justice, Office of Justice Programs.
2. Di Maio, V. and DiMaio, D. 2001. *Forensic Pathology*. 2nd edn. Boca Raton, FL: Taylor & Francis.

Nature of Latent Fingerprints

6

With dramatic suddenness he struck a match, and by its light exposed a stain of blood upon the whitewashed wall. As he held the match nearer, I saw that it was more than a stain. It was the well-marked print of a thumb.

Sherlock Holmes[1]

Key Terms

- Ridge flow
- Latent fingerprints
- Patent fingerprints
- Plastic fingerprints
- Matrix
- Substrate
- Latent print examiner (LPE)
- Eccrine gland
- Sebaceous sweat (sebum)
- Touch DNA

Learning Objectives

- Define the key terms.
- Describe and give an example of latent, patent, and plastic fingerprints.
- Explain the duties of a latent fingerprint examiner.
- List the components of latent fingerprint residue.
- Explain why fingerprints cannot be aged.
- Understand touch DNA and how to avoid contamination during collection.

6.1 Latent Fingerprints

Fingerprints recovered from crime scenes are known as *latent fingerprints*. The word "latent" is a Latin word meaning "hidden." The Merriam-Webster dictionary defines it as follows: "present and capable of emerging or developing but not now visible, obvious."[2] Latent fingerprints are invisible, and they are also of unknown origin. Unlike exemplar fingerprints, latent prints are fingerprints from an unknown source. Unknown fingerprints are often referred to simply as *latents*.

Figure 6.1 Fingerprints developed from a crime scene with fingerprint powder.

When one imagines fingerprints at crime scenes, what images come to mind? A crime scene investigator diligently twirling a brush coated in black fingerprint powder across a surface, revealing a fingerprint? This image, though accurate, is only one segment of fingerprint analysis. There are many ways to recover invisible fingerprints from items of evidence or from surfaces at a crime scene using both powders and chemical reagents (Figure 6.1).

Not all fingerprints found at crime scenes are invisible, however. *Patent* fingerprints are fingerprints visible to the naked eye. The word "patent" means "readily visible or intelligible: obvious."[2] Patent prints are visible because they are recorded in a visible medium such as blood, paint, or grease. Though patent prints are visible, they may require chemical processing to improve visibility and contrast. For example, a bloody fingerprint is often light brown or rust in color. A chemical reagent is applied to turn the light brown fingerprint a blue/black color so it is easier to see and photograph (Figure 6.2). A grease fingerprint may also be enhanced with the use of chemical reagents.

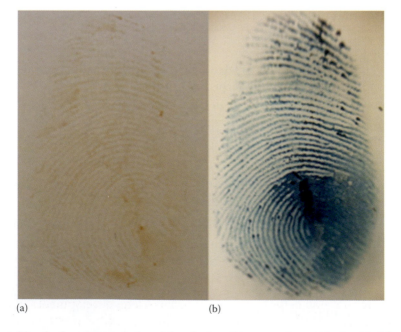

(a)   (b)

Figure 6.2 A bloody fingerprint before (a) and after (b) processing with Amido black.

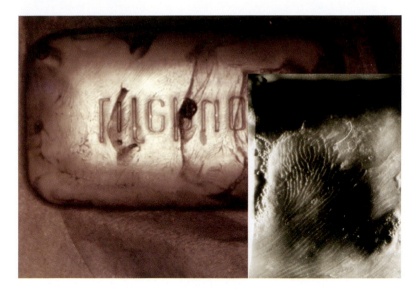

Figure 6.3 A patent print on a bar of soap identified to a suspect in a homicide.

Plastic fingerprints are those left in a soft material such as clay, glue, wax, soap, or tacky paint. The ridge detail is visible, but must be photographed to capture the details (Figure 6.3).

Regardless of whether the fingerprints are latent, patent, or plastic, a *latent print examiner (LPE)* is responsible for analyzing the unknown print and, if possible, identifying it to a source. LPEs are forensic scientists who compare latent prints to the fingerprints of known individuals to determine whether or not they came from the same source. They may also recover those latent fingerprints from crime scenes and/or items of evidence in a laboratory. If the suspect is unknown, an LPE may choose to search the fingerprint in the fingerprint computer known as the Automated Fingerprint Identification System (AFIS).

6.2 Matrix

Latent fingerprints are left on a surface when friction ridges coated with a substance such as sweat or contaminants are deposited on a *substrate*, or surface. This is analogous to an ink pattern left by a rubber stamp. The rubber stamp is coated with ink, and the ink is pressed to a surface, thereby duplicating the stamp pattern. The substance coating friction ridges is made up mostly of sweat, but may also be any combination of lotion, grease, soap, or anything else an individual touched. These substances are known collectively as the fingerprint matrix.

The fingerprint matrix is predominantly comprised of sweat. An average of 2–4 L of fluid is secreted per hour from the sweat pores of the body.[3] Most of the sweat evaporates. Sweat is produced in coiled up glands in the skin (Figure 6.4). A gland is a "tubular shaped structure with a duct portion that coils in helical fashion down deep into the dermis layer."[3] The glands found in the friction skin, known as *eccrine* glands, form during embryological development. They develop between 8 and 32 weeks of fetal development.[3] There are three types of sweat glands in the human body that produce three different types of sweat: apocrine, sebaceous, and eccrine.

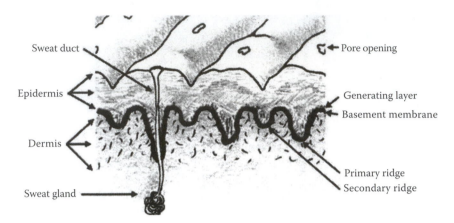

Figure 6.4 Cross section of the primary components of friction ridge skin, including the sweat gland, which conducts sweat through the sweat duct to the pore opening on the friction ridge. (Reprinted from Wertheim, K. and Maceo, A., *J. Forensic Identif.*, 52(1), 37, 2002. With permission.)

Each of these glands is produced in different parts of the body. *Apocrine* sweat is found in the genital and armpit regions. *Sebaceous* sweat is associated with regions of the body containing hair follicles, including the face and scalp. When the face or hair is touched, the friction ridges are coated with sebaceous sweat. The third type of sweat, eccrine sweat, is associated with friction ridge skin.

Eccrine sweat is secreted from pores found along the friction ridges of the hands and feet. There are 3–4 million eccrine sweat glands in the human body.[4] An individual doing strenuous exercise in a warm environment may secrete up to 10 L of sweat from his eccrine glands.[4] Eccrine sweat is over 98% water. The remaining components are excretory products including the following organic and inorganic compounds: ammonia, magnesium, iodide, bromide, fluoride, cobalt, manganese, sulfur, mercury, phosphate, sulfate, iron, zinc, copper, lead, molybdenum, tin, urea, sodium lactate, proteins, lipids, cholesterol/fatty acids, and 22 amino acids.[3,5]

Sebaceous sweat, known as *sebum*, is secreted from pores associated with hair follicles. Sebum is composed of mostly lipids. De Paoli et al. identified more than 300 components of sebum in sebaceous fingerprints.[4] The lipid constituents include fatty acids, wax esters, squalene, and cholesterol.[5] Latent fingerprints often contain a mixture of eccrine and sebaceous sweat, but they also include other contaminants from surfaces touched during the day. Contaminants may include lotions, cosmetics, soap, or grease.

The composition of fingerprints is especially important when determining which chemical reagent to use to visualize latent fingerprints. Most fingerprint reagents react with amino acids, lipids, or sodium lactate.[6] Regardless of the chemical or physical development method used, latent prints must be visualized to compare them with exemplars.

6.3 Substrate

The *substrate* is the surface the latent print is deposited on. Substrates are variable in texture and contour. A substrate may be smooth or rough, flat or curved, porous or nonporous.

Figure 6.5 A fingerprint on a manila envelope developed using the chemical reagent ninhydrin.

Porous surfaces are absorbent: permeable to gases or liquids. Examples of porous surfaces include paper, cardboard, and unfinished woods. Nonporous items are nonabsorbent. Examples of nonporous surfaces include glass, plastic, or metal.

Rough or highly textured surfaces are not ideal for fingerprint collection with chemical reagents or fingerprint powders. When a latent fingerprint is deposited on a rough surface, such as the grip of a gun or a window screen, the minutiae are not recorded in detail. The pattern is interrupted by the texture of the surface.

When friction ridges come into contact with a nonporous item, a fingerprint may be deposited on the surface. It will stay on the surface unless it is wiped off or obliterated by environmental or other physical forces. That makes fingerprints on nonporous surfaces fairly fragile. Both chemical reagents and fingerprint powders are used to develop fingerprints on nonporous substrates. Since fingerprints are mostly composed of sweat, they are easily absorbed into porous substrates. Therefore, they are more stable than latent prints deposited on nonporous items. These fingerprints are developed using chemical reagents that permeate the substrate (Figure 6.5).

6.4   Aging Latent Prints

In some cases, an investigator may want to know how long the latent fingerprint has been on a surface. For example, a fingerprint recovered from the interior of a stolen vehicle is identified to a suspect. The suspect insists he did not steal the car. Instead, he asserts he test-drove that exact car a year prior. How can we test his assertion? Is it possible to "age" fingerprints or determine how long they have persisted on a surface? As of the publication date of this text, there is no scientific method for directly dating latent print residues.

Sometimes, it is possible to date a latent print indirectly because of the circumstances in which it is deposited. For example, a patent print left in blood must have been made while the source of the blood was still wet after the wound was made. Thinly deposited blood will dry within minutes. In another example, a small piece of broken glass at a crime scene is found to have the suspect's thumb on one side and index finger on the opposite side. The only way that could happen is if the suspect picked up the fragment after the glass was broken (see Chapter 15).

There are many factors that contribute to how long a latent print will persist on a surface, including the chemical composition of the latent print, the nature and condition of the substrate, and the environment. Immediately after a latent fingerprint is placed on a surface, it begins to change. The chemical compounds in sweat degrade. There are hundreds of chemical compounds present in eccrine and sebaceous excretory deposits. The components and ratios of these compounds are unique to the individual and are based on many different factors, including diet, age, sex, health, metabolism, occupation, and stress. The environmental factors that affect latent print persistence include temperature, humidity, exposure to sunlight, and weather. Surfaces may also have an impact on the persistence of latent prints. Some of those variables include surface texture, cleanliness, shape, porosity, and temperature.

Research projects have focused on finding a stable component of latent print residue and determining how the optical, electrostatic, and chemical properties change over time.[3,7–12] Some of those components identified are saturated fatty acids and wax esters.[3,8–10] Research continues in the area of aging latent fingerprints. A challenge researchers face is the number of variables involved in this process, only some of which are listed earlier. However, new technologies with better sensitivity may allow researchers to control for most of the aforementioned variables and find a nondestructive method of aging latent fingerprints on a surface.

6.5 DNA from Fingerprints

Just like fingerprints, DNA recovered from crime scenes and evidentiary items can be identified to an individual. Advances in DNA analysis have made it possible to obtain DNA evidence from items that have been touched, regardless of the substrate they are deposited on. Whether the substrate is rough or smooth, porous or nonporous, fingerprints can be sampled for DNA. This type of DNA is known as *touch DNA*.[13]

Since the 1980s, samples of biological evidence from crime scenes have been analyzed for DNA. Initially, biological material could only yield a DNA profile if the sample size was 250 ng or more or visible to the human eye.[14] Over time, the technology and sensitivity of DNA analysis improved allowing for the collection of smaller samples from crime scenes and evidentiary items. Biological evidence no longer needs to be visible to be collected for DNA analysis.

When an individual touches a surface, skin cells are shed and may adhere to the surface. Humans shed tens of thousands of skin cells daily.[13] Skin cells are invisible to the naked eye. A sample with a mass of less than 100 pg can yield a DNA profile.[15] (1 pg is one trillionth of a gram.) Extensive research has shown that touch DNA can successfully be recovered from latent fingerprints on various surfaces, as well as from weapons, vehicles, clothing, wood, fabric, glass, briefcase handles, pens, car keys, locker handles, telephone

Figure 6.6 A forensic scientist swabs the grip of a weapon to obtain a sample for DNA analysis.

handsets, doorbells, chocolate bars, electrical cords, knife handles, glass, gloves, paper, and other items.[13-18]

Touched surfaces that are rough or otherwise unsuited to preserving fingerprint patterns are excellent sample areas for collecting touch DNA evidence. Examples of unsuitable surfaces include textured gun and knife grips, clothing, and rough, unfinished wood. These areas are swabbed with a wet sterile swab, the epithelial cells are lifted from the material with adhesive tape, or the area is scraped with a sterile razor blade (Figure 6.6).[9] However, one does not have to choose whether to collect fingerprints or DNA from a surface. With the increased sensitivity of DNA, fingerprint examiners have the option of swabbing latent fingerprints that have no value for identification. Any unusable, smudged, or poor quality fingerprint can be swabbed for DNA with a sterile swab wetted with distilled water.

Because touch DNA requires so little material to be viable, it is particularly subject to contamination. Even the act of breathing on an item can result in DNA transference. Where it appears that DNA processing may be utilized, fingerprint examiners and crime scene technicians must take great care to change gloves frequently, wear particulate masks to cover the mouth, and limit handling of evidentiary items. Even the act of dusting a crime scene for fingerprints using a standard fiberglass fingerprint brush and fingerprint powder may contaminate the scene. Disposable powder packets and fingerprint brushes are used to avoid contamination.[15]

The analysis of touch DNA is not a common practice nor is it entirely reliable. Because of the minute amount of DNA present in touch samples, it is subject to both false-positive and false-negative results. It is also subject to contamination. The vast majority of laboratories do not analyze touch DNA. However, as research on the topic progresses, it may be used as an investigative tool more frequently in the future.

6.6   I Had a Case: Aging Latent Fingerprints

(Submitted by Ken Moses, Forensic Identification Services [retired, San Francisco Police Department])

Burglars in San Francisco broke into the Harley Davidson Motorcycle shop late on Sunday night. Entry had been gained by sawing through the sheetrock wall of an adjacent shop. The safe in the office was forcibly entered with chisels and sledgehammers that were then left at the scene. Due to all the dirty and greasy surfaces, the only latent print found by investigators was on a compartment door inside the safe. When dusted with powder, this print looked dark and "fresh" and lifted off easily with tape.

The next day, the print from the safe was searched in AFIS and identified to the right thumb of a suspect. When investigators contacted the Harley Davidson store to ask them if they know this suspect, the owner stated, "Yes, he used to work here but he died six years ago." The death was confirmed, but for some reason, the person's fingerprints were never purged from the system.

The lesson learned is that it is most often impossible to state when a particular latent print was deposited on a surface, even though it may look "fresh."

6.7   Chapter Summary

There are three types of unknown fingerprints found at crime scenes: latent, patent, and plastic fingerprints. Plastic prints are fingerprint molds in a soft material such as clay or wax. Patent prints are fingerprints that are visible to the naked eye where the matrix is a visible material such as blood or paint. Latent fingerprints are invisible fingerprints formed when a matrix deposits a friction ridge pattern on a substrate. The matrix is composed of eccrine sweat from the friction ridge pores, sebaceous sweat from touching other parts of your body such as your face and hair, and/or contaminants from the environment such as lotions, cosmetics, or grease. Latent fingerprints must be developed, or processed, to make them visible. It is not possible to determine how long the fingerprint has been on a surface. It is possible to extract touch DNA from latent fingerprints.

Review Questions

1. How is a patent fingerprint different from a plastic fingerprint? Give an example of each.
2. What are the duties of an LPE?
3. What is the fingerprint matrix?
4. What are the possible components of latent fingerprint residue?
5. What is eccrine sweat composed of?
6. Is it possible to determine how long a latent fingerprint has been present on a surface? Why, or why not?
7. What is touch DNA?
8. How is touch DNA collected from an item?
9. How can the LPE avoid DNA contamination when searching for, processing, collecting, and analyzing fingerprint evidence?

References

1. Doyle, AC. 1903. The adventure of the Norwood builder. In *The Return of Sherlock Holmes*. London, U.K.: The Strand Magazine.
2. *Merriam-Webster Dictionary*. 2013. s. v. "rigor mortis". www.merriam-webster.com. Accessed June 4, 2014.
3. Ramotowski, R. 2001. Composition of latent print residue. In Lee, HC. and Gaensslen, R.E. (eds.), *Advances in Fingerprint Technology*, 2nd edn. Boca Raton, FL: Taylor & Francis.
4. Fawcett, D. and Jensh, R. 2002. *Bloom and Fawcett's Concise Histology*, 2nd edn. London, U.K.: Hodder Arnold.
5. DePaoli, G. et al. 2010. Photo- and thermal-degradation studies of select eccrine fingerprint constituents. *J. Forensic Sci.* 55(4): 962–969.
6. Fregeau, C., Germain, O., and Fourney, R. 2000. Fingerprint enhancement revisited and the effects of blood enhancement chemicals on subsequent *Profiler Plus*™ fluorescent short tandem repeat DNA analysis of fresh and aged bloody fingerprints. *J. Forensic Sci.* 45(2): 354–380.
7. Menzel, E. 1992. Fingerprint age determination by fluorescence. Letter to the editor. *J. Forensic Sci.* 37(5): 1212–1213.
8. Mong, G., Petersen, C., and Clauss, T. 1999. *Advanced Fingerprint Analysis Project: Fingerprint Constituents, PNNL-13019*. Richland, WA: Pacific Northwest National Laboratory.
9. Wertheim, K. 2003. Fingerprint age determination: Is there any hope? *J. Forensic Identif.* 53(1): 42–49.
10. Koenig, A., Girod, A., and Weyermann, C. 2011. Identification of wax esters in latent print residues by gas chromatography-mass spectrometry and their potential use as aging parameters. *J. Forensic Identif.* 61(6): 652–676.
11. Watson, P. et al. 2011. Imaging electrostatic fingerprints with implications for a forensic timeline. *Forensic Sci. Int.* 209(1–3): 41–45.
12. Ronny, M. et al. 2012. On non-invasive 2D and 3D chromatic white light image sensors for age determination of latent fingerprints. *Forensic Sci. Int.* 222(1–3): 52–70.
13. Williamson, A. 2011. Touch DNA: Forensic collection and application to investigations. *J. Assoc. Crime Scene Reconstr.* 2012(18): 1–5.
14. Wickenheiser, R. 2002. Trace DNA: A review, discussion of theory, and application of the transfer of trace quantities of DNA through skin contact. *J. Forensic Sci.* 47(3): 442–450.
15. Kopka, J. et al. 2011. New optimized DNA extraction protocol for fingerprints deposited on a special self-adhesive security seal and other latent samples used for human identification. *J. Forensic Sci.* 56(5): 1235–1240.
16. Daly, D., Murphy, C., and McDermott, S. 2012. The transfer of touch DNA from hands to glass, fabric and wood. *Forensic Sci. Int. Genet.* 6(1): 41–46.
17. Azoury, M., Zamir, A. et al. 2002. The Effect of 1,2-Indanedione, a latent fingerprint reagent on subsequent DNA profiling. *J. Forensic Sci.* 47(3): 586–588.
18. Van Oorschot, R. and Jones, M. 1997. DNA fingerprints from fingerprints. *Nature* 387(6635): 767.
19. Wertheim, K. and Maceo, A. 2002. The critical stage of friction ridge pattern formation. *J. Forensic Identif.* 52(1): 37.

Biometrics
Livescan and AFIS

7

Names can be fraudulently changed; faces can be altered, identities hidden, histories covered. Fingerprints, however, do not change. Fingerprints link a person to a history, even if the history states that there is no history.

Peter Komarinski[1]

Key Terms

- Biometrics
- Automated Fingerprint Identification System (AFIS)
- Livescan terminal
- Next Generation Identification (NGI)
- Integrated Automated Fingerprint Identification System (IAFIS)
- Tenprint examiner
- Coding
- Feature extraction
- Candidates
- Unsolved latent database

Learning Objectives

- Define the key terms.
- Explain biometrics and give examples of modern applications of biometrics.
- Describe how computers have revolutionized the forensic sciences.
- Explain why it is important to take high-quality, comprehensive exemplar fingerprints.
- Describe AFIS and explain how it was developed.
- Explain the role of the tenprint examiner and the latent print examiner.
- Describe how latent prints are searched in AFIS.
- List the future developments that will improve AFIS.

7.1 Biometrics

Criminal identification has come a long way since the days of Bertillonage and its anatomical measurement methods. Anthropometry was the first method of criminal identification using biological characteristics. Fingerprints soon replaced anthropometry as more reliable means of individualization. Fingerprints are an example of a *biometric. Biometrics* (from the root words "bio" meaning life and "metric" meaning measure) refers to using unique biological measurements or features to identify individuals.

Computers not only have made fingerprint acquisition, comparison, and storage more efficient and effective but have also expanded the field of biometrics to a wide array of biological measurements beyond fingerprints. There are many examples of forensic biometrics other than fingerprints you may be familiar with: handwriting, odontology (examining the unique features of teeth), anthropology, and DNA. Examples of modern digital biometrics include the following: iris scans, retinal scans, facial recognition, voiceprint identification, gait pattern, hand geometry, and vascular patterns.[2–6] Iris scans capture the unique patterns in the pigmented section of the eye (Figure 7.1). Retinal scans detect the vascular patterns in the interior rear surface of the eye. Facial recognition software analyzes the contours of the face. Voiceprint identification captures the unique patterns of speech. Gait pattern analysis captures the unique patterns in the way we walk. Hand geometry captures the unique shapes of our hands. And vascular pattern biometrics measures the pattern of veins and capillaries in various parts of the hand.

A photograph on a driver's license or passport is a simple biometric used to confirm your identity. A driver's license with a photograph can be forged. If a fingerprint is attached to that driver's license, it becomes a more potent form of identification. It is possible to embed biometrics such as fingerprints to all types of identification cards. Biometrics is the future of personal security and fraud prevention.

As shown earlier, biometrics are not limited to forensic analysis. Walt Disney World in Orlando, Florida, requires its pass holders to scan their fingerprints to prove their identity upon entry to the park (Figure 7.2). All foreign visitors entering the United Arab Emirates at Abu Dhabi airport are subjected to iris scans to ensure that previously expelled individuals or individuals on a watch list or wanted list do not enter the country illegally.

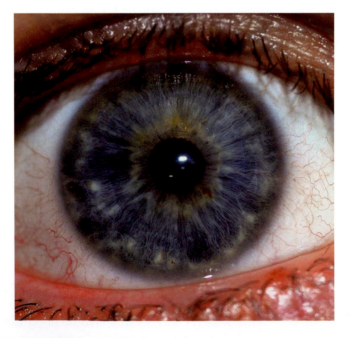

Figure 7.1 The iris, or colored portion, of the eye contains unique patterns that can be used for identification, similar to a fingerprint.

Figure 7.2 Biometric fingerprint scanners at Walt Disney World in Orlando, Florida.

Schools and retailers are testing the possibility of using fingerprint scanners to pay for food and other items. Biometrics can be used to combat illegal activities such as fraud, forgery, and identity theft. Biometrics are the future of secure, efficient, and convenient access to all types of services we use in our daily lives.

Fingerprints are still the most common biometric used for criminal identification around the world. Fingerprints were the first biometric to be digitized for analysis by a computer. The computer system that stores the fingerprint databases and searches for matches both to known and to unknown fingerprints is known as the *Automated Fingerprint Identification System (AFIS)*. AFIS is used not only to identify criminals but also to perform criminal background checks on job applicants, teachers, taxi drivers, etc.[1] There are two main purposes of AFIS as a law enforcement tool. One purpose is to determine if an individual has been arrested before, regardless of the name or history they provide. The other purpose is to search for matches to latent fingerprints collected from crime scenes.

7.2   Livescan

In order for the AFIS to perform its duties, the fingerprints must first be captured and converted to a language the computer can read. If an inked tenprint card is available, that card can be scanned into the AFIS computer on a flatbed scanner. As mentioned in Chapter 5, a livescan device can also be used to capture the necessary fingerprint images digitally. The livescan is similar to a document scanner in that it creates a digitized replica of the fingerprint. The fingerprint will appear on the screen in black and white and will appear similar to a tenprint card, with black ridges on a white background (Figure 7.3). The fingerprints are taken using the same process for inked tenprint cards. Each finger is

Figure 7.3 A fingerprint scanned at a livescan terminal appears on the screen of the computer monitor.

rolled, starting with the number one finger, from nail to nail. Then the flats and thumbs are recorded.

Many law enforcement agencies have *livescan terminals*. These may simply consist of a scanner for recording fingerprint images, a computer monitor to view the images, and a keyboard for recording demographic and criminal information. There are many vendors who build and maintain different types of terminals. While they look different, most of these terminals function similarly.

The image must be recorded at a high-enough resolution to result in a high-quality reproduction. Taking a comprehensive record of the known fingerprints, either with ink or via a livescan, is the most crucial step for successfully utilizing AFIS technology. If the initial acquisition is poor, if the prints are not rolled nail to nail, if the hands are transposed, or if the quality of the images is poor, then a latent fingerprint may never be identified to the corresponding suspect record prints. The latent may be any portion of friction ridge skin from any part of the finger, finger joint, or palm.

There is some debate among the fingerprint community about whether inked tenprint cards are better than livescan prints. Many latent fingerprint examiners prefer inked prints. They argue that inked prints have more detail and look better under a magnifying glass. Livescan images are made up of pixels, which are essentially tiny monochromatic squares. When magnified, the images may appear "pixelated." The same thing happens when you zoom in on a small picture file, resulting in a blurry, indistinct image. Livescan proponents argue that newer versions of livescan, which record the prints at a high resolution, have negated this problem.

There are several advantages to livescan. The records are stored electronically, so there is no longer a need for warehouses with filing cabinets full of tenprint cards (Figure 7.4). The process is also faster than inking individual tenprint cards since no medium is necessary to record the friction ridges. This also makes it a cleaner process. The fingers are

Figure 7.4 Filing cabinets for tenprint cards.

simply rolled across the scanner. The fingerprints are immediately shared with other agencies and departments. City, county, state, and federal agencies receive copies of the fingerprint record electronically. It is no longer necessary to ink several copies of a tenprint card to mail off to other agencies. There is some quality control in that the computer can reject prints that are not adequate, though no computer can replace human decision making in this regard.

As with most technology, the quality and efficiency of these livescan devices have improved over the years and will continue to improve. Computers have historically become better, faster, more portable, and cheaper with time. This is true for personal computers, which were at one time prohibitively expensive. Many people now carry smart phones, which are essentially handheld computers. Similarly, livescan technology has become increasingly available to law enforcement agencies that may not have been able to afford the technology in the recent past.

7.3   History of AFIS

The current, efficient use of fingerprints as a biometrics is only possible due to the advent of the silicone microchip, and consequently the computer, in the early 1970s.[1,7] A computer is a device that can be programmed to carry out complex arithmetic equations or logical sequences much faster than a human can and with greater accuracy. It can also perform multiple functions at the same time. The computer therefore showed great promise for solving the problem of the overwhelming volume of tenprint cards that required humans to classify, file, and search by hand.

Law enforcement agencies' identification bureaus employed fingerprint examiners who were responsible for classifying, filing, and searching for tenprint cards by hand. The FBI's identification bureau, known as the Identification Division, was established in 1924 "to provide a central repository of criminal identification data for law enforcement agencies. The original collection of fingerprint records contained 810,188 records."[7] The technicians employed in the Identification Division were responsible for classifying, filing, and searching approximately 30,000 tenprint cards submitted by law enforcement agencies around the country every day. The manpower necessary to sustain this ever-expanding repository would soon reach critical mass.

The AFIS computer was developed to address this problem. A computer can store an abundance of information in a small space. It can perform simultaneous functions, unlike a human who has to perform one task at a time. It can work quickly and efficiently 24 h per day, 7 days per week, 365 days per year. As of 2012, the FBI's criminal fingerprint database known as *Next Generation Identification (NGI)*, formerly known as *Integrated Automated Fingerprint Identification System (IAFIS)*, contained more than 70 million criminal files: over 700 million individual fingerprints. And it gets bigger every day. Identification bureaus would have had to employ tens of thousands of individuals to keep up with the volume of work.

The United States, France, Canada, the United Kingdom, and Japan all developed computer systems to address the needs of overwhelmed and unsustainable identification bureaus.[1,7] The Royal Canadian Mounted Police put a system into place in 1977.[1] The city of San Francisco was the first jurisdiction to use the AFIS on a routine basis in the United States (Figure 7.5).

When the citizens of San Francisco were asked whether they wanted a fingerprint computer, they approved the ballot proposition with an 80% majority.[7] An AFIS system was installed in 1983 and a new unit, called Crime Scene Investigations, was formed.[7] Crime scene investigators were trained in the use of the system and searched their own cases when they recovered fingerprints from crime scenes. Over the next 2 years, the "San Francisco experiment" resulted in a dramatic increase in fingerprint identifications.[7] Ten times as many fingerprints found at crime scenes were identified to suspects over 2 years.[7] The burglary rate decreased by 26% over the next 4 years.[7]

The experiment was a great success that resulted in the proliferation of AFIS systems in law enforcement agencies nationwide and around the world. In 1992, IAFIS imported 32 million fingerprint cards into its database. In 1997, the United Kingdom installed its own national AFIS database. Thirty years after the advent of AFIS, most law enforcement

Figure 7.5 A San Francisco Police Department Crime Scene Investigations Unit patch.

agencies use the system routinely, and few fingerprint examiners are trained to classify prints using the Henry system.

7.4   Tenprint Searches

One of the main functions of AFIS is to store, classify, and search tenprint records from arrests. When an individual is arrested, his fingerprints are taken either in ink on a tenprint card or by a livescan. The suspect's palm prints and mug shot may also be taken at this time. Demographic and other identifying information are recorded. Descriptions of other individualizing marks such as scars, marks, and tattoos may also be recorded and/or photographed. The fingerprints will then be classified, or coded, by the computer and searched in the database. If the computer locates a candidate file with matching fingerprints, a *tenprint examiner* will confirm the match. A tenprint examiner is an individual whose job is to confirm tenprint matches by the AFIS computer and manage the database.

One of the most important aspects of this function is the *coding* of the fingerprint by the computer. The fingerprint is coded when the computer picks out the minutiae in the fingerprint. This is known as *feature extraction*. The AFIS computer is programmed with an algorithm that recognizes minutiae. It can also recognize the direction of ridge flow, the distance between ridges, and how many ridges are between minutiae. The computer searches through the database and returns candidates that have similar features in similar positions. There can be 100 or more minutiae in a rolled fingerprint. In a latent print, however, there are far fewer minutiae since it is deposited unintentionally on a variety of substrates. A latent fingerprint may be a fingertip, delta, palm print fragment, or an entire hand.

7.5   Latent Print Searches

The second major function of AFIS is to enter, code, and search latent fingerprints against the tenprint database (as well as the unsolved latent [UL] database). A latent print, unlike a rolled fingerprint, is deposited unintentionally. The fingerprint may be of poor quality, smudged, or distorted. It may have been left on a curved or rough surface. It may be the side of a finger or a fingertip. If a latent print is recovered from a crime scene, but there is no suspect to compare it to, it can be searched in the AFIS database. It is up to the latent print examiner to determine whether a latent fingerprint will be searched in AFIS.

In order to search a latent print against the AFIS tenprint database, the database of all known fingerprint records in a given jurisdiction, the latent print must be first entered into the computer. The fingerprint can be either scanned on a document scanner or photographed. The latent print will appear on the computer screen. The latent print examiner will enter the case number, agency, and any other data pertaining to the case at hand. The latent print examiner can also instruct the computer which finger or hand to search, if known, and can also tell the computer what fingerprint pattern type to search for.

The latent print examiner rotates the fingerprint so it is in the proper position with the top of the finger at the top of the screen. The latent print is centered. In some systems, the core and delta(s) are selected. Next, the computer codes the fingerprint minutiae. The latent

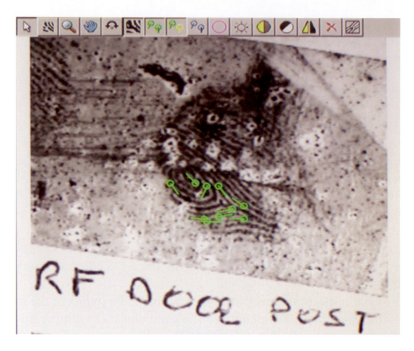

Figure 7.6 This latent lift card was scanned into AFIS. The minutiae (green circles) were selected by the latent print examiner. The green lines indicate the directionality of the minutiae.

print examiner double checks the minutiae picked out by the computer. The examiner choose to add more minutiae the computer missed. Or she may deselect minutiae the computer picked that may be questionable or inaccurate (Figure 7.6).

When the latent print examiner is satisfied with the latent print, the search is launched. The computer will return a list of *candidates*. A candidate is an individual whose exemplar fingerprint is recognized by the computer as having a similar arrangement of minutiae as the latent fingerprint. The latent print examiner then compares the latent print to the known prints of each candidate. If a match is found, it is recorded, and another latent print examiner verifies the match (Figure 7.7). It is important to know that the latent print examiner, not the computer, decides whether an AFIS record matches an unknown fingerprint from a crime scene.

If the latent fingerprint does not match any records in the AFIS database, the latent print examiner can then choose to search it against the *UL database*. This database stores all unidentified latent fingerprints entered into the database. While this may not result in identification to a suspect, it may lead to information linking several crime scenes. If the latent print does not match another unidentified latent print, it can be saved, along with the accompanying case data, into the UL database for future searches. Every new tenprint card entered into AFIS is searched against the UL database. If the computer finds a match, the case will be forwarded to a latent print examiner who will verify the identification. Approximately 10%–15% of all cases and 2%–3% of latent print searches result in a fingerprint match.[1]

An increase in tenprint records entered into AFIS will not necessarily increase the probability of a fingerprint match. With AFIS, the quality of the tenprint records is

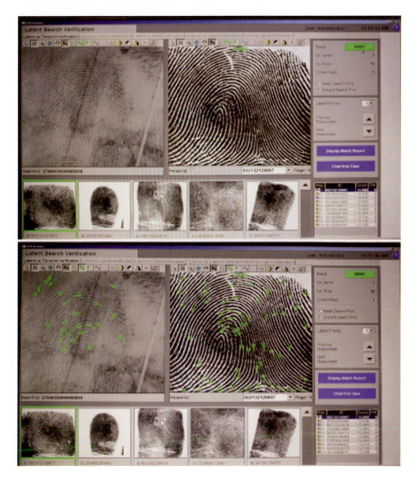

Figure 7.7 This latent lift was scanned into AFIS and identified to a suspect. The identification is shown with (bottom) and without (top) minutiae selected.

more important than the quantity of records in the system. If a latent fingerprint is the left side and left delta of the right thumb, but the thumbprint on the tenprint card was not recorded "nail to nail," that latent fingerprint may never be identified and the case never solved. This is why it is so important to record quality, comprehensive known fingerprints.

7.6   Future of AFIS

As we rely more and more on computing in our daily lives, we must remember that the technology is only as good as the people who build the systems, write the algorithms, run the machines, and conduct the analyses of the data. As with all computers, the future of AFIS is smaller, faster, and more accurate systems (Figure 7.8). Coding algorithms will improve, resulting in improved minutiae selection by the computer. Just as the computer became more affordable with time, allowing individuals to own personal computers, so too do the AFIS computers become more affordable for agencies that may not have been able to afford previous systems.

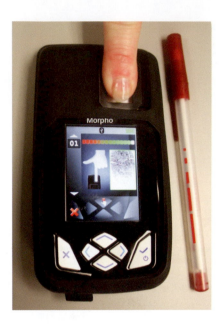

Figure 7.8 A mobile ID unit.

It is certain that as the population of the world increases, so will the number of arrests. AFIS systems will have to keep up with this trend with faster turnaround times for searches and larger database capacities. One way to increase the effectiveness and accuracy of AFIS is to provide extensive training and retraining to anyone who uses AFIS: latent print examiners, law enforcement officers, tenprint examiners, etc. This will ensure that the images captured are of the highest quality, rolled from nail to nail, and that the input of data is thorough and consistent.

The success of AFIS depends on the people who use it every day. Only a fingerprint analyst can identify a latent fingerprint. A computer cannot make the final determination about whether a latent fingerprint and a known fingerprint come from the same source. It is also important to remember that there are people behind these fingerprints: people with lives and families who may depend on them. Just because a fingerprint is identified through the AFIS criminal database does not mean that an individual is guilty of that particular crime. A guiding tenet of our criminal justice system is that all people are innocent until proven guilty.

7.7   Chapter Summary

Biometrics refers to using unique biological measurements or features for personal identification. Digital records can be recorded, codified, and searched by computers. The most utilized biometric in the criminal justice system is the fingerprint. Fingerprint exemplars captured via a livescan device or with ink must be comprehensive and of good quality. If the initial record acquisition is poor, if the prints are not rolled nail to nail, if the hands are transposed, or if the quality of the images is poor, then a latent fingerprint may never be identified to the corresponding suspect record prints. The AFIS was developed after the advent of the computer. This system can digitally analyze, store, and search for fingerprints. Its two main functions are to store, classify, and search tenprint records from arrests and to enter, code, and search latent fingerprints against the tenprint database and UL database. Both functions require specialized personnel and are not performed by the computer alone.

Review Questions

1. What is biometrics?
2. What are some examples of forensic biometrics? What are some examples of modern digital biometrics?
3. What is a livescan terminal, and what is its use in the criminal justice system?
4. Why is it important to take high-quality, comprehensive exemplar fingerprints?
5. What is AFIS?
6. What invention of the twentieth century made AFIS possible?
7. What are the two main functions of AFIS?
8. What is the future of AFIS?

References

1. Komarinski, P. 2005. *Automated Fingerprint Identification Systems (AFIS)*. New York: Elsevier Academic Press.
2. Jain, A. and Pankanti, S. 2001. Automated fingerprint identification and imaging systems. In Henry, L. and Gaensslen, R.E. (eds.), *Advances in Fingerprint Technology*, 2nd edn. Boca Raton, FL: Taylor & Francis, pp. 275–326.
3. Jain, A., Ross, A., and Nandakumar, K. 2011. *Introduction to Biometrics*. New York: Springer.
4. Van Der Lugt, C. et al. 2006. Earprints. In Sue, B. and Tim, T. (eds.), *Forensic Human Identification*, Boca Raton, FL: Taylor & Francis.
5. Hardy, J. 2006. Odontology. In Sue, B. and Tim, T. (eds.), *Forensic Human Identification*, Boca Raton, FL: Taylor & Francis.
6. Grant, M. 2006. Gait. In Sue, B. and Tim, T. (eds.), *Forensic Human Identification*, Boca Raton, FL: Taylor & Francis.
7. Moses, K. 2011. Automated fingerprint identification system. In *The Fingerprint Sourcebook*. The Scientific Working Group on Friction Ridge Analysis, Study and Technology (SWGFAST) et al. Washington, DC: National Institute of Justice, U.S. Department of Justice, Office of Justice Programs.

Fingerprint Processing

II

Introduction to Processing Methods

8

Key Terms

- Eccrine glands
- Sebaceous glands
- Porous
- Nonporous
- Semiporous
- Sequential processing methods
- Physical processing methods
- Chemical processing methods
- Material safety data sheet (MSDS)
- Safety data sheets (SDSs)
- Nitrile gloves
- Safety glasses
- Particulate or ventilated mask
- Fume hood
- Downflow workstation
- Flammables cabinet
- Sequential processing
- Standard operating procedures (SOPs)

Learning Objectives

- Define the key terms.
- Understand how fingerprint residues react with porous, nonporous, and semiporous substrates.
- Explain physical and chemical processing methods.
- Describe health and safety concerns and how to avoid exposure.
- Understand how to handle evidence properly.
- Understand how fingerprint reagents affect DNA processing.

8.1 Matrices and Substrates

Because latent fingerprints are invisible, they must be processed, or developed, to make them visible. Once they are visualized, they are documented and analyzed. There are four major limitations that affect the quality of prints recovered from the crime scene or items of evidence:

- Condition of the substrate (texture and permeability)
- Environmental effects (dry, humid, rain, wind, etc.)
- Quantity of latent print material deposited
- Method(s) of development, documentation, and collection

Recall that latent fingerprint deposits are composed of 98% water, lipids (fatty acids, cholesterol, squalene, and triglycerides), amino acids and proteins, environmental contaminants (lotions, soaps, cosmetics, etc.), and the products of environmental chemical reactions following deposition.[1–4] The majority of these components are metabolic excretory products from the pores of *eccrine glands*, which are the sweat glands most abundant along friction ridge structures. Champod et al. state, "Secretions from eccrine and apocrine glands are mixtures of inorganic salts and water-soluble organic components that result in a water-soluble deposit (WSD). Secretions from sebaceous glands consist of a semisolid mixture of fats, waxes and long-chain alcohols that result in a non-water-soluble deposit (NWSD)."[5] *Sebaceous glands*, associated with hair follicles, are most abundant on areas of the skin that perspire, especially the scalp and face.[1,4] When one touches the face or scalp, the oils from these areas are transferred to the friction ridges of the fingers and palms.[4]

A latent fingerprint generally consists of both water-soluble and water-insoluble material. After a latent is placed on a surface, it is subject to environmental effects, and its composition begins to change. The water constituent begins to evaporate when exposed to the air. A latent print can lose nearly 98% of its original weight within 72 h of deposition. Arid, hot, and windy climates can speed up this process. Rain can dilute or obliterate a latent. Inorganic latent components may also produce a chemical reaction with the substrate, such as an oxidation reaction that may cause a fingerprint to be etched onto a metal surface. The substrate the latent is deposited on also contributes to the "staying power" as well as the changes in composition that occur. *Porous* substrates such as paper, cardboard, or raw wood are absorbant. Just as a sheet of paper will absorb water, so too will a sheet of paper absorb latent print deposits. As soon as the latent print is absorbed into the material, the water begins to evaporate, but the residual components remain in the fibrous matrix of the porous substrate (Figure 8.1).[6]

On *nonporous* substrates such as glass, metal, or plastic, latent prints remain on the surface (Figure 8.2).[6] They are therefore exposed to the elements and are more fragile than latent fingerprint deposits that are absorbed into the substrate. *Semiporous* items such as magazines, wax-coated paper cups, photographs, glossy paint, or painted/varnished wood absorb the water-soluble deposits much more slowly than porous items.[5] The water-insoluble components sit on the surface.[5] In this way, semiporous surfaces have the properties of both porous and nonporous substrates.

8.2   Fingerprint Development

Latent fingerprints are made visible using a variety of optical, chemical, and physical development procedures. These development techniques initially arose from trial and error.[3] As science progressed, specializations developed in the form of numerous subdisciplines

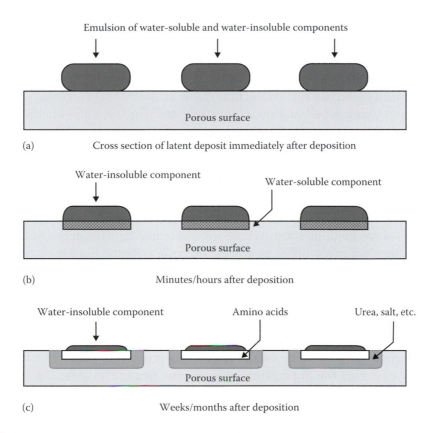

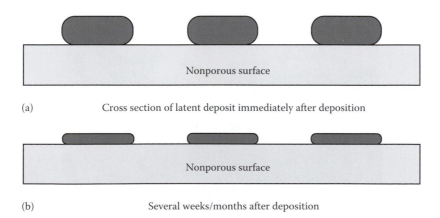

Figure 8.1 A cross section of fingerprint residues deposited on a porous substrate such as paper. When the fingerprint is deposited on the surface (a), the water-soluble components are absorbed into the substrate (b) and the water-insoluble components remain on the surface (c). (Reprinted from Champod, C., *Fingerprints and Other Ridge Skin Impressions*, Taylor & Francis, Boca Raton, FL, 2004, Figure 4.1. With permission.)

Figure 8.2 A cross section of fingerprint residues deposited on a nonporous substrate such as glass. When the fingerprint is deposited on the surface (a), both the water-soluble and water-insoluble components remain on the surface (b). (Reprinted from Champod, C., *Fingerprints and Other Ridge Skin Impressions*, Taylor & Francis, Boca Raton, FL, 2004, Figure 4.2. With permission.)

dedicated to addressing increasingly specific issues with latent fingerprint development. Contributions from these scientific subdisciplines have led to improved methods for developing latents. This burgeoning sophistication has both improved existing methods of development and generated novel techniques.[4]

There are many powders and chemical reagents available for processing latent fingerprints on porous, semiporous, and nonporous surfaces. There are also chemical reagents available for enhancing patent (visible) fingerprints in blood or grease. The type of processing method you choose will depend on the condition and type of substrate as well as the composition of the latent fingerprint.

Research in the field of fingerprint analysis is focused on finding chemical reagents that react with the various components of eccrine and sebaceous sweat to develop latent fingerprints and make them visible. The resulting visible fingerprint may produce a specific color, or it may be fluorescent, visible with alternate light sources (ALSs) or lasers (Figure 8.3). There are many different processing options. Some have proven superior to others, and many historically popular chemical reagents are no longer in common use. Most items of evidence can be processed with multiple chemical reagents, as long as those reagents are used in a specific order. See Appendix A for a list of *sequential processing methods* for various types of evidence.

Fingerprint development techniques are often broken down into *physical processing methods* and *chemical processing methods*. Physical processing implies that the scientist physically enhances the fingerprint using various fingerprint powders and brushes. Chemical processing refers to the use of chemical reagents. This text further subdivides fingerprint development techniques into four categories: physical processing methods, chemical processing methods on porous substrates, chemical processing methods on nonporous substrates, and "other" chemical processing methods. "Other" chemical processing methods will address how to develop bloody or greasy fingerprints, fingerprints on firearms, fingerprints on the adhesive side of tape, and other processing methods such as vacuum metal deposition. See Appendix B for a list of formulations for fingerprint reagents.

Figure 8.3 An ALS.

8.3 Health and Safety

It is important to remember health and safety considerations when any physical or chemical development technique is used. Even the use of the ALS or laser requires attention to safety protocols. Exposure may not have immediate effects, but may cause injury or illness after prolonged use if safety procedures and protocols are not followed. It is easy to get comfortable with the use of many of these methods and thereby become complacent. Your safety should be your number one priority at a crime scene or in a laboratory.

Many black fingerprint powders are made of carbon. Carbon powder is not inherently harmful unless you inhale large amounts of airborne powder on a regular basis, as coal miners do. Coal miners may suffer from a disease called pneumoconiosis, commonly known as "black lung," as a result of carbon dust exposure. Pneumoconiosis is "a disease of the lungs characterized by fibrosis and caused by the chronic inhalation of mineral dusts."[7] The size of the particle determines how deep the inhaled dust penetrates into the lungs and thus how harmful the dust is (Table 8.1).[7–10]

Dust particles less than 5 μm (0.005 mm) in diameter can penetrate all the way to the alveoli, the small sacs deep in the lungs that are responsible for oxygen and carbon dioxide gas exchange.[7] As shown in Table 8.2, most fingerprint powders are greater than 5 μm in width and therefore are unlikely to penetrate deep enough to accumulate in the alveolar sacs. However, extra care must be taken to avoid inhalation when working with white and fluorescent powders. While there has been no link between frequent exposure to fingerprint powders and pneumoconiosis, it is important to be aware of the potential health risks when using fingerprint powders on a regular basis or in a confined area.

Fingerprint powders are not all composed of variations of carbon powder. There are various colors (black, blue, red, white, etc.) and types of fingerprint powders (granular, magnetic, metallic, or fluorescent) that are mixtures of various organic and inorganic components (Figure 8.4). Some fingerprint powders that have historically been available by commercial forensic suppliers contain the following toxic inorganic chemicals: lead,

Table 8.1 Depositional Location of Water-Insoluble Inorganic Particles upon Inhalation

Particle Size (μm)	Deposition Location after Inhalation
>15	Outer nasal passages
10–15	Nasal turbinates and pharynx (the areas just behind the nasal cavity)
5–10	Major airways, trachea, and major stem bronchi
<5	Penetration to alveoli

Table 8.2 Average Particle Sizes for Common Fingerprint Powder Types

Fingerprint Powder Type	Particle Size (Average in μm)
Black	20–33
Black magnetic	11–18
White	0.55–0.85
Fluorescent	1–2.5
Metal flake	10

Figure 8.4 Bronze, gold, and silver fingerprint powder.

mercury, cadmium, copper, silicon, titanium, and bismuth, though it is uncommon to find these powders today.[1] Most known hazardous ingredients are no longer used to make commercial powders; however, one must still exercise caution in order to avoid chronic health issues. Several organic powder formulations have been developed from nontoxic components such as starch, fern spores, calcium sulfate, gum Arabic, Rhodamine B, turmeric, and fluorescein solution (also a bloodstain reagent and a component of many cosmetic products touted to give you a "glow").[1,11,12]

Most of the chemical reagents are not toxic unless absorbed through the skin, ingested, splashed into the eyes, or inhaled. Adherence to basic laboratory safety procedures negates these hazards. Potential health hazards and environmental hazards are listed in the applicable *material safety data sheet (MSDS)* or *safety data sheets (SDSs)* (which will replace the MSDS by 2015 under the new guidelines of the Globally Harmonized System). Reagents such as Rhodamine 6G, crystal violet, and Ardrox are possibly carcinogenic. Cyanoacrylate ester, or superglue, is potentially hazardous as it may release hydrogen cyanide and cyanide gas at high temperatures above 200°C (392°F).[13] Ninhydrin, the most commonly used reagent for developing fingerprints on porous materials, has been used in surgical marking pens and was found to cause eczema or allergic reactions.[14–16]

The general rule when working with chemicals is to limit exposure and adhere to all safety precautions. *Nitrile gloves* should be worn at all times (Figure 8.5). (Remember that even gloved hands can wipe away delicate fingerprints from a nonporous surface if the item is handled on fingerprint-bearing surfaces.) *Safety glasses* with side shields or chemical-resistant safety goggles will protect the eyes (Figure 8.6). A laboratory coat with long sleeves will protect the skin (Figure 8.7). A *particulate or ventilated mask* will prevent excess inhalation (Figure 8.8). Proper ventilation through the use of a *fume hood* (when working with chemical reagents) or *downflow workstation* (when working with powders) will also prevent inhalation. A downflow workstation is similar to a fume hood, but instead of pulling air up through the unit into a filtration system, it pulls air down through a

Figure 8.5 Nitrile glove.

Figure 8.6 Safety glasses.

Figure 8.7 A forensic scientist handles chemical reagents with gloves and a long-sleeved laboratory coat.

Figure 8.8 A particulate mask protects a forensic scientist from inhaling particles such as fingerprint powders.

perforated work surface (Figure 8.9). As soon as fingerprint processing is complete, the hands should be washed thoroughly with soap and water. Clothes should be laundered as soon as possible. These same precautions can also protect you from potentially harmful pathogens from biological evidence. It also protects the evidence from contamination by preventing the transfer of DNA to the evidence.

Chemicals and powders should always be stored properly in a cool, dry place away from open flame. Flammable materials should be stored in a *flammables cabinet* (Figure 8.10). Chemicals should all be properly labeled and MSDS or SDS made available for all reagents

Figure 8.9 A downflow workstation is a fume hood that pulls air and fingerprint dust down through a perforated work surface.

Figure 8.10 Flammable reagents are stored in a flammables cabinet.

used. All chemicals should be disposed of properly. Spills should be cleaned up as recommended by the appropriate MSDS or SDS. Equipment such as fume hoods, eye wash stations, and drench showers should be regularly tested and maintained. Common sense and attentiveness, as well as a general working knowledge of chemistry, should diminish the possibility of exposure or long-term detrimental effects.

Light sources of varying intensities and wavelengths are used extensively in many forensic subdisciplines, and fingerprint analysis is no exception. Just because exposure to light does not immediately cause acute health problems or pain does not mean it is harmless. You have experienced the detrimental effects of ultraviolet (UV) radiation if you have ever experienced sunburn after sitting on the beach too long. ALSs and lasers can cause eye and skin damage. Light of different wavelengths should always be viewed through the appropriate colored filter. Gloves and long-sleeved laboratory coats should be worn at all times. Prolonged skin exposure may lead to skin cancer in the same way that skin cancer may be caused by too much tanning. Regardless of the fingerprint processing or visualization technique used, personal safety is a matter of both education and due diligence.

8.4 General Approach to Evidence Processing

Most items can be processed using more than one chemical reagent or a variety of both physical and chemical processing methods. Some chemical reagents have to be used in a specific order. We call this *sequential processing*, which means the processes must be done in a particular sequence. Some chemicals may inhibit other chemicals. Also, some chemicals are more successful than others and should be used first. Examples of these sequences will be presented in the chapters that follow.

A vast majority of forensic laboratories do not use all the processes described in this text. In fact, most laboratories use only a few reagents. Forensic scientists have preferences based on their professional experience. Laboratories are restricted by their limited budgets. Some laboratories do not have access to certain reagents. Other laboratories have standard operating procedures (SOPs) that outline specific techniques that are used in specific circumstances. Or they are limited by time and have too heavy of a caseload to spend time processing items with multiple reagents. The most commonly utilized development techniques are superglue fuming, fingerprint powdering, and a chemical reagent called ninhydrin. All of these development techniques, and many more, will be described in subsequent chapters. Regardless of the processing method chosen, be it physical or chemical, there are procedures that are used in order to protect the integrity of the evidence and ensure success. Examiners from other disciplines should be consulted prior to processing certain items to prevent damage to or loss of other forensic evidence such as DNA, toolmarks, or trace evidence.

It is important to document every step when you process evidence for fingerprints. Documentation includes taking thorough laboratory notes, taking photographs, filling out the necessary forms, and writing final reports based on your actions and analyses. These documentation methods are discussed in Chapter 14. How you document your cases depends on your agency's *SOPs* and protocols, which vary from one agency to another. The following is an example of general steps that should be followed:

- Remove the evidence from its packaging.
- Photograph the item before processing.
- Visually inspect the surface of interest with optical techniques such as white light, oblique lighting, ALS, laser, and/or reflective ultraviolet imaging system (see Chapter 9).
- Photograph any visible fingerprints.
- Process #1.
- Photograph any visible fingerprints.
- Process #2.
- Photograph any visible fingerprints.
- Process #3.
- Photograph any visible fingerprints.
- Repackage in the original evidence bag or box and seal the package.

8.5 DNA

As DNA technology becomes more and more sensitive, fingerprint examiners must be more careful not to contaminate or degrade a possible source of DNA evidence. Gloves should always be worn and changed frequently. Particulate masks should be worn if the examiner might breathe, sneeze, or cough on the evidence. And only chemical processing methods that will not degrade or destroy DNA evidence should be used if the item will be sent for DNA analysis following fingerprint processing.

Extensive research has been done to examine the effects of each fingerprint reagent on DNA. Recent studies have found that current methods of fingerprint development do not have detrimental effects on DNA. While the yield of DNA may be lower following fingerprint processing, a DNA analyst can still obtain enough DNA for forensic analysis following development with the following common fingerprint reagents: ninhydrin, 1,8-diazafluoren-9-one (DFO), vacuum metal deposition, Amido black, and cyanoacrylate (superglue) fuming.[18–26] DNA recovered after indanedione processing, however, must be done within 6 days.[23] After that time period, DNA is not viable. Most ALSs also had no detrimental effect on DNA processing with the exception of shortwave UV radiation, which is known to degrade DNA.[26] Physical developer, a process for processing fingerprints on porous surfaces, degrades DNA. Physical developer should not be used if DNA analysis is to follow.[26]

8.6 Chapter Summary

The limitations on the quality of fingerprints recovered from the crime scene or items of evidence include the texture and permeability of the substrate, the quantity of material deposited, the composition and age of the latent fingerprint, environmental effects, and the method of development, documentation, and collection. Latent print deposits are mixtures of water-soluble and water-insoluble deposits. Fingerprints placed on porous substrates are absorbed, while fingerprints placed on nonporous substrates sit on the surface and are more easily obliterated.

It is important to adhere to your laboratory's safety procedures and protocols and to educate yourself about all potential hazards. Regardless of the processing method you use, be it physical or chemical, there are procedures you must use in order to protect the integrity of the evidence. This includes handling the evidence responsibly and documenting every step of your analysis. If an item of evidence might be submitted for DNA analysis following fingerprint processing, do not use physical developer or expose the item to shortwave UV radiation.

Review Questions

1. What are four limitations to the quality of prints recovered from the crime scene or items of evidence?
2. Secretions from which glands contribute the most water-insoluble material to the latent print deposit?
3. Secretions from which glands contribute the most water-soluble material to the latent print deposit?
4. Name three or more common porous evidentiary items you may find at a crime scene.
5. Name three or more common nonporous evidentiary items you may find at a crime scene.
6. Name two or more common semiporous evidentiary items you may find at a crime scene.
7. What is one example of a physical processing method?
8. What are three important items of personal protective equipment that must be worn at all times when working in a laboratory environment?
9. What additional item must be worn if you are concerned with DNA contamination or if you are working with biological evidence?

10. What are the general steps that are taken when processing items of evidence for fingerprints?
11. Which two processes commonly used in fingerprint development must not be used if the item is to be submitted for DNA analysis?

References

1. Ramotowski, R. 2001. Composition of latent print residue. In Lee, H.C. and Gaensslen, R.E. (eds.), *Advances in Fingerprint Technology*, 2nd edn., Boca Raton, FL: Taylor & Francis.
2. Bramble, S.K. 1995. Separation of latent fingermark residue by thin-layer chromatography. *J. Forensic Sci.* 400(6): 969–975.
3. Voss-DeHaan, P. 2006. Physics and fingerprints. *Contemp. Phys.* 47(4): 209–230.
4. Moses, H. 2009. A critical comparison of black fingerprint powder formulations to improve latent fingerprint clarity and contrast on common substrates. Masters of Science Thesis, Forensic Sciences Graduate Group. University of California, Davis, CA.
5. Champod, C. et al. 2004. *Fingerprints and Other Ridge Skin Impressions.* Boca Raton, FL: Taylor & Francis.
6. Thomas, G.L. 1978. The physics of fingerprints and their detection. *J. Phys. E. Sci. Instrum.* 1978(11): 722–731.
7. Lang, H. Pneumoconiosis—A disease of the lungs characterized by fibrosis and caused by the chronic inhalation of mineral dusts, especially silica and asbestos. Lecture, West Virginia University, Morgantown, WV, 2008.
8. Bourdon, J.A. et al. 2012. Carbon black nanoparticle instillation induces sustained inflammation and genotoxicity in mouse lung and liver. *Part. Fibre Toxicol.* 2012(9): 5.
9. Kamata, H. et al. 2011. Carbon black nanoparticles enhance bleomycin-induced lung inflammatory and fibrotic changes in mice. *Exp. Biol. Med.* 236(3): 315–324.
10. Jackson, P. et al. 2012. Pulmonary exposure to carbon black by inhalation or instillation in pregnant mice: Effects on liver DNA strand breaks in dams and offspring. *Nanotoxicology* 6(5): 486–500.
11. Yamashita, B. and French, M. 2011. Latent print development. In The Scientific Working Group on Friction Ridge Analysis, Study and Technology (SWGFAST) et al. *The Fingerprint Sourcebook.* Washington, DC: National Institute of Justice, U.S. Department of Justice, Office of Justice Programs.
12. Garg, R., Kumari, H., and Kaur, R. 2011. A new technique for visualization of latent fingerprints on various surfaces using powder from turmeric: A rhizomatous herbaceous plant (*Curcuma longa*). *Egypt. J. Forensic Sci.* 1(1): 53–57.
13. Fung, T. et al. 2011. Investigation of hydrogen cyanide generation from the cyanoacrylate fuming process used for latent fingermark detection. *Forensic Sci. Int.* 1(2011): 143–149.
14. Schlacke, K. and Fuchs, T. 1989. Allergic contact eczema to ninhydrin. *Derm. Beruf. Umwelt.* 37(5): 179–180.
15. Hytonen, M. et al. 1996. Occupational IgE-mediated rhinitis caused by ninhydrin. *Allergy* 51(2): 114–116.
16. Pirila, P. et al. 1997. Rhinitis caused by ninhydrin develops into occupational asthma. *Eur. Respir. J.* 10(8): 1918–1921.
17. Duncan, G.T. et al. 1986. Effects of superglue, other fingerprint developing agents and luminol on bloodstain analysis. *J. Assoc. Off. Anal. Chem.* 69(4): 677–680.
18. Bowen, K. and Wickett, S. 1988. The effects of fingerprinting techniques on bloodgrouping. *Can. Soc. Forensic Sci.* 21(1,2): 29–40.
19. Lee, H. et al. 1989. The effect of presumptive test, latent fingerprint and some other reagents and materials on subsequent serological identification, genetic marker and DNA testing in bloodstains. *J. Forensic Identif.* 39(6): 339–357.

20. Bhoelai, B. et al. 2011. Effect of common fingerprint detection techniques on subsequent STR profiling. *Forensic Sci. Int.-Gen.* 3(1): 429–430.
21. Zamir, A., Oz, C., and Geller, B. 2000. Threat mail and forensic science: DNA profiling from items of evidence after treatment with DFO. *J. Forensic Sci.* 45(2): 445–446.
22. Schultz, M. et al. 2004. Ninhydrin-dyed latent fingerprints as a DNA source in a murder case. *J. Clinical Forensic Med.* 11(4): 202–204.
23. Azoury, M. et al. 2002. The effect of 1,2-indanedione, a latent fingerprint reagent on subsequent DNA profiling. *J. Forensic Sci.* 47(3): 586–588.
24. Presley, L., Baumstark, A., and Dixon, A. 1993. The effects of specific latent fingerprint and questioned document examinations on the amplification and typing of the HLA DQ alpha gene region in forensic casework. *J. Forensic Sci.* 38(5): 1028–1036.
25. Andersen, J. and Bramble, S. 1997. The effects of fingermark enhancement light sources on subsequent PCR-STR DNA analysis of fresh bloodstains. *J. Forensic Sci.* 42(2): 303–306.
26. Shipp, E. et al. 1993. Effects of argon laser light, alternate source light, and cyanoacrylate fuming on DNA typing of human bloodstains. *J. Forensic Sci.* 38(1): 184–191.

Forensic Light Sources

9

Bloodstains, semen, bruises, bone fragments, questioned documents, flammable residues, fibers and fingerprints all merit examination with a forensic light source or laser.[1]

Key Terms

- Oblique lighting
- Visible spectrum
- Atomic number
- Atomic mass
- Photon
- Luminescence
- Fluorescence
- Phosphorescence
- Incident light
- Reflected light
- Scattered light
- Barrier filter
- Forensic light source
- Laser
- Alternate light source
- Reflective ultraviolet imaging system (RUVIS)
- Intensifier

Learning Objectives

- Define the key terms.
- Understand the importance of visually examining evidence.
- Understand the physics of light and how it interacts with matter.
- Distinguish between and understand the applications of the alternate light source, laser, and reflective ultraviolet imaging system.

9.1   Visual Examination

Light is one of the forensic scientist's most potent tools. Regardless of the substrate, matrix, or circumstance, all evidentiary items and surfaces must be visually examined before any chemical or physical process is initiated. Visual examination is a nondestructive

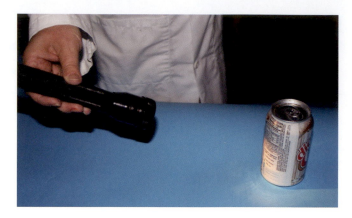

Figure 9.1 A forensic scientist examines an item of evidence with oblique lighting.

process. It allows visible fingerprints to be documented before fingerprint powder or chemicals are applied.

A visual examination is not just performed under white overhead lights or in natural lighting conditions. A variety of light sources are used. A simple flashlight can be used to shine light at various angles to create light and shadow across a surface. *Oblique lighting* is often the best way to see both latent, plastic and patent fingerprints on an object (Figure 9.1). Light is shone at a low angle in order to see details on the surface where light and shadow create contrast. Oblique lighting is used throughout the forensic sciences to observe details in shoe and tire impressions, firearm evidence, toolmarks, and various other types of evidence.

If a thorough visual examination of the surface reveals a fingerprint, that print is photographed. Only then may a fingerprint analyst proceed with chemical and physical processing methods. Visual examination is a nondestructive process. There are several other stages of fingerprint processing when the fingerprint analyst uses light as a nondestructive technique to reveal fingerprints. Besides white light, the fingerprint analyst uses different colors of light, ultraviolet (UV) light, and infrared light to view evidence without obliterating fingerprints.

9.2   Physics of Light

Forensic scientists use light of different colors to see details and view luminescent chemical reagents. Light is a form of electromagnetic energy that travels in waves. Light energy is only one portion of a spectrum, or range, of wavelengths that includes x-rays, gamma rays, and radio waves (Figure 9.2). Wavelengths are measured in nanometers (nm). A wavelength can range from picometers (1×10^{-12} m) to many meters in length (such as radio waves). The shorter the wavelength of light, the greater the energy it produces.

The way humans perceive light and color is based on how light interacts with matter. When light hits a surface, it is reflected, transmitted, or absorbed by the surface (Figure 9.3). If it is absorbed, it is perceived as black in color. Most of the light that passes through translucent or transparent objects is transmitted. Most of the light that is reflected bounces off

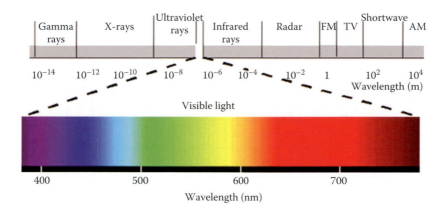

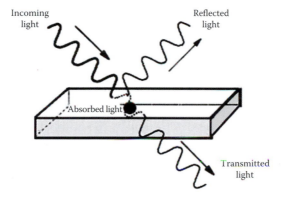

Figure 9.2 The color spectrum (the range of colors visible to the human eye) is a narrow range of wavelengths within the electromagnetic spectrum.

Figure 9.3 A schematic drawing demonstrating how light is reflected, absorbed, and/or transmitted when it interacts with a surface.

a surface in different ways. Depending on the texture and reflectivity of the surface, the human eye sees that light as a color.

The spectrum of colors that makes up a rainbow is the same range of wavelengths humans can perceive with the naked eye. This range, known as the *visible spectrum*, contains light of wavelengths between 390 and 700 nm. Each color of the rainbow represents a short range of wavelengths within the visible spectrum of light; for example, green light is between about 490 and 575 nm. The color we see is a result of the wavelength of light reflecting off the surface. A red rose reflects light at wavelengths between 620 and 700 nm. What we perceive as white light is in fact a mixture of colors. Black objects absorb light and therefore do not reflect light at a wavelength within the visible color spectrum.

9.3 Fluorescence and Phosphorescence

Each element in the periodic table has a unique *atomic number*. The atomic number is the number of protons or electrons in an atom. For example, oxygen has an atomic number of eight, indicating it has eight protons and eight electrons (Figure 9.4). Protons have a

Periodic Table of the Elements

1A																	8A
1 **H** 1.00794	2A											3A	4A	5A	6A	7A	2 **He** 4.002602
3 **Li** 6.941	4 **Be** 9.012182											5 **B** 10.811	6 **C** 12.0107	7 **N** 14.0067	8 **O** 15.9994	9 **F** 18.9984032	10 **Ne** 20.1797
11 **Na** 22.989769	12 **Mg** 24.3050	3B	4B	5B	6B	7B	——— 8B ———		1B	2B		13 **Al** 26.9815386	14 **Si** 28.0855	15 **P** 30.973762	16 **S** 32.065	17 **Cl** 35.453	18 **Ar** 39.948
19 **K** 39.0983	20 **Ca** 40.078	21 **Sc** 44.955912	22 **Ti** 47.867	23 **V** 50.9415	24 **Cr** 51.9961	25 **Mn** 54.938045	26 **Fe** 55.845	27 **Co** 58.933195	28 **Ni** 58.6934	29 **Cu** 63.546	30 **Zn** 65.38	31 **Ga** 69.723	32 **Ge** 72.64	33 **As** 74.92160	34 **Se** 78.96	35 **Br** 79.904	36 **Kr** 83.798
37 **Rb** 85.4678	38 **Sr** 87.62	39 **Y** 88.90585	40 **Zr** 91.224	41 **Nb** 92.90638	42 **Mo** 95.96	43 **Tc** [98]	44 **Ru** 101.07	45 **Rh** 102.90550	46 **Pd** 106.42	47 **Ag** 107.8682	48 **Cd** 112.411	49 **In** 114.818	50 **Sn** 118.710	51 **Sb** 121.760	52 **Te** 127.60	53 **I** 126.90447	54 **Xe** 131.293
55 **Cs** 132.9054519	56 **Ba** 137.327	57-71 Lanthanides	72 **Hf** 178.49	73 **Ta** 180.94788	74 **W** 183.84	75 **Re** 186.207	76 **Os** 190.23	77 **Ir** 192.217	78 **Pt** 195.084	79 **Au** 196.966569	80 **Hg** 200.59	81 **Tl** 204.3833	82 **Pb** 207.2	83 **Bi** 208.98040	84 **Po** [209]	85 **At** [210]	86 **Rn** [222]
87 **Fr** [223]	88 **Ra** [226]	89-103 Actinides	104 **Rf** [267]	105 **Db** [268]	106 **Sg** [271]	107 **Bh** [272]	108 **Hs** [270]	109 **Mt** [276]	110 **Ds** [281]	111 **Rg** [280]	112 **Cn** [285]	113 **Uut** [284]	114 **Uuq** [289]	115 **Uup** [288]	116 **Uuh** [293]	117 **Uus** [294]	118 **Uuo** [294]

57 **La** 138.90547	58 **Ce** 140.116	59 **Pr** 140.90765	60 **Nd** 144.242	61 **Pm** [145]	62 **Sm** 150.36	63 **Eu** 151.964	64 **Gd** 157.25	65 **Tb** 158.92535	66 **Dy** 162.500	67 **Ho** 164.93032	68 **Er** 167.259	69 **Tm** 168.93421	70 **Yb** 173.054	71 **Lu** 174.9668
89 **Ac** [227]	90 **Th** 232.03806	91 **Pa** 231.03588	92 **U** 238.02891	93 **Np** [237]	94 **Pu** [244]	95 **Am** [243]	96 **Cm** [247]	97 **Bk** [247]	98 **Cf** [251]	99 **Es** [252]	100 **Fm** [257]	101 **Md** [258]	102 **No** [259]	103 **Lr** [262]

Figure 9.4 The periodic table of the elements.

positive charge and electrons have a negative charge. The charge is balanced in its ground, or normal, state. The *atomic mass* is determined by the number of protons plus the number of neutrons in the nucleus, the core of the atom. Neutrons are neutral. They have no charge. Isotopes are elements that have the same atomic number but different numbers of neutrons and therefore different atomic masses.

Light not only travels in waves but also acts on matter as a unit of energy known as a *photon*. A photon acts on surfaces at the atomic level. An atom or molecule absorbs the photon's energy and changes from its natural ground state to a more energetic, "excited" state. The atom is naturally inclined to seek its ground state. In order to restore the balance of energy within the particle, it emits that absorbed energy as a photon. The energy absorbed and emitted by the particle is known as electromagnetic radiation whether it is visible light, UV, infrared, x-ray, microwaves, or radio waves.

When the molecule absorbs energy, some of that energy is transferred to surrounding molecules. Because some of the energy is used up in this process, the emitted electromagnetic radiation has less energy than the absorbed electromagnetic radiation. As was mentioned earlier, light waves with longer wavelengths have lower energy. Light waves with shorter wavelengths have higher energy. When light is absorbed at one wavelength, and loses energy as it interacts with matter, the atom or molecule emits light at a longer wavelength than the absorbed light (Figure 9.5). This process creates *luminescence*.

Luminescence includes both *fluorescence* and phosphorescence. When molecules are excited by a specific color, or wavelength, of light, they luminesce in a way that is specific to the chemical composition of that molecule. Surfaces and chemicals that fluoresce will only glow when energy is constantly applied to the surface. For example, if a chemical fluoresces only under yellow light, it will stop fluorescing as soon as that yellow light is removed. 1,8-diazafluoren-9-one (DFO) and Rhodamine 6G are fluorescent chemicals that fluoresce under green light (Figure 9.6). When the green light is removed, the chemical no longer glows.

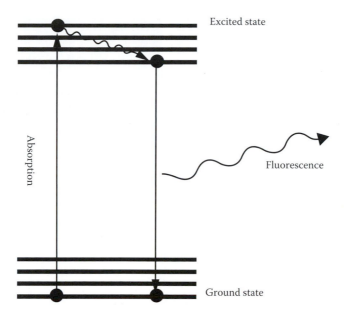

Figure 9.5 Fluorescence is observed when light is absorbed, loses energy as it interacts with matter, and is emitted at a longer wavelength.

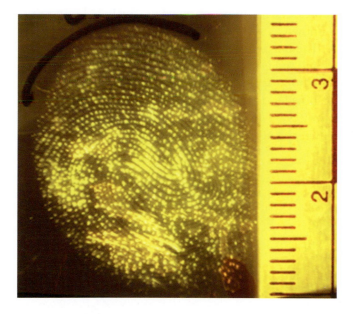

Figure 9.6 A fingerprint developed with Rhodamine 6G.

Phosphorescence occurs when the surface continues to glow even after the energy source is removed. Luminol is a chemical used to visualize latent bloodstains and enhance patent bloodstains at crime scenes (Figure 9.7). When the chemical is sprayed onto a surface, it reacts with the iron in hemoglobin and glows blue. Luminol continues to glow on its own for approximately 30 s without applying any constant energy source. This phosphorescence is only visible in the dark. Though phosphorescence is used in forensics, fingerprint analysts use fluorescent compounds in the laboratory.

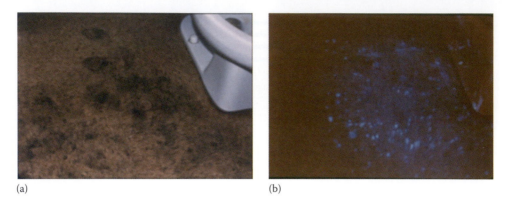

(a)   (b)

Figure 9.7 The bathroom floor at a crime scene (a) before and (b) after treatment with luminol. (Photographs courtesy of Wilson Sullivan.)

Fluorescence is most often not viewed with the naked eye. The light that comes from the forensic light source is known as *incident light*. When the incident light hits the substrate, it is reflected. This is known as *reflected light*. The angle at which the incident light hits the surface (the angle of incidence) is equal to the angle at which it is reflected off the surface (the angle of reflection). When incident light hits the friction ridges that have been treated with fluorescent chemicals or powders, the light bounces off in many different angles. This light is known as *scattered light*. A *barrier filter* is placed between the human eye and the surface. The barrier filter blocks the reflected light, while the scattered light passes through the filter and is perceived as fluorescence (Figure 9.8).

Filters are often laboratory safety glasses of different colors that are specific to the chemical reagent or powder, the color of the light source, and the color of the fluorescent emission (Figure 9.9). Filters block the light source and only allow the fluorescing light from the fingerprints to pass through. Yellow filters are used with blue light.

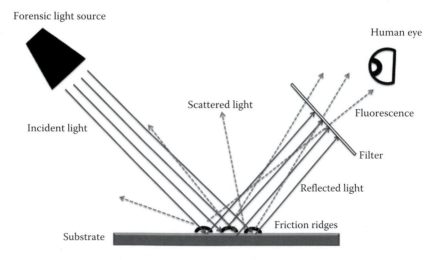

Figure 9.8 This schematic demonstrates how incident light from a fluorescent light source interacts with a latent print treated with a fluorescent chemical reagent. The incident light reflects off the surface and is observed through the barrier filter as fluorescence.

Figure 9.9 Colored safety glasses are worn as filters in conjunction with forensic light sources.

Table 9.1   Wavelengths, Colors of Light, and Their Associated Filters and Fluorescent Fingerprint Reagents

Wavelength (nm)	Light Color	Filter Color	Fluorescent Fingerprint Reagent/Powder
350–400	UV	UV (clear)/yellow	Ardrox, basic yellow 40, RAM
400–445	Blue	Yellow	Yellow/green fluorescent powder, acid yellow 7
445–515	Blue/green	Orange	Acid yellow 7, orange fluorescent powder, Rhodamine 6G, MBD [7-(p-methoxybenzylamino)-4-nitrobenzene-2-oxa-1,3-diazole] and RAM (a mixture of Rhodamine 6G, Ardrox and MBD dye stains)
515–575	Green	Red	RAM, Rhodamine 6G, DFO, indanedione, Redwop (red fluorescent powder)

Orange safety glasses are used with blue/green light. Red glasses are used with green light. Table 9.1 illustrates the most common fluorescent reagents used in the fingerprint laboratory, the corresponding wavelengths/colors of light used to excite the chemicals, and the barrier filters used to view the resulting fluorescence. Fluorescent reagents are especially useful when the background substrate is too dark or patterned to see the colored products of visible reagents (Figure 9.10). Fluorescence creates contrast, which is

Figure 9.10 Ninhydrin fingerprints developed on a check.

necessary in order to see minutiae in the developed fingerprint. However, if the substrate the fingerprint is placed on is itself fluorescent, the fingerprint will not stand out against the background.

Forensic light sources are also useful tools for visualizing blood on various surfaces. Hemoglobin absorbs light energy. Bloody fingerprints will therefore absorb long-wave UV light, some visible and near-infrared light. Because it absorbs light, the blood will appear black against the background. Blood can thus be enhanced through nondestructive means by simply viewing it under various colors of light with various filters. The blood should not be exposed to light energy for too long, as it may degrade the DNA.[2]

Colored glasses, or filters, are not only used to see the fluorescence. They are also used to protect the eyes from electromagnetic radiation. It is also important to protect skin. Any exposed skin should be covered with nitrile gloves and a long-sleeved lab coat. Higher-energy, shorter-wavelength light is especially hazardous. Therefore, great care should be taken especially when using shortwave UV light.

9.4   Lasers and Alternate Light Sources

In the 1930s, researchers developed a fingerprint powder that fluoresced under UV light.[3] *Forensic light sources* were first introduced to the forensic community at large in the late 1970s when Dalrymple et al. published a paper on the inherent fluorescence of fingerprint residue.[4] Some of the compounds in fingerprints glow under different wavelengths of light without the aid of chemical processing. However, items are not often viewed with forensic light sources prior to processing because inherent fluorescence is usually very weak and does not occur frequently.[5-7]

Fingerprints treated with fluorescent reagents or powders luminesce strongly under various wavelengths of light. The light source utilized in the initial research studies was an argon ion laser. *Laser* stands for light amplification by stimulated emission of radiation. In the 1980s, companies in Australia, Great Britain, and Canada developed for an sick light sources that could be dialed to different monochromatic wavelengths.[8] These units are known as *alternate light sources* (ALSs) (Figure 9.11).

Over the years, with advances in technology such as light-emitting diodes, portable lasers and ALSs have been developed.[3] ALS units are now so portable they can be carried throughout a crime scene. Flashlight versions have been developed with interchangeable heads for different colors of light (Figure 9.12). Forensic light sources are routinely used in the forensic laboratory as part of almost every processing sequence to develop fingerprints on a wide variety of substrates.

9.5   Reflective Ultraviolet Imaging System

The reflective (or reflected) ultraviolet imaging system (RUVIS), pictured in Figure 9.13, is a type of forensic light source that utilizes UV light in a narrow band of the UV spectrum to visualize friction ridges (Figure 9.13). The system requires a shortwave UV light source and the RUVIS unit itself, a cylindrical device known as an *intensifier*. The intensifier has a UV filter at one end and a monocular eyepiece at the other end. The analyst looks through the eyepiece to view the friction ridges under UV light.

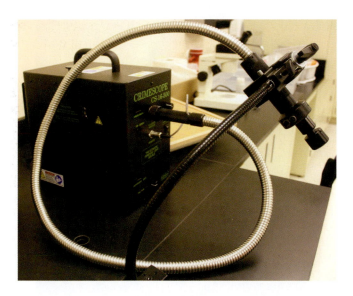

Figure 9.11 An ALS.

Figure 9.12 The Spectroline® Optimax™ Multi-Lite is a handheld ALS with interchangeable heads providing single-wavelength UV, blue, green, orange, red, and white illumination. (Reprinted with permission from Safariland, Inc. http://www.forensicssource.com/ProductDetail.aspx?ProductName=Spectroline-Optimax-Multi-Lite)

Figure 9.14 demonstrates how fingerprints are imaged with the RUVIS (Figure 9.14). A shortwave UV light source is used to shine 254 nm UV light on the substrate. Unlike laser light and white light, most of the shortwave UV light is absorbed by the substrate. Only the scattered light is visualized. The scattered UV light passes through a UV band-pass filter, which only lets UV light in a narrow spectrum pass through. All other wavelengths of light are blocked.

Because only a narrow band of scattered UV light penetrates the filter, the signal must be converted to visible light and amplified to be visible to the naked eye. This is the function of the intensifier. It intensifies the signal 70,000×, much like night vision technology, making a faint image easily visible to the human eye (Figure 9.15).[9] Because only the scattered light is viewed, the light source must be shone at various angles onto the substrate to

Figure 9.13 The RUVIS pictured comprises an intensifier on a stand and a shortwave UV light.

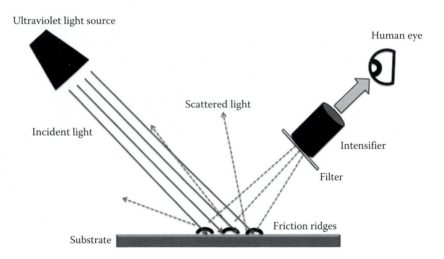

Figure 9.14 This schematic demonstrates how the incident light from a shortwave UV light source interacts with a latent print. The scattered light is observed through the intensifier.

obtain the best image. A fingerprint that is visible when the light is directed at the surface at a 45° angle might be invisible when the light is held at a 30° angle. The laboratory analyst must wear yellow laboratory safety glasses in order to view the RUVIS image.

RUVIS is a nondestructive process that can be used prior to any physical or chemical processing techniques. It has been used since the late 1980s in many forensic applications. It can be used to highlight indentations or irregularities in a surface, such as wounds, bite marks, and bruising on live and deceased victims; biological fluids such as semen and

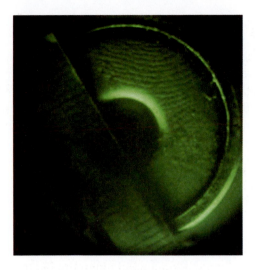

Figure 9.15 A RUVIS fingerprint on a magnet.

saliva; indented writing and ink analysis in questioned documents; and trace evidence such as fibers and hairs.[9,10] While RUVIS has been shown to illuminate untreated latent fingerprints, it provides significant contrast when used on superglue fingerprints.[11]

Only fingerprints on the surface of an item are detected, regardless of the type of substrate they are detected on or the color of the substrate. If the fingerprint residue is not deposited on the surface, the RUVIS will not be effective. Porous items, therefore, cannot be analyzed with a RUVIS since the matrix is absorbed into the substrate. Similarly, highly reflective items are not conducive to RUVIS. Another limitation to RUVIS is the texture of the surface. If a surface is textured, the light will scatter more and the print will not be readily visible on the surface.

A complete RUVIS may also include a charge-coupled device camera attached to the intensifier that provides a live feed of the image to an attached monitor. This allows the image to be viewed on a screen instead of through the eyepiece giving the analyst a larger, clearer view of the evidence. The RUVIS intensifier is portable and battery powered. It can be hand-carried throughout the laboratory or crime scene.

RUVIS has been used in many applications and has proven successful on postblast explosive materials, such as improvised explosive devices (IEDs) and vehicle-borne IEDs (VBIEDs).[12,13] Fingerprints were visualized before and after superglue fuming.[12] Gardner states, "Based on the reported results, it is believed the RUVIS UV imager could be used to quickly (and safely) locate and capture latent prints on ordnance (explosive materials) and associated materials prior to on-site demolition. Obtaining these latent prints would assist in identifying those responsible for the construction, storing, emplacement and use of IEDs."[12]

The shortwave UV light used with RUVIS is especially harmful and all skin surfaces should be covered at all times. The short wavelength corresponds to high-energy electromagnetic radiation. A face shield and/or neoprene hood can provide extra protection for the face and neck. Regardless of the forensic light source used, proper personal protective equipment (PPE) and yellow safety glasses must be worn at all times when working with ALSs and lasers.

9.6   Chapter Summary

Visual examination is the first step for processing evidence. Oblique lighting—light shone at a shallow angle—creates contrast with light and shadow. Light travels in waves. A shorter wavelength of light is higher in energy than a longer wavelength of light. Light energy with wavelengths between 390 and 700 nm is visible as color to the human eye. Fluorescence is the light emitted when material is illuminated by a certain wavelength. Fluorescent materials glow only when energy (such as a forensic light source or laser) is applied. Fluorescence is viewed with special colored glasses and filters. Yellow filters are used with blue light. Orange glasses are used with blue/green light. Red glasses are used with green light. Fluorescent dye stains adhere to superglue and give fingerprints greater contrast under fluorescent light sources. Superglue fingerprints can be viewed with a RUVIS.

Review Questions

1. Why is it necessary to visually inspect any surface before processing it for fingerprints?
2. What is the best tool for examining a surface with oblique lighting?
3. What is color?
4. What is fluorescence?
5. Name three fluorescent compounds used for fingerprint processing.
6. True or false: Light from a forensic light source passes through a barrier filter.
7. Which color barrier filters (or safety glasses) are used in conjunction with the following colors of incident light?
    a. Blue light
    b. Blue/green light
    c. Green light
8. What does ALS stand for?
9. What type of light is used with the RUVIS? What color filter is used?
10. Why is the RUVIS a useful forensic light source?
11. How does the RUVIS work?

References

1. Yamashita, B. and French, M. 2011. Latent print development. In *The Fingerprint Sourcebook*. The Scientific Working Group on Friction Ridge Analysis, Study and Technology (SWGFAST) et al. Washington, DC: National Institute of Justice, U.S. Department of Justice, Office of Justice Programs.
2. Sears, V. 2012. Enhancement techniques for fingerprints in blood. In Ramotowski, R. (ed.), *Advances in Fingerprint Technology*, 3rd edn. Boca Raton, FL: Taylor & Francis.
3. Bleay, S. et al. 2012. *Fingerprint Source Book*. Centre for Applied Science and Technology. London, UK: United Kingdom Home Office.
4. Dalrymple, B., Duff, J., and Menzel, E. 1977. Inherent fingerprint luminescence—Detection by laser. *J. Forensic Sci.* 22(1): 106–115.
5. Menzel, E. and Duff, J. 1979. Laser detection of latent fingerprints—Treatment with fluorescers. *J. Forensic Sci.* 24(1): 96–100.
6. Dalrymple, B. 1979. Case analysis of fingerprint detection by laser. *J. Forensic Sci.* 24(3): 586–590.

7. Menzel, E. 1979. Laser detection of latent fingerprints—Treatment with phosphorescers. *J. Forensic Sci.* 24(3): 582–585.
8. Champod, C. et al. 2004. Fingerprints and other ridge skin impressions. Boca Raton, FL: Taylor & Francis.
9. West, M. et al. 1990. Reflective ultraviolet imaging system (RUVIS) and the detection of trace evidence and wounds on human skin. *J. Forensic Identif.* 40(5): 249–255.
10. Misner, A. 1991. Ultraviolet light sources and their uses. *J. Forensic Identif.* 41(3): 171–175.
11. Saferstein, R. and Graf, S. 2001. Evaluation of a reflected ultraviolet imaging system for fingerprint detection. *J. Forensic Identif.* 51(4): 385–393.
12. Gardner, E. 2010. Using a reflected ultraviolet imaging system to recover friction ridge impressions on post-blast material. *J. Forensic Identif.* 60(1): 104–118.
13. McCarthy, D. 2012. Latent fingerprint recovery from simulated vehicle-borne improvised explosive devices. *J. Forensic Identif.* 62(5): 488–516.

Physical Processing Methods   10

Key Terms

- Fiberglass brushes
- Fingerprint lifting tape
- Hinge lifter
- Silicone rubber lift material
- Gelatin lifters
- Latent lift cards
- Granular powders
- Bichromatic powder
- Dual-contrast powder
- Magnetic powders
- Magna brush
- Fluorescent powders
- Metallic flake powders
- Powder suspensions
- Small particle reagent (SPR)
- Adhesive-side powder

Learning Objectives

- Define the key terms.
- Describe the components of fingerprint powders.
- Describe the four main types of fingerprint powders and their applications.
- Understand the procedure for processing dry, nonporous surfaces at crime scenes.

10.1 Fingerprint Powder

Fingerprint powders are a fast, effective, and low-cost method of latent print development. Fingerprint powders are used on dry, nonporous surfaces. The powder particles adhere to the lipid and water constituents of latent print residue. They are most often used at crime scenes where large areas and fixed objects such as furniture, windows, and railings must be processed quickly and thoroughly (Figure 10.1). While "dusting for prints" is a common technique, it is also the least sensitive technique compared to chemical processing methods. This is why powdering is not recommended for items that can be safely transported to a laboratory for chemical processing in a controlled environment.

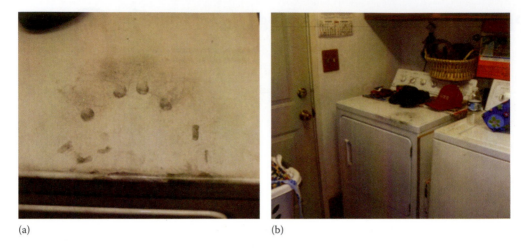

(a)   (b)

Figure 10.1 Black powdered fingerprints (a) were developed on a clothes dryer (b) at a burglary crime scene.

Fingerprint powders are most effective on fresh fingerprints. The longer a latent print remains on a surface, the drier it gets as the water evaporates. Even though the oils are still present, there is less material for the powder to adhere to. Regardless of its insensitivity as a technique, fingerprints recovered with fingerprint powder account for about 50% of the 60,000 fingerprint identifications each year in the United Kingdom.[1]

10.2   Compositions of Fingerprint Powders

Fingerprint powders were first developed experimentally in the nineteenth century. The first fingerprint powders were composed of ground chalk and mercury.[2] Mercury was a common ingredient through the 1980s.[3] Lead was found in gray powders through the 1990s in concentrations reaching 40% or more.[3] While the formulations of fingerprint powders have changed throughout the years, most of the powders we use today were developed by the mid-nineteen hundreds.[1,4]

Most nonmagnetic fingerprint powders are composed of a pigment and an adhesive carrier particle and/or a filler material.[5,6] The adhesive component is often a rosin extract, such as dragon's blood (powdered rosin of the *Daemonorops draco* plant), stearic acid, cornstarch, raven powder, *Acacia* powder, or *Lycopodium* powder.[1,5,7]

Lycopodium powder is derived from the spores of the stag's horn club moss or Christmas tree fern (*Lycopodium clavatum*). The *Lycopodium* spores that form the powder are fine in texture, extremely lightweight, smooth, and round.[1,5,8] The spores do not stick together in powder form. The powder was first used in the 1930s and 1940s by Carlson and Kornei to make the first electrostatic copies of documents.[8]

Stearic acid is a hydrophobic fatty acid. Its prevalence and hydrophobic qualities make it another suitable adhesive component for fingerprint powders. *Acacia* powder, also known as gum arabic, is a common nontoxic adhesive.[9] It is commonly used as a food binder.[9] Similarly to stearic acid, it is a hydrophobic binder in any oil/water interface.[9,10] Raven powder is a fine carrier powder also used in a wide range of industries. It is found in past homeopathic literature and is commonly used as a fine powder lubricant on automobile parts and as a powder coating on latex gloves.

Fingerprint powders also contain filler materials, most commonly fine to medium mesh pumice. Pumice is a volcanic rock, rich in silica (SiO), with a crystalline structure similar to that of glass.[11] The SiO_2 forming the vesicles in solid pumice—approximately 90% porosity—accounts for pumice's low density.[11] This makes it ideal as a lightweight filler material.[12] Pumice is used as an abrasive or as a lightweight filler in wall insulation, plaster, soil conditioner, filtration, beauty products, cement, ceramics, paint, rubber, electroplating, automotive finishing, leather finishing, lithography, and other industrial applications.[12,13] In fingerprint powder formulations, fine mesh pumice is used as lightweight, anticaking filler material and as a carrier particle for pigments and adhesive elements. As a component of fingerprint powders, these features ensure even dispersal of the powder over a surface.

There are many different colors and formulations of fingerprint powders. The powder you choose will depend on the condition, texture, and color of the substrate. The color you choose should contrast with the color of the surface. For most reflective, transparent, and light-colored surfaces, black fingerprint powder is sufficient. If the background is multicolored or dark, a light-colored or fluorescent powder should be used. There are four common types of fingerprint powders:

1. Granular powder (black, white, and bichromatic)
2. Magnetic powder (black, bichromatic, and/or fluorescent)
3. Fluorescent powder (many colors available)
4. Metallic flake powder (aluminum, copper)

How well the powder adheres to the latent depends on the size and shape of the powder particles, the surface chemistry of the powder, the condition of the latent print, and the adhesive properties of the powder.

10.3   Fingerprint Powder Processing

Fingerprint powders are applied using fingerprint brushes. Brushes come in several styles and are made of natural or synthetic materials. Granular powders are typically applied with *fiberglass brushes* such as the Zephyr® brush, composed of thousands of bundles of soft glass fibers, each about 12 μm in diameter (Figure 10.2).[1] Other brushes are made from polyester, animal hair (such as camel or squirrel), or feathers. Magnetic powders are applied with a special magnetic applicator.

Once the fingerprint is developed, it is typically lifted with an adhesive fingerprint tape. *Fingerprint lifting tape* is a transparent clear or frosted adhesive tape available in 1–2 in. rolls or in 4 in. rolls for lifting simultaneous fingerprint impressions (more than one finger at a time) or palm print impressions (Figure 10.3). Fingerprint tape rolls are pressure-wound to eliminate bubbles that may obscure fingerprint features.

Another type of adhesive lifting device is known as a *hinge lifter*. Hinge lifters are clear, hinged polymer sheets precut to different sizes. One side of the hinged device is coated with an adhesive, and the other side is either white or black in color or transparent.

Figure 10.2 The Zephyr® fingerprint brush was developed in 1956 and is still used extensively at crime scenes today.

Figure 10.3 Rolls of frosted fingerprint lifting tape are available in 2″ and 4″ widths.

The hinge lifter is used to lift and seal powder prints quickly and easily. However, case data and sketches cannot be recorded on most hinge lifters.

Fingerprints can be found on many surfaces, and not all are smooth and flat. Some surfaces are textured or curved, which makes lifting fingerprints difficult. Friction ridges developed on textured or curved surfaces cannot be easily or successfully lifted with regular fingerprint tape or hinge lifters. Instead, it is possible to lift the developed fingerprint using silicone casting material or gelatin lifters. The *silicone rubber lift material* is made up of a white casting material with a consistency of toothpaste and a catalyst (a chemical

Figure 10.4 Mikrosil™ casting putty is a common silicone casting material used to lift powdered fingerprints from curved or textured surfaces.

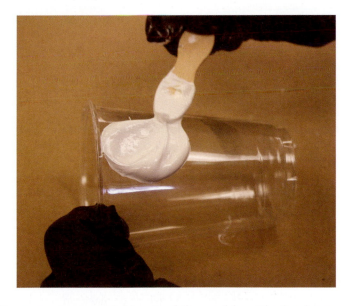

Figure 10.5 Silicone casting material is mixed thoroughly with a hardener catalyst and spread over a powdered fingerprint.

that initiates the hardening reaction) (Figure 10.4). The casting material is mixed with a catalyst and applied gently over a powdered fingerprint (Figure 10.5). After a few minutes, it hardens into a flexible rubbery cast similar to Silly Putty™ that can be lifted from the surface (Figure 10.6).

Gelatin lifters are lightly adhesive rolls or flat sheets with a layer of gelatin that makes them thicker and more pliable than lift tapes. Gelatin lifters are applied and pressed into

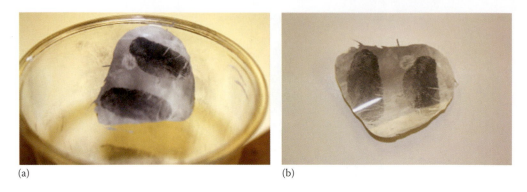

(a)   (b)

Figure 10.6 After the silicone casting material hardens (a), it is removed from the surface (b).

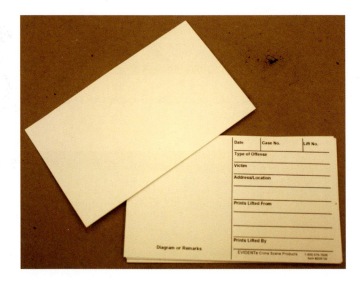

Figure 10.7 Latent lift cards.

surfaces that are rough or curved. Often, a rubber roller is used to roll out air bubbles while the gelatin lifter is pressed onto the surface where the latent of value is found. Gelatin lifters are also used to lift shoeprints, dust patterns, and trace evidence.

Fingerprints lifted with fingerprint tape are typically mounted onto *latent lift cards*. Fingerprint lift cards not only preserve the print but also allow for documentation of the fingerprint's original location on the surface and other case information. Lift cards, also known as latent print backing cards, are glossy white or black on one side and have a non-glossy reverse side (Figure 10.7). The reverse side is preprinted for filling out case information and sketching the surface. Light powders are lifted onto black fingerprint cards, while dark powders are lifted onto standard white fingerprint cards.

The following procedure should be used to process dry, nonporous surfaces at crime scenes with granular powders:

1. Visually inspect the surface of interest with oblique white light.
2. Photograph any visible prints in situ (in place).
3. Pick a color powder that contrasts with the surface.

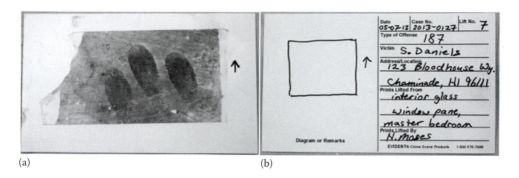

(a)   (b)

Figure 10.8 Latent lift card front (a) and back (b) demonstrating directionality, case info, and sketch from the location where the latent print was developed.

4. Put a light layer of powder onto a fingerprint brush and shake off the excess.
5. Lightly pass the brush over the surface until friction ridges are visualized.
6. Photograph the visible fingerprints.
7. Lift the fingerprints onto a contrasting fingerprint card using fingerprint lift tape.
8. Fill out all known case info, complete a sketch, and note the "up" direction of the print as shown in Figure 10.8.

10.4   Varieties of Fingerprint Powders

Granular powders are composed of large asymmetrical particles. Black fingerprint powder is a carbon-based granular powder most commonly used in the United States at crime scenes. Black powder is used on light-colored surfaces such as windows, mirrors, light-colored cars, and highly lacquered woods (Figure 10.9). Black granular powder is applied with a fiberglass fingerprint brush and lifted with fingerprint tape onto white fingerprint lift cards or with hinge lifters.

Granular powders also come in several other colors, most commonly white, gray, and bichromatic. White and gray powders are insensitive and result in a significant amount

Figure 10.9 Black granular fingerprint powder.

Figure 10.10 Bichromatic fingerprint powder.

of "background noise," which makes it difficult to distinguish the details of the print. *Bichromatic powder* (from "bi" meaning two and "chromatic" meaning color), also called *dual-contrast powder*, is a mixture of black granular powder and aluminum powder. This powder is especially useful on dark surfaces since the aluminum particles show up silver on the dark background (Figure 10.10). The prints are lifted with fingerprint tape onto standard white latent print cards.

Magnetic powders have particles that are smaller than granular powders, mixed in with magnetic metallic particles. Iron particles are blended with the powder to makes the mixture magnetic. Magnetic powder is available in many colors and may be fluorescent. Magnetic powders are applied with a magnet-tipped applicator. The applicator, which resembles a pen, is dipped into the magnetic powder. A "brush" of magnetic powder is formed on the end of the applicator, also referred to as a *magna brush* or magnetic brush (Figure 10.11). The powder is gently passed across the surface to develop the prints. To release the excess powder back into the container, the internal magnet is pulled up into the applicator, thereby releasing the powder (Figure 10.12). The empty wand can then be used to "clean up" excess magnetic powder from the print and surrounding area. Magnetic fingerprint powder can be lifted with standard fingerprint lift tape, hinge lifters, gelatin lifters, or with silicone rubber casting material.

There are many advantages to using magnetic powders. For one, they are more sensitive than black granular powders, so they produce less "background noise." Because the "brush" formed on the tip of the applicator is made of powder, there are no bristles that might inadvertently wipe away important details in the latent fingerprint. Fiberglass brushes cannot be used on greasy or dirty surfaces that might soil the brush, making it unusable in the future. Because magnetic applicators do not have brush tips, magnetic powders can be used on greasy surfaces such as fast-food cups and wrappers. Magnetic powders can also be used on Styrofoam™ (Figure 10.13). Magnetic powder is also cleaner to use than black granular powder because the unused or spilled powder can be gathered up with the magnetic applicator and returned to the original container.

Figure 10.11 Magnetic fingerprint powder on the tip of a magna brush.

Figure 10.12 Pulling up the opposing end of the magna brush retracts the magnet in the magna brush and releases the magnetic fingerprint powder.

There are some disadvantages to using magnetic fingerprint powder. For one, it cannot be used on large areas because of the sensitivity of the technique. It is also difficult to use on vertical or steeply angled surfaces because the powder end is pulled down by gravity. Black magnetic powders cannot be used on ferric metal surfaces (surfaces containing iron) because the magnetic particles will be attracted to the surface and will obliterate the fingerprint.

Figure 10.13 A fingerprint developed with black magnetic fingerprint powder on Styrofoam™.

Figure 10.14 Fluorescent fingerprint powders of various colors with a feather duster applicator brush.

Fluorescent powders are very small fluorescent particles mixed with cornstarch or *Lycopodium* powder carrier particles. They are either granular or magnetic and are available in many colors including black, pink, red, orange, green, and yellow (Figure 10.14). The fluorescent components of these powders are dyes such as Phloxine B, Rhodamine 6G, and fluorescein.[1,14,15] Fluorescent powders are a very sensitive fingerprint development method. They are useful for delicate dusting or on items that cannot get wet with chemical reagents such as computers, electronics, and cell phones. It is also used on surfaces that are multicolored and therefore do not provide contrast with any visible magnetic or granular powders.

Fluorescent powders glow under a specific wavelength of light, such as UV light or green light. Alternate light sources (ALSs) can be used to visualize these fluorescent prints in a dark room using the appropriate filter or goggle color. For example, orange fluorescent

Figure 10.15 Feather duster fingerprint brush.

powder is visualized under green light (using an ALS or laser) with orange goggles. ALS will be discussed in detail in Chapter 13. Fluorescent powders are used very sparingly with a feather duster brush (Figure 10.15). The powders are lightly applied to the surface, visualized, photographed, and lifted onto black fingerprint cards.

Metallic flake powders are composed of flattened flakes of aluminum, zinc, iron, or copper.[1,16] They are also available in magnetic form. Aluminum flake powder is most commonly used on smooth, dry surfaces. When a surface does not provide sufficient contrast with the aluminum flake powder, such as a silver vehicle, copper flake powder can be used. Metallic flake powders are the most commonly used powders in Europe. Several researchers over four decades have determined that it is the most effective powder for fingerprint development because the flattened flakes are deposited in layers over the latent and result in high-contrast prints with minimum background noise.[16–25]

Fingerprint powders are useful on most nonporous, dry surfaces. So how would you process a nonporous surface that is wet or has been wetted by environmental exposure such as rain or snow? Or an item that has condensation on it, such as a recently opened soda can? Aqueous powder suspensions are available for this purpose. *Powder suspensions* are mixtures of insoluble fine powder particles in a dilute detergent solution such as Kodak Photo-Flo™ (originally used as a wash to protect developed film from dust and scratches) or Liquinox™.[1,25,26] The powder suspension is applied as a spray, painted or dipped and rinsed with water. The powder particles selectively adhere to the sebaceous fingerprint residue, since the water-soluble components have been washed away.

A common powder suspension is *small particle reagent (SPR)*. SPR is a formulation of molybdenum disulfide in water and Photo-Flo™. It is available in a dark gray, white, or fluorescent formulation. SPR has proved successful in laboratory studies on wet vehicles, cardboard, metal, rusty metal, rocks, concrete, plastic, vinyl, wood, glass, and adhesive surfaces.

Another type of powder suspension used commonly in fingerprint development is *adhesive-side powder*. There are several commercially available black and white powder suspensions (Figure 10.16). Each of these products is brushed, dipped, or sprayed onto the surface. Then the surface is rinsed with water. More development methods for processing the adhesive side of the tape will be discussed in Chapter 12.

Figure 10.16 A fingerprint developed on black electrical tape with a white powder suspension.

10.5 Chapter Summary

Fingerprint powder dusting is a fast, low-cost method for developing latent fingerprints on clean, dry, nonporous surfaces. Because it is an insensitive technique, it should only be used at crime scenes on large areas or fixed objects such as furniture, windows, and railings. Fingerprint powder particles adhere to the water and oily components of the latent print residue. In addition to dry fingerprint powders, there are liquid powder suspensions available that are used to process wet surfaces and the adhesive side of tape.

There are four main types of fingerprint powders: granular, magnetic, fluorescent, and metallic. Granular fingerprint powders, the least sensitive of the fingerprint powders, are brushed onto a surface with a fiberglass fingerprint brush and lifted with fingerprint tape onto fingerprint lift cards. Magnetic fingerprint powder is more sensitive than granular powder and is applied with a magnetic applicator. The resulting prints are lifted with tape, gelatin lifters, or casting material. Fluorescent powders are applied sparingly with a feather brush and lifted onto black fingerprint cards. Metallic aluminum fingerprint powder is the most effective of all the fingerprint powders.

Review Questions

1. What is the first step in processing a surface with fingerprint powder?
2. What must be done before the powder-enhanced print is lifted?
3. What surface features should be taken into consideration before deciding what fingerprint powder and lifting method to use?
4. What are the advantages to magnetic fingerprint powder?

5. What are the disadvantages to magnetic fingerprint powder?
6. Which powder is most effective according to research?
7. What lifting method(s) is used to lift powdered fingerprints from curved or rough surfaces?
8. What is bichromatic fingerprint powder?
9. How are fluorescent fingerprint powders visualized?
10. On what surfaces are fluorescent fingerprint powders used?

References

1. Bandey, H., Bleay, S., and Gibson, A. 2012. Powders for fingerprint development. In Ramotowski, R. (ed.), *Advances in Fingerprint Technology*, 3rd edn. Boca Raton, FL: Taylor & Francis.
2. Thomas, G.L. 1978. The physics of fingerprints and their detection. *J. Phys. [E]*. 1978(11): 722–731.
3. Van Netten, C. and Teschke, K.E. 1990. Occupational exposure to elemental constituents in fingerprint powders. *Arch. Environ. Health*. 45(2): 123–128.
4. Champod, C. et al. 2004. *Fingerprints and Other Ridge Skin Impressions*. Boca Raton, FL: Taylor & Francis.
5. Moses, H. 2009. A critical comparison of black fingerprint powder formulations to improve latent fingerprint clarity and contrast on common substrates. Masters of Science Thesis, Forensic Sciences Graduate Group. University of California, Davis, CA.
6. Yamashita, B. and French, M. 2011. Latent print development. In *The Fingerprint Sourcebook*. The Scientific Working Group on Friction Ridge Analysis, Study and Technology (SWGFAST), et al. Washington, DC: National Institute of Justice, U.S. Department of Justice, Office of Justice Programs.
7. Voss-DeHaan, P. 2006. Physics and fingerprints. *Contemp. Phys.* 47(4): 209–230.
8. Owen, D. 2004. Copies in seconds: How a lone inventor and an unknown company created the biggest communication breakthrough since Gutenberg—Chester Carlson and the birth of the xerox machine. New York: Simon & Schuster.
9. Williams, P.A. and Phillips, G.O. 2002. *Gums and Stabilisers for the Food Industry*. Cambridge, U.K.: Royal Society of Chemistry Special Publication; Tyne and Wear, U.K.: Athenaeum Press Ltd.
10. Nussinovich, A. 1997. *Hydrocolloid Applications: Gum Technology in the Food and Other Industries*. London, U.K.: Chapman & Hall, Blackie Academic and Professional.
11. Hoffer, J. 1994. *Pumice and Pumicite in New Mexico*. Socorro, NM: New Mexico Bureau of Mines and Mineral Resources, New Mexico Institute of Mining and Technology. *Bulletin 140*.
12. Wilson, H.S. 1981. *Lightweight Aggregates—Vermiculite Perlite, Pumice-for Insulating Concretes*. Minerals Research Program, Ottawa, Ontario, Canada: Mineral Science Laboratories, Canada Centre for Mineral and Energy Technology. *CanMet Report 81–15E*.
13. Chesterman, C. 1956. *Pumice, Pumicite and Volcanic Cinders in California*. San Francisco, CA: Department of Natural Resources, Division of Mines. *Bulletin 174*.
14. Sodhi, G.S., Kaur, J., and Garg, R. K. 2004. Fingerprint powder formulations based on organic, fluorescent dyes. *J. Forensic Identif.* 54(1): 4–8.
15. Saroa, J.S. et al. 2006. Evaluation of fingerprint powders. *J. Forensic Identif.* 56(2): 186–197.
16. James, J.D., Pounds, C.A., and Wilshire, B. 1991. Flake metal powders for revealing latent fingerprints. *J. Forensic Sci.* 36: 1368–1375.
17. Thomas, G.L. 1973. The physics of fingerprints. *Criminology* 8: 21–38.
18. Thomas, G.L. 1975. The resistivity of fingerprints. *J. Forensic Sci. Soc.* 15: 133–135.
19. Thomas, G.L. 1978. The physics of fingerprints and their detection. *J. Phys. [E]*, 11: 722–731.
20. James, J.D., Pounds, C.A., and Wilshire, B. 1991. Obliteration of latent fingerprints. *J. Forensic Sci.* 36: 1376–1386.

21. James, J.D., Pounds, C.A., and Wilshire, B. 1991. Magnetic flake fingerprint technology. *J. Forensic Identif.* 41: 237–247.
22. James, J.D., Pounds, C.A., and Wilshire, B. 1992. New magnetic applicators and magnetic flake powders for revealing latent fingerprints. *J. Forensic Identif.* 42: 531–542.
23. James, J.D., Pounds, C.A., and Wilshire, B. 1993. Magnetic flake powders for fingerprint development. *J. Forensic Sci.* 38: 391–401.
24. Fieldhouse, S. 2011. An investigation into the use of a portable cyanoacrylate fuming system (SUPERfume®) and aluminum powder for the development of latent fingermarks. *J. Forensic Sci.* 56(6): 1514–1520.
25. Bleay, S.M. et al. 2012. Chapter 3: Finger mark development techniques within scope of ISO 17025. In *Fingerprint Source Book*. London, UK: United Kingdom: Home Office.
26. Jasuja, O.P., Singh, G.D., and Sodhi, G.S. 2007. Small particle reagent: A saponin-based modification. *J. Forensic Identif.* 57(2): 244–251.

Chemical Processing Methods
Porous Substrates

11

Key Terms

- Porous
- Amino acids
- Sublimate
- Iodine fuming
- Silver nitrate
- Ninhydrin
- Triketohydrindene hydrate
- Ruhemann's purple
- Analogs
- 1,8-Diazafluoren-9-one (DFO)
- 1,2-Indanedione
- Physical developer (PD)
- Cationic surfactant
- Hydrophilic
- Hydrophobic
- Micelle
- Stock solution
- Working solution

Learning Objectives

- Define the key terms.
- Define and recognize porous substrates.
- Understand how fingerprint residues react when deposited on porous substrates.
- Describe the sequential processing method for porous substrates.
- Understand the reaction mechanisms and developmental results of treating porous items with ninhydrin, 1,8-diazafluoren-9-one (DFO), indanedione, and physical developer (PD).

11.1 Porous Substrates

In our daily lives, we are surrounded by and interact with objects that are both natural and synthetic: objects of different sizes, shapes, colors, and materials. Any of these objects may have significance at a crime scene. Items of evidence may have a variety of properties. Each item has to be considered individually before it is processed for fingerprints. One of the first things that must be determined is whether the item is porous or nonporous. *Porous* items are processed with a specific set of reagents. Nonporous items are processed with a different set of reagents.

Porous refers to a surface "containing pores" or small spaces within a substrate, like a sponge. Porous materials are permeable to liquids and gases. The most common porous substrates at crime scenes are paper, cardboard, and unfinished wood. Wood fibers are the basic raw materials for making paper. Wet pulp of mashed-up cellulose fibers from wood is mixed with fillers and dyes, pressed in screens to extract the water from the mash, dried, and cut into sheets. The overlapping cellulose matrix is a porous material, even though some commercial papers feel smooth to the touch.

Porous substrates absorb the fingerprint matrix. When fingerprints are deposited on a porous surface, they permeate the fibers. The water-soluble components of the fingerprint residue (amino acids, sodium chloride, urea, etc.) are absorbed into the surface, while the non-water-soluble components (lipids, waxy compounds, etc.) sit on the surface until they are wiped away or destroyed by environmental factors (Figure 11.1).[1] While the water evaporates, the other components remain embedded in the fibers. In a study of 15 paper samples, Almog et al. found that fingerprint residues do not penetrate into smoother (less porous) papers as thoroughly as more porous papers.[2] They also found that deeper penetration of fingerprint residues results in higher-quality processed prints.

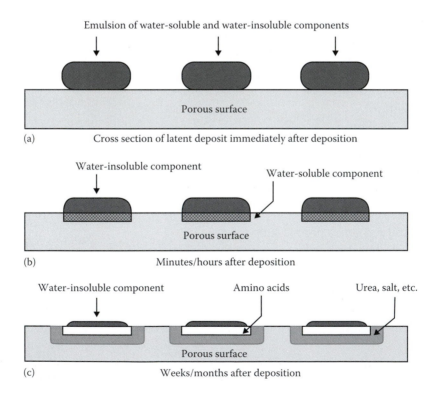

Figure 11.1 A cross section of fingerprint residues deposited on a porous substrate such as paper. When the fingerprint is deposited on the surface (a), the water-soluble components are absorbed into the substrate (b) and the water-insoluble components remain on the surface (c). (Reprinted from Champod, C., *Fingerprints and Other Ridge Skin Impressions*, Taylor & Francis, Boca Raton, FL, 2004, Figure 4.1. With permission.)

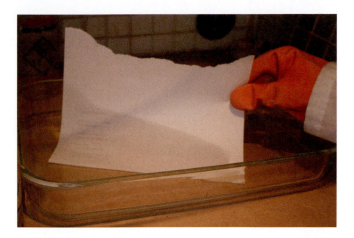

Figure 11.2 A fingerprint analyst dips a sheet of paper in a ninhydrin solution.

Latent prints in porous substrates are developed with chemical reagents. *Amino acids*—the building blocks of proteins—in the latent print residue bind strongly to the cellulose fibers and remain there unless the item gets wet.[3] If the item gets wet, the amino acids may be diluted or washed away. Most chemical reagents for porous materials react with amino acids, though there are reagents that react with the sodium chloride and lipid components. Chemical fingerprint reagents are applied to the porous item by dipping or spraying so the reagent can penetrate the fibers (Figure 11.2). With some reagents, invisible latent fingerprints change color and become visible. Other fingerprint reagents for porous materials make the fingerprint fluorescent. The latent prints will glow under an alternate light source or laser.

11.2   Sequential Processing

There are several chemical reagents available for processing porous items. The choice of chemical reagent will depend on the situation and the condition of the item. What color is the item? Is the item now or has it ever been wetted? How porous is the item? There may be patent prints visible on the surface. All visible fingerprints are photographed prior to using any processing method. During the chemical development process, the fingerprint analyst should wear personal protective equipment such as a laboratory coat, laboratory goggles or protective glasses, and gloves.

Regardless of the chemicals used, they must be applied in a particular sequence in order to be effective (see Appendix A). The application of the chemical reagents in sequence may reveal more fingerprints than each process alone or may enhance the quality of previously developed fingerprints. However, because some reagents inhibit or decrease the effectiveness of others, the processes you use must be applied in a particular sequence in order to be effective. After each process, any fingerprints that are revealed are photographed before moving on to the next process. The following is the porous processing sequence proposed in this and other texts:

1. Visual examination
2. Indanedione

3. Laser or ALS
4. DFO
5. Ninhydrin
6. PD

11.3   Historical Chemical Reagents

This chapter will concentrate on the most effective chemical reagents available to date. However, there are several reagents that are infrequently employed but are still available to the fingerprint analyst. These historic processing methods include iodine fuming and silver nitrate staining.

Iodine fuming is a technique that has been used for over 150 years.[4] This process involves blowing air into a tube containing calcium chloride crystals and iodine crystals.[5] The iodine crystals warm and *sublimate* (change from a solid to a gas) and the vapor is blown across the surface. It reacts with the fatty and oily components of fingerprints. The latent fingerprints turn a yellowish-brown color. The colored product is not permanent unless it is fixed with iodine fixing solution.

Iodine vapors are toxic and corrosive, and accidental inhalation is possible, so great care must be taken when processing fingerprints using this method. Iodine fuming may also be done in a fuming cabinet to negate this possibility. The items are suspended in a sealed chamber. Iodine crystals placed in the cabinet are heated, sublimating the iodine and creating the fumes to develop the fingerprints.

Silver nitrate is a chemical reagent that has been used to develop fingerprints on porous items since 1877.[4,9] Silver nitrate ($AgNO_3$) reacts with the sodium chloride (NaCl) in the fingerprint deposits to form silver chloride (AgCl), which is a photosensitive compound. A photoreduction reaction converts the silver chloride to elemental silver.[3] A solution of 1%–10% silver nitrate in distilled water is applied to the paper by brushing or dipping. The item is air-dried and exposed to long-wave UV radiation or sunlight until dark-colored fingerprints appear. Fingerprints must be photographed immediately as the background will continue to develop as it is exposed to light, decreasing the contrast over time.[5] Due to its insensitivity, background staining, and tendency to deteriorate, the method is not commonly used today.

There are many other chemicals used for fingerprint processing on porous surfaces. These include ninhydrin, indanedione, oil red O, DFO, and PD. The most common and current fingerprint reagents in use today in forensic laboratories nationwide are ninhydrin, indanedione, DFO, and PD.

11.4   Ninhydrin

Ninhydrin was discovered by chance in 1910 by a chemist named Siegfried Ruhemann. Ninhydrin, also known as *triketohydrindene hydrate*, is both water soluble and alcohol soluble. In solid form, it is a yellowish crystalline structure (Figure 11.3).[3] Ruhemann observed that the chemical reacts with proteins and amino acids to form a purple color, thereafter known as *Ruhemann's purple*.[3–5] It was originally used in chemistry to test for proteins in biological samples and to locate amino acids on chromatograms (snapshots of molecules separated via chromatography).[3] In 1954, a pair of chemists suggested the aqueous solution of ninhydrin be used to develop fingerprints:[6]

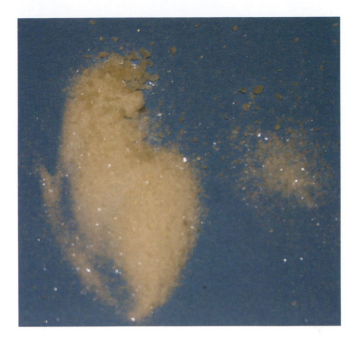

Figure 11.3 Ninhydrin crystals.

In connexion with some recent legal proceedings, a new method for detecting fingerprints has been discovered by one of us (S. O.). The method involves the well-known Ninhydrin test for amino-acids, often used in chromatography. In this method, fingerprints on paper have always been considered a great nuisance, and one is often recommended to use forceps "to avoid fingerprints".[7] In our opinion, the new method will be most suitable for detecting fingerprints on paper and similar materials.

Ninhydrin reacts with amino acids and other amine-containing compounds in fingerprint residues. Figure 11.4 demonstrates the mechanism for the reaction between ninhydrin and an amino acid. In this reaction, the nitrogen from the amino acid binds to the central ketone groups of two ninhydrin molecules, linking them together in a complex.[3]

As the treated fingerprints develop, the amino acids and proteins in the latent fingerprint turn purple (Figure 11.5). Because amino acids are stable in paper fibers over time, fingerprints may be developed on paper long after they are deposited. In some instances, fingerprints deposited on student notebooks were developed with ninhydrin 40 years after they were last handled.[9]

Ninhydrin can be applied in a fume hood by thoroughly saturating the paper by dipping, spraying, or painting. Ninhydrin "recipes" all include a polar solvent and a carrier solvent (see Appendix B).[1] Some contain acetic acid. The polar solvent is often ethanol or methanol, though methanol is a hazardous chemical.[1] The acetic acid is included because the reaction occurs more efficiently under slightly acidic conditions.[1] The most current formulation of ninhydrin uses HFE 7100™ as an inflammable carrier solvent with low toxicity. HFE 7100™ (hydrofluoroether 1-methoxynonafluorobutane) is supplied by the 3M™ company and may be purchased from any forensic supplier.[8] HFE 7100™ has proven superior to previous carrier solvents because it does not cause ink to run if there is writing on the paper, though it is cost prohibitive for many departments and agencies.

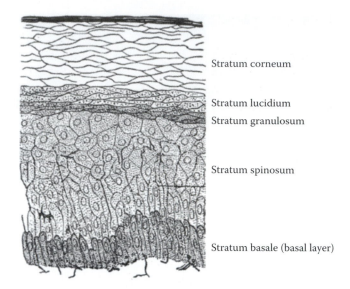

Stratum corneum

Stratum lucidium
Stratum granulosum

Stratum spinosum

Stratum basale (basal layer)

Figure 11.4 The mechanism for the reaction between ninhydrin and an amino acid to form Ruhemann's purple. (Reprinted from Proteins and amino acids. *UC Davis ChemWiki.* University of California, Davis. Creative Commons Attribution-Noncommercial-Share Alike 3.0 United States License. http://creativecommons.org/licenses/by-nc-sa/3.0/us/)

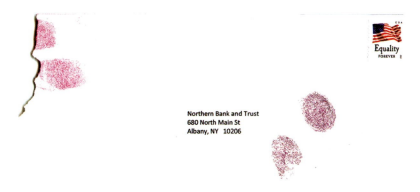

Northern Bank and Trust
680 North Main St
Albany, NY 10206

Figure 11.5 Fingerprints developed with ninhydrin on a white envelope.

In situations where the subject matter of the document is important—such as a suicide letter, threat letter, or forgery—the text must be preserved for the questioned document examiner.

Once the item is treated with ninhydrin, it is air-dried at room temperature in a fume hood. The item should be left to develop for 24–48 h at room temperature for maximum development.[1] Heat and humidity speed up the development process, but excessive humidity may cause the fingerprints to "bleed." If this occurs, the ridges may appear diffuse rather than well defined. A clothing steam iron is sometimes used to steam the porous item, but this causes the background to be stained and the ridges to appear diffuse. Background staining results in poor contrast between the developed fingerprints and the background. If the evidence must be developed immediately, the UK Home

Office suggests developing the treated items at 80°F for 5–10 min at 65% relative humidity in an incubator.[9]

Research has shown that ninhydrin fingerprints can be enhanced by metal salt treatments. A zinc nitrate solution will turn the purple fingerprints orange, while a cadmium nitrate solution will turn the purple fingerprints red.[1] The metallic elements form a complex with Ruhemann's purple. This complex not only results in a color change to enhance contrast in white light but also results in a luminescent compound that may be viewed under various light sources. The luminescence emission for the zinc nitrate treatment occurs at ~550 nm (green/yellow light).[1] The luminescence emission for the cadmium nitrate treatment occurs at ~590 nm (orange light).[1] These treatments are especially beneficial when ninhydrin alone results in a visible fingerprint with poor contrast. For example, a purple ninhydrin fingerprint on a blue, purple, or pink substrate is not as well defined as a fluorescent fingerprint that glows in contrast with a dark background.

Ninhydrin has been the workhorse for porous items in the forensic laboratory since the 1950s, and it still is today. It is likely that ninhydrin's staying power is due to the fact that it creates a visible product that is relatively straightforward to photograph, scan, or photocopy. The fingerprints are generally of good quality and are stable over time. There is also limited background noise observed. Over time, many other chemicals have been tested as possible fingerprint reagents. Most of these are fluorescent in nature and are not readily seen with the naked eye. The most commonly used fluorescent fingerprint reagents for porous materials are DFO and indanedione.

11.5 DFO

Another chemical reagent commonly used in the forensics laboratory is called DFO (1,8-diazafluoren-9-one). DFO was developed as a "highly fluorescent" fingerprint reagent in the 1980s.[9,10,20] Just like ninhydrin, DFO reacts with the amino acids in fingerprint residues. The reaction mechanism is similar to that of ninhydrin. Unlike ninhydrin, DFO produces a strong fluorescent fingerprint that is not readily seen with the naked eye (Figure 11.6). This makes it more difficult to photograph. Fluorescent fingerprints are also easier to see on multicolored or dark backgrounds where purple ninhydrin fingerprints may not be visible.

Just like the ninhydrin process, DFO is applied in a fume hood by thoroughly saturating the paper by dipping, spraying, or painting. The following is a common formulation for DFO working solution using HFE7100™ as a carrier solvent (see Appendix B). The treated item is dried in a fume hood. Items processed with DFO are heated in an incubator at 100°C for 20 min. Unlike the ninhydrin process, which is enhanced by humid environments, the DFO process must be completed in a dry environment. The processed items are viewed with an alternate light source or laser set to 530–570 nm (green light). The items must be viewed through orange or red goggles and photographed with an orange or red barrier filter.

DFO has been shown to be a superior fingerprint reagent as compared with ninhydrin in multiple studies. In some cases, it developed twice as many fingerprints as ninhydrin.[1,3,10–12] Instead of choosing one chemical over the other, fingerprint analysts can use both chemicals in sequence. DFO is always used before ninhydrin. One chemical may develop fingerprints, while the other does not. Or both chemicals may develop the same print, but one may be clearer than the other. Even with the success of DFO, researchers

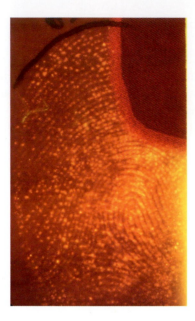

Figure 11.6 A DFO fingerprint developed on a printed document.

continued to search for chemical reagents that developed better-quality, higher-contrast fingerprints. One of those chemical reagents is known as indanedione.

11.6   Indanedione

Research into other chemical reagents for processing porous items for fingerprints focused on *analogs* of ninhydrin. An analog is "a chemical compound that has a similar structure and similar chemical properties to those of another compound, but differs from it by a single element or a group."[9] Analogs are commonly developed in medical research laboratories to create drugs that either work better than the original drugs or work in a slightly different way. Examples of analogs are the antibiotics penicillin and amoxicillin. Both antibiotics come from the mold *Penicillium*. Penicillin was historically used to treat most bacterial infections. Amoxicillin was developed from penicillin as an improved antibiotic.

Indanedione (*1,2-indanedione*) (indanedione–zinc) is a ninhydrin analog that is still emerging in forensic laboratories around the world. The reagent was developed in the mid- to late 1990s. It has since been tested and improved over time by dozens of scientists and research groups. Indanedione reacts with the amino acids in fingerprint residues. The fingerprints it produces are both visible (like ninhydrin fingerprints) and fluorescent (like DFO fingerprints) (Figure 11.7). The visible fingerprints are pink in color and are lighter than Ruhemann's purple.

Indanedione (in its indanedione–zinc form) has been shown to develop fingerprints better than DFO or ninhydrin alone. It also performed better on its own than with DFO and ninhydrin in sequence.[13–19] It has been suggested that indanedione replace the current DFO–ninhydrin sequence, though many fingerprint analysts have simply added

(a)   (b)

Figure 11.7 A fingerprint developed with indanedione on paper is visible under white light (a) and fluorescent under green light from a forensic light source (b).

indanedione to the sequence. If used in sequence, it is used first, followed by DFO, and finally ninhydrin. One limitation to indanedione is that preliminary research suggests it may degrade DNA. If DNA analysis is requested on a particular item, it must be done within 6 days of processing with indanedione.

Just like the ninhydrin and DFO processes, indanedione is applied in a fume hood by thoroughly saturating the paper by dipping, spraying, or painting. A common formulation for indanedione working solution using HFE7100™ as a carrier solvent is listed in Appendix B. The item is dried in a fume hood. Like DFO, indanedione must be heated after the treated item is dried. The best results develop when the items are heated with a heat press set at 165°C for 10 s.[18] However, since most forensics laboratories do not have a heat press available, the dried items can be heated in an incubator at 100°C for 20 min at 65% relative humidity. The processed items can be viewed with an alternate light source or laser set to ~520 nm (green light). The items must be viewed through orange or red goggles and photographed with an orange or red barrier filter. The indanedione process is fast and easy and results in high-quality visible and fluorescent fingerprints.

11.7 Physical Developer

Amino acid reagents are relatively fast, easy, and sensitive processes for developing fingerprints on porous items. However, if the items have been wetted—through exposure to the elements, a garbage can, kitchens or bathrooms, or humid conditions—the amino acids and water-soluble compounds in the fingerprint residue will dissipate. A different reagent must be used: one that reacts with the water-insoluble, sebaceous components of latent prints that remain on the surface or slightly embedded in the porous substrate. There are several reagents that have been tested over the years. The most common reagent is PD. Its name is a misnomer, as PD is not actually a physical process but a chemical one. PD is not only sensitive to lipids and oils in fingerprint residues, but it can also develop very old fingerprints. In one case, it developed 30-year-old fingerprints and has been reported to develop fingerprints over 50 years old.[9,21]

PD is a fingerprint processing technique adapted from photographic development reagents. In a photo lab where photographs are developed by hand, the photo paper is placed in a tray with a chemical reagent and agitated, or gently rocked, until an image appears. PD is a similar technique. The item of evidence is gently agitated in a chemical reagent until dark gray or black fingerprints appear. It was first developed in the 1970s in the United Kingdom as a result of research contracted by the British Home Office through the Atomic Weapons Research Establishment.[1,21,22]

PD can be used in sequence with the amino acid reagents, but it must be used last. The complete sequence is as follows: indanedione–zinc or DFO, ninhydrin, and PD. However, if the item has been wetted, it is preferable to use PD on its own. If the item is wet when it is received, it does not have to be dried before the PD process is used.

Many different formulations have been researched over the years. Regardless of the method used, the complicated set of chemical processes result in silver metal deposits along the ridges of the latent fingerprints. The silver comes from a silver nitrate solution that is used to make the PD. All PD formulations have four steps: a presoak in an acidic solution, development in the PD working solution, a rinse in water followed by bleach solution, and a drying stage.

The first step is to soak the porous item in an acid: traditionally maleic acid. This acid has several functions. It removes the calcium carbonate from the paper to avoid creating nucleation sites for the silver particles. The acid will also ensure the pH of the solution does not become too basic and lower the acidity of the material.[22] The reaction works best in an acidic environment. It minimizes the background staining and increases contrast between the gray/black fingerprints and the background.[21]

The second step in the process is to agitate the now acidic item in the PD working solution for anywhere from 10 to 60 min, depending on how quickly and completely the fingerprints appear. The silver deposits all over the surface but adheres more strongly to latent print residues. The PD solution requires silver and iron ions in a slightly acidic buffer with a cationic surfactant.[1,21,22] A *cationic surfactant* is a detergent (soap) with a *hydrophilic* (water binding) head and a *hydrophobic* (lipid binding) tail. The surfactant is used to keep too much silver from being deposited on the substrate by binding some of the silver in a *micelle* structure with the silver ions held in the center of a circular structure of alternating hydrophilic and hydrophobic ends (Figure 11.8).[1,5,22] The surfactant also stabilizes the solution to give it a longer shelf life.[22]

Three separate stock solutions are made separately then combined together to form the PD working solution. *Stock solutions* are the individual aqueous components of the reagent that must be mixed together to make a working solution. A *working solution* is the reagent used to develop the fingerprints. The first solution is the redox solution (oxidation–reduction agent). The second solution is the surfactant, or detergent, solution. The third solution is the silver nitrate solution, which consists of 10 g silver nitrate and 50 mL distilled water. The final working solution is a mixture of all three stock solutions (see Appendix B). The working solution should be prepared only when it is going to be used, as it has a shorter shelf life than each stock solution alone.

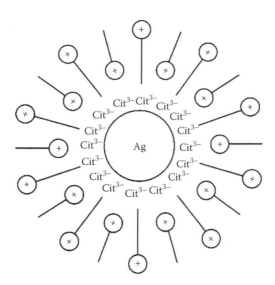

Figure 11.8 Cationic surfactant molecules with hydrophobic "tails" and hydrophilic "heads" (in the diagram, the latter are represented by circles containing positive charges) surround a small amount of silver. The citrate ions surrounding the silver are absorbed during treatment with a citric acid solution. (Reprinted from Cantu, A. and Johnson, J., Methods of latent finger-print development, in *Advances in Fingerprint Technology*, Taylor & Francis, Boca Raton, FL, 2001. With permission.)

After the fingerprints are developed in the PD working solution, the porous item is either rinsed in water or immersed in a posttreatment of 1:1 household bleach to water. The bleach solution fades the background staining. It also causes silver oxide to form along the silver fingerprint to darken it. If the background staining on the item is significant, bleaching is suggested. If the background staining is minimal, a water rinse should be sufficient. Finally, the item must be thoroughly dried.

While PD is effective, it is a cumbersome process that requires several processing steps and the preparation of multiple reagents. The process takes up to an hour to complete after the reagents are prepared. Soaking the paper in an acidic solution weakens the paper, which can tear easily. Also, the silver may be deposited in any creases, marks, or indentations on the evidence or in cracked or abraded glassware used to hold the working solution. Care must be taken to avoid creasing the porous item and to use clean, scratch-free glassware that has been rinsed in distilled water. The PD reagents are expensive. The process is also destructive as it permanently stains any surface it comes into contact with, so few processes can be used afterwards. Because of these negative points, many forensic laboratories do not use PD as part of their regular processing sequence.

11.8 I Had a Case: Operation Pendennis

(Submitted by Rick Sinclair, Detective Senior Sergeant, Fingerprint Operations, Identification Services Branch, Forensic Services Group, New South Wales Police Force)

Since the 9/11 attacks on the World Trade Center in New York, city, state, and federal law enforcement agencies around the world have invested more resources to investigate "home-grown" terrorists. In July of 2004, a joint investigation into two suspected terror cells began in Sydney and Melbourne, Australia. The New South Wales Police, Victoria Police, Australian Federal Police, and Australian Security Intelligence Organisation initiated an extensive 16-month operation—Operation Pendennis—to gather intelligence and evidence against these terrorist cells, members of whom were loosely connected both with Al Qaeda and the Southeast Asian terrorist organization Lashkar-e-Taiba.

The individuals under investigation had organized several terrorist training camps in the Australian Outback. They were in possession of beheading videos, weapons, ammunition, diagrams for building improvised explosive devices, electrical timers, circuitry, railway detonators, and jihadi propaganda. In addition to the intelligence and physical evidence, investigators of the Sydney cell developed a latent fingerprint on a bank deposit slip. The fingerprint, developed with indanedione, turned out to be critical forensic evidence linking a suspect to financial transactions in support of the cell's planning to commit a terrorist act in Sydney. Fingerprint evidence plays a critical role not only in local police investigations but also in homeland security operations worldwide.

11.9   Chapter Summary

Porous items are items that are permeable to liquids and gases because they contain pores. Examples of porous items include paper, cardboard, and wood. When fingerprints are deposited on a porous surface, they permeate the fibers. The water-soluble components of the fingerprint residue are absorbed into the surface, while the non-water-soluble components sit on the surface until they are wiped away or destroyed by environmental factors.

Aqueous chemical reagents can be applied to porous items in particular sequence to develop both visible and fluorescent products. The chemical reagents that react with amino acids are indanedione, DFO, and ninhydrin. Indanedione must be used first. It produces visible pink-colored fingerprints as well as highly fluorescent fingerprints. DFO produces a fluorescent product. Ninhydrin is used after indanedione and/or DFO and produces highly visible purple fingerprints. The most common chemical reagent that reacts with the sebaceous components of fingerprint residues is PD. PD must be used last in the sequence.

Review Questions

1. List at least five porous items you encounter in your daily life.
2. Why is it important to use the chemical reagents in a particular sequence?
3. Put the following reagents in order of how they should be used in sequence:
   a. DFO
   b. PD
   c. Ninhydrin
   d. Indanedione
4. Which reagents react with the amino acids in fingerprint residues?
5. What is the name of the colored dye product that results from a chemical reaction between ninhydrin and amino acids?
6. Why should ninhydrin-treated items be allowed to sit at room temperature to develop for 24–48 h even though the process can be sped up with heat and humidity?

7. If ninhydrin-processed items must be developed immediately, what is the suggested method of development?
8. Why are the fluorescent fingerprints developed with DFO often preferable to the visible fingerprints developed with ninhydrin?
9. How are DFO-processed fingerprints developed and visualized?
10. Why is indanedione an improved method of fingerprint development when compared with DFO and ninhydrin?
11. What is one limitation to using indanedione on evidence?
12. How are fingerprints developed and visualized using indanedione?
13. What are the four steps for processing a wet piece of paper using PD?
14. What are the five undesirable traits of PD development?

References

1. Champod, C. et al. 2004. *Fingerprints and Other Ridge Skin Impressions.* Boca Raton, FL: Taylor & Francis.
2. Almog, J., Azoury, M. et al. 2004. Fingerprints' third dimension: The depth and shape of fingerprints penetration into paper—Cross section examination by fluorescence microscopy. *J. Forensic Sci.* 49(5): 981–985.
3. Yamashita, B. and French, M. 2011. Latent print development. In The Scientific Working Group on Friction Ridge Analysis, Study and Technology (SWGFAST) et al. *The Fingerprint Sourcebook.* Washington, DC: National Institute of Justice, U.S. Department of Justice, Office of Justice Programs.
4. Olsen, R.D. 1978. *Scott's Fingerprint Mechanics.* Springfield, IL: Charles C. Thomas.
5. Cantu, A. and Johnson, J. 2001. Methods of latent fingerprint development. In Lee, H.C. and Gaensslen, R.E. (eds.), *Advances in Fingerprint Technology,* 2nd edn. Boca Raton, FL: Taylor & Francis.
6. Oden, S. and von Hofsten, B. 1954. Detection of fingerprints by the ninhydrin reaction. *Nature* 173(4401): 449–450.
7. Levy, A.L. and Chung, D. 1953. Two-dimensional chromatography of amino acids on buffered papers. *Anal. Chem.* 25(3): 396–399.
8. 3M Electronics Markets Materials Division. 2009. 3M™ Novec™ 7100 engineered fluid. Product information. Accessed June 05, 2013. http://multimedia.3m.com/mws/mediawebserver?mwsId=SSSSSufSevTsZxtU4Y_G5x_eevUqevTSevTSevTSeSSSSSS—&fn=prodinfo_nvc7100.pdf.
9. Ramotowski, R. 2012. Amino acid reagents. In Ramotowski, R. (ed.), *Advances in Fingerprint Technology,* 3rd edn. Boca Raton, FL: Taylor & Francis.
10. Pounds, C.A., Grigg, R., and Mongkolaussavaratana, T. 1990. The use of 1,8-diazafluoren-9-one (DFO) for the fluorescent detection of latent fingerprints on paper. A preliminary evaluation. *J. Forensic Sci.* 35(1): 169–175.
11. McComiskey, P. 1990. DFO: A Simple and quick method for the development of latent fingerprints. *Fingerprint Whorld.* 16: 64–65.
12. Masters, N., Morgan, R., and Shipp, E. 1991. DFO, Its Usage and Results: A study of treatment on various paper substrates and the resulting fluorescence under a variety of excitation wavelengths. *J. Forensic Identif.* 41(1): 3–10.
13. Almog, J. 2012. Fingerprint development by ninhydrin and its analogues. In Ramotowski, R. (ed.), *Advances in Fingerprint Technology,* 3rd edn. Boca Raton, FL: Taylor & Francis.
14. Almog, J., Hirshfeld, A., and Klug, J.T. 1982. Reagents for the chemical development of latent fingerprints: Synthesis and properties of some ninhydrin analogues. *J. Forensic Sci.* 27(4): 912–917.

15. Almog, J. et al. 1999. Latent fingerprint visualization by 1,2-indanedione and related compounds: Preliminary results. *J. Forensic Sci.* 44(1): 114–118.
16. Roux, C. et al. 2000. Evaluation of 1,2-Indanedione and 5,6-methoxy-1,2-Indanedione for the detection of latent fingerprints on porous surfaces. *J. Forensic Sci.* 45(4): 761–769.
17. Wiesner, S. et al. 2001. Chemical development of latent fingerprints: 1,2-Indanedione has come of age. *J. Forensic Sci.* 46(5): 1082–1084.
18. Wallace-Kunkel, C. et al. 2007. Optimisation and evaluation of 1,2-Indanedione for use as a fingermark reagent and its application to real samples. *Forensic Sci. Int.* 168(1): 14–26.
19. Bicknell, D.E. and Ramotowski, R.S. 2008. Use of an optimized 1,2-indanedione process for the development of latent prints. *J. Forensic Sci.* 53(5): 1108–1116.
20. Berdejo, S., Rowe, M., and Bond, J. 2011. Latent fingermark development on a range of porous substrates using ninhydrin analogs—A comparison with ninhydrin and 1,8-diazofluoren. *J. Forensic Sci.* 57(2): 509–514.
21. Phillips, C.E., Cole, D.O., and Jones, G.W. 1990. Physical developer: A practical and productive latent print developer. *J. Forensic Identif.* 40(3): 135–147.
22. Wilson, J.D. et al. 2007. Examination of the steps leading up to the physical developer process for developing fingerprints. *J. Forensic Sci.* 52(2): 320–329.

Chemical Processing Methods
Nonporous Substrates

12

Key Terms

- Nonporous
- Superglue® fuming
- Cyanoacrylate ester (CA)
- Vaporization
- Polymerization
- Monomers
- Polymer
- Polycyanoacrylate
- Nucleophile
- Fuming chamber
- Vacuum chamber
- Dye staining
- Luminescent
- Fluorescence
- Barrier filter
- RAM
- Rhodamine 6G (R6G)
- Ardrox
- Basic yellow 40 (BY 40)
- MBD
- Vacuum metal deposition (VMD)
- Semiporous

Learning Objectives

- Define the key terms.
- Give examples of nonporous and semiporous items.
- Understand the sequential processes for nonporous substrates.
- Describe the vaporization and polymerization of cyanoacrylate.
- Describe the two most common methods of Superglue fuming.
- Describe the most common dye stains and the mechanism of their reaction with cyanoacrylate.
- Understand the vacuum metal deposition (VMD) process.
- Describe the sequential processing methods for semiporous substrates.

12.1   Nonporous Substrates

In this digital age, many of the objects we handle in our daily lives are nonporous. Most items are manufactured from metal, plastic, and glass. These surfaces are considered *nonporous*: not permeable to gases and liquids. Examples of nonporous items include cell phones, drinking glasses, plastic bags, and vehicle exteriors. When a fingerprint is deposited on a nonporous substrate, the matrix does not penetrate the surface. Over time, the water in the fingerprint residue evaporates, leaving behind the water-insoluble components (lipids, waxy compounds, etc.) and the components that do not evaporate with the water (amino acids, sodium chloride, urea, etc.).

Unlike fingerprints on porous objects, the fingerprints on nonporous objects remain on the surface (Figure 12.1).[6] This makes them very fragile. These fingerprints can easily be wiped off if the object is handled improperly. Crime scene technicians must avoid handling any surfaces that may contain latent prints. Items that will be processed for fingerprints can be handled on any heavily textured or rough surface where friction ridge detail cannot be successfully developed and recorded. If the item is completely smooth, it can be handled by the edges. It is also important to take care when packaging nonporous items of evidence for that same reason. Fingerprints may be rubbed off in transit by the action of evidence bags rubbing up against the item or if it is secured in a package that is too small.

The durability of latent fingerprints is affected not only by the actions of those people handling evidentiary items but also by environmental factors such as wind, rain, temperature, and humidity. Rain can obliterate fingerprints. Wind and dry weather can dry prints out quickly, as can exposure to direct sunlight. Leaves, dirt, or sand may blow across the surface, obliterating the prints. A fingerprint in the shade in humid weather may survive much longer than a fingerprint in full sun in a desert environment.

Fingerprint powders and powder suspensions such as small particle reagent (see Chapter 10) are the traditional methods for developing fingerprints on nonporous surfaces. However, these processing methods are not sensitive. Powders adhere to the oils and aqueous components of fingerprints. Fingerprint powders are used on fixed objects or large

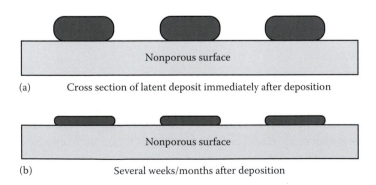

(a)   Cross section of latent deposit immediately after deposition

(b)   Several weeks/months after deposition

Figure 12.1 A cross section of fingerprint residues deposited on a nonporous substrate such as glass. When the fingerprint is deposited on the surface (a), both the water-soluble and water-insoluble components remain on the surface (b). (Reprinted from Champod, C., *Fingerprints and Other Ridge Skin Impressions*, Taylor & Francis, Boca Raton, FL, 2004, Figure 4.2. With permission.)

surfaces at crime scenes. Smaller items and items containing aged latent prints should be carefully collected, packaged, and submitted for fingerprint processing.

12.2 Sequential Processing

Chemical reagents are available for processing nonporous items, just as they are for processing porous items. The fingerprint examiner must ask similar questions to those she would ask if the item were porous. What color is the item? Is the item fluorescent? Is the item now or has it ever been wetted? How porous is the item? There may be patent prints visible on the surface. Those fingerprints should be photographed prior to processing. During the chemical development process, the fingerprint examiner should wear personal protective equipment such as a laboratory coat, laboratory goggles or safety glasses, and gloves.

Just like the chemicals used to process porous items, chemical reagents for nonporous items are applied in a particular sequence in order to be effective (see Appendix A). Following each process, any fingerprints that are revealed are photographed before moving on to the next process.

One of the most common methods for developing fingerprints on nonporous surfaces is Superglue fuming. (Cyanoacrylate ester [CA] is the chemical name for Superglue, which is a registered trademark.) *Superglue fuming* involves vaporizing CA in an enclosed chamber. This technique is always the first chemical process used to develop latent prints on nonporous items. The process "fixes" the latent print so that it can be further developed. The object is then treated with a dye stain that selectively adheres to the CA residue. Another alternative is to use VMD between the cyanoacrylate fuming step and the dye staining step. The following is the sequence proposed in this and other texts:

1. Visual examination
2. CA (Superglue) fuming
3. Dye staining
4. Laser or alternate light source (ALS)
5. Fingerprint powder
6. VMD

12.3 Cyanoacrylate Ester: Superglue Fuming

In the 1970s, it was discovered that cyanoacrylate fumes cause latent fingerprints to turn white and become visible.[1,2] The Japanese National Police Agency developed this technique around the same time it was being examined in the United Kingdom.[3] In 1982, Ed German, a forensic scientist with the U.S. Army Criminal Investigation Laboratory in the Pacific (USACIL-Pacific), introduced the cyanoacrylate fuming technique to forensic science laboratories in the United States.[1-3] As with many other accidental discoveries, this discovery made an impact on the field of fingerprint analysis and changed the way forensic laboratories process evidence. CA fuming has become a routine process for fingerprint laboratories worldwide.

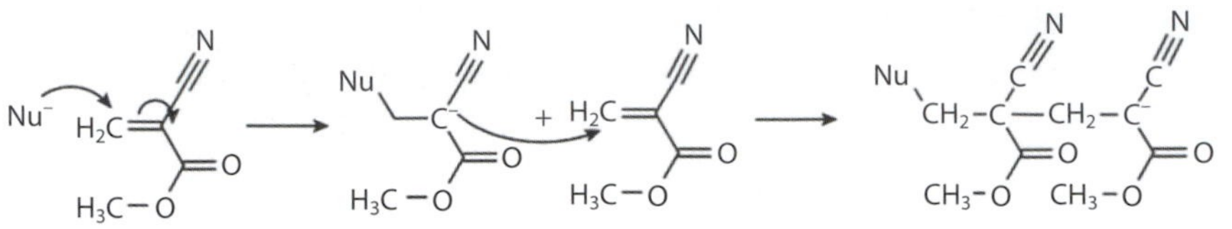

Figure 12.2 The cyanoacrylate polymerization reaction.

Cyanoacrylate fumes selectively adhere to latent print residues. The result is white, 3D fingerprints. The process effectively "glues" fingerprints to the surface of an object, making them more durable (though not indestructible). Extensive and continuing research has demonstrated that cyanoacrylate fuming develops fingerprints on any nonporous surface, including the following: plastic bags, tape, plastic, Styrofoam™, carbon paper, firearms, metal, glass, coated papers, finished and painted wood, aluminum foil, cellophane, rubber bands, and even smooth rocks.[1-3]

The mechanisms for this process are *vaporization* and *polymerization*. Vaporization is the conversion of a liquid to a gas. Polymerization occurs when individual molecules (called *monomers*) link together to form a chain. That long-chain molecule is called a *polymer*. In the case of cyanoacrylate fuming, a monomer of cyanoacrylate is attracted to the latent print residue. It binds to the residue. Other monomers of cyanoacrylate bind to it. This causes a chain of cyanoacrylate molecules to form along the friction ridges, resulting in white ridges of polymerized cyanoacrylate. Figure 12.2 shows the polymerization reaction for cyanoacrylate resulting in a product known as *polycyanoacrylate*.[7]

The specific mechanism for these molecular interactions is still unclear. In order for the polymerization reaction to occur, the cyanoacrylate monomer needs something to react with to initiate polymerization. This "initiator" is known as a *nucleophile*. A nucleophile is a molecule that donates electrons to form chemical bonds. Various components of the latent print residue have been suggested as initiators. Water molecules, amino acids, and sodium lactate can all act as nucleophiles, and all have been proposed by researchers as possible initiators of polymerization.[3,4]

Other variables that may affect the polymerization reaction include the temperature of the surface of the item and the environment, the humidity of the fuming chamber and the laboratory prior to processing, and the age of the latent print.[1-6] It is suggested that low pH, high humidity, warm temperatures, and fresh latent prints are ideal settings for developing fingerprints using the cyanoacrylate fuming method.[1-6] As of the publication date of this chapter, research into this polymerization reaction continues.

There are many different methods for processing items of evidence with cyanoacrylate. The two most popular methods are the fuming chamber method and the vacuum chamber method. Both methods cause the liquid cyanoacrylate to vaporize so the fumes can interact with the latent print residues. In the cyanoacrylate fuming chamber, the liquid cyanoacrylate is heated until it vaporizes. In the vacuum chamber, a pump pulls air from the chamber to reduce the pressure, resulting in the immediate vaporization of the cyanoacrylate without heat.

A *fuming chamber* can be any container that can be sealed shut. The chamber's job is to contain the fumes. A plastic box, a fish tank, a vehicle, or even a Ziploc™ bag can act as a fuming chamber. Heating the cyanoacrylate requires a heat source. A heat source can be a mug warmer, hot plate, alcohol lamp, hair dryer, light bulb, or even the sun.[1]

Figure 12.3 This photograph shows a cyanoacrylate fuming chamber constructed from a fish tank, Plexiglas lid, and mug warmer. The string and clips suspend the evidence to allow the vaporized cyanoacrylate to reach every surface.

The Superglue fuming process can work with a simple setup consisting of the items listed previously (Figure 12.3). However, it works better in a humid environment. The simple addition of a cup of hot water can serve to humidify the chamber. Homemade Superglue chambers are still found in forensics labs and universities today. A sealable fish tank containing a hot plate and a string of rods with clips for hanging items of evidence is a simple and inexpensive Superglue fuming setup.

There are also commercial fuming chambers available for purchase from forensic vendors (Figure 12.4). These chambers have many advantages over homemade versions.

Figure 12.4 Mystaire® Misonix CA-3000 cyanoacrylate fuming chamber. (Reprinted with permission from Mystaire Misonix. http://www.mystaire.com/forensic/cyanoacrylate-chambers. Accessed June 4, 2014.)

They have built-in temperature-controlled heat sources. The temperature cannot be easily controlled with some heat sources such as light bulbs or hot plates. If the glue gets too hot (above 205°C–220°C), it releases toxic hydrogen cyanide gas.[3] Commercial equipment prevents the overheating of cyanoacrylate. Many of the commercial chambers also have internal fans to circulate the cyanoacrylate fumes throughout the chamber. This ensures even distribution of the vapors. Some also have built-in humidifiers or the option to attach an external humidifier in order to control the relative humidity inside the chamber. The ideal humidity for the polymerization process is 60%–80%.[3,4] Many commercial fuming chambers also have built-in fume hoods with special filters to evacuate all harmful fumes from the chamber at the end of the cycle. The downside of these commercial units is that they are often prohibitively expensive for many smaller forensic labs and police departments.

Regardless of the chamber and heat source used, the process is relatively straightforward. Evidentiary items are suspended or placed in the chamber (Figure 12.5). If multiple items are fumed at the same time, there should be enough space between the items to allow the vapors to circulate. A source of humidity, such as a cup of hot water, is placed in the chamber. Several drops of cyanoacrylate (~0.5 g) are placed on an aluminum tray over a heating element (Figure 12.6).[7] The chamber is then sealed and the heating element turned on. The items should be allowed to fume for anywhere from 5 to 60 min. The time it takes to process is dependent on many factors including the type of item, age of the print, humidity of the chamber, and size of the chamber.

Since the timing is critical for successful cyanoacrylate development, it is good practice to include a control sample with your evidentiary items. The control can be a glass slide or a black latent lift card with a fingerprint deliberately deposited on it. The control sample should be similar to the type of evidence that will be processed. The control print should be sebaceous sweat. Fingers can be "charged" with sebaceous sweat by rubbing a thumb on the forehead or side of the nose, then lightly pressing the thumb to the control surface. When you begin to see white ridges developing on the control, the process is complete

Figure 12.5 An AK-47-type rifle is placed in the cyanoacrylate fuming chamber.

Figure 12.6 Cyanoacrylate is added to an aluminum tray on the heating element of the cyanoacrylate fuming chamber.

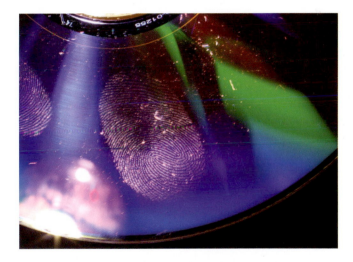

Figure 12.7 A cyanoacrylate fingerprint developed on a CD.

(Figure 12.7). If the control sample does not show signs of development, it should be processed with cyanoacrylate dye stains (see Section 12.4) as the prints may be faint and not readily visible. Latent prints must be successfully developed on a control substrate before evidence is processed in any cyanoacrylate chamber.

You may not always see well-defined, white fingerprints on your items of evidence when they are removed from the fuming chamber. This is preferable to the alternative: overprocessing the item. A reliability test should be performed prior to using any fingerprint development process. Overprocessing is a serious problem. Once the item is coated with cyanoacrylate, the glue cannot be removed. If the item is left in the chamber too long, the background and the furrows of the ridges will be coated with cyanoacrylate along with the friction ridges. This not only results in poor contrast between the friction ridges and the background but also causes the dye stains to adhere to the background as well as

Figure 12.8 A cyanoacrylate vacuum chamber.

the latent print. The end result is an indistinct fingerprint with poor contrast. There are other problems encountered when the fuming chamber is used. Watkin et al. state, "the path of the (cyanoacrylate) fumes produced cannot be controlled or predicted, sometimes resulting in uneven coverage of an exhibit."[8] They also emphasize the health and safety threat inherent with exposure to large amounts of cyanoacrylate fumes.

Items processed in cyanoacrylate vacuum chambers do not have the same problem with overfuming if an item is left in the chamber too long. They also utilize minimal amounts of cyanoacrylate vapor. A *vacuum chamber* is a thick metal chamber with a lid that creates a tight seal with a rubber O-ring (Figure 12.8). Heat is not used in the chamber. Instead, the glue is placed in the chamber on a metal tray or coated on foil to increase the surface area of the glue. The items of evidence are placed in the chamber, and the lid is sealed. A vacuum pump evacuates air from the chamber, decreasing the atmospheric pressure to less than 1 torr. One torr is equal to 0.001 atmospheres of pressure or 0.02 lbs/in.^{2}. The reduced pressure causes the glue to vaporize quickly. The vapor is evenly dispersed throughout the chamber without the pressure of air filling the chamber. The pump is then turned off and the items are left to develop at room temperature in the reduced-pressure environment. The items are left to fume for 20–30 min.

When processed in a cyanoacrylate vacuum chamber, the resulting fingerprints are not white in appearance. They are usually very faint, if visible at all. The polymerization process creates a thin coat of cyanoacrylate that is often translucent. Research has found that the vacuum chamber fuming method is a superior process when latent fingerprints are further developed with dye stains.[8] The drawbacks to vacuum fuming are that you cannot put wet items or items under pressure (such as unopened soda cans or bottles) in the chamber. Also, the equipment can be prohibitively expensive to purchase and maintain.

Besides the heat/humidity and vacuum fuming methods, there are also devices available known as fuming wands. These were developed as portable units for use at crime scenes. The wand is a handheld device that generates heat with butane, similar to a cigarette lighter. A glue cartridge is attached to the tip of the device. As the wand

Figure 12.9 A cyanoacrylate fuming wand. (Reprinted with permission from Safariland, Inc. http://forensicssource.com/CategoryDetail.aspx?CategoryName=Cyanoacrylate-Fuming-Supplies. Accessed June 4, 2014.)

heats up, the glue vaporizes and is expelled from the tip. The glue vapor is passed over an area of interest or an item of evidence (Figure 12.9). While this device is convenient and portable, it is not recommended. It is easy to overdevelop latent prints using this method. It is difficult to control the vapor. It also exposes the user to a significant amount of hazardous vapor.

Another method of cyanoacrylate fuming is the chemical acceleration method. This method can be used when a heat source is unavailable. The process involves soaking a cotton ball or cotton pad with sodium hydroxide (2 g NaOH in 100 mL H_2O). The cotton is then dried and stored. When chemical acceleration is necessary, a few drops of cyanoacrylate are applied to the dried cotton. This causes an exothermic (heat-producing) reaction that immediately vaporizes the cyanoacrylate.

This method may be used to create vapors in a fuming chamber. Other methods of development are available, such as thin aluminum sheets coated with cyanoacrylate. These packets are peeled apart and used in vacuum chambers, cars, tents, or other enclosed areas. The thin layer of cyanoacrylate in these packets provides a greater surface area of cyanoacrylate for more efficient fuming.

Regardless of the method, equipment, or initiation process used, cyanoacrylate fuming is always the first step in the nonporous processing sequence following optical, nondestructive methods such as ALS, laser, and reflective UV imaging systems (RUVIS). However, the white or translucent fingerprints are not easy to see with the naked eye. What prints are visible should be photographed. They can also be examined and photographed using a RUVIS, which is a nondestructive visualization technique using shortwave UV radiation (see Chapter 9). Following the documentation step, further enhancement is required to improve the contrast of the fingerprint.

12.4   Cyanoacrylate Dye Stains

Once an item is processed with cyanoacrylate, it is either treated immediately with a dye stain or left to sit overnight to allow the polymerization to set.[3] A dye stain is then applied to the item. This process is known as *dye staining. Luminescent* (glowing) dye stains selectively adhere to the cyanoacrylate polymer deposited along the friction ridges. The theory

Figure 12.10 Application of R6G dye stain.

Figure 12.11 Monochromatic laser light viewed without a barrier filter.

of dye staining is that "dye molecules get stuck in the polymer by filling voids in the compound."[3]

Dye stains are easy to use. They are prepared by dissolving the material in a solvent or mixture of solvents. They are applied by spraying or dipping, rinsed with an alcohol solvent or water, and dried (Figure 12.10). The resulting *fluorescence* is viewed with an ALS, UV lamp, or laser depending on the dye stain. The light source shines a powerful beam of light set to a specific wavelength (color) onto the dye-stained item (Figure 12.11). This step is performed in a darkened room.

A *barrier filter* allows fluorescent fingerprints to be seen with the naked eye. It allows light of a certain wavelength range to be viewed and blocks the rest of the light. Barrier filters are colored safety glasses, camera filters, or Plexiglas sheets (Figure 12.12).

Figure 12.12 Colored safety glasses worn as barrier filters in conjunction with a forensic light source.

High contrast is observed with yellow or orange fingerprints "glowing" on a dark background. Different colors of light and barrier filters are suggested for each dye stain. Depending on the background color and luminescence of the items processed, items treated with the same dye stain may display different levels of contrast when viewed with different wavelengths of light.

There have been many dye stains proposed over the years. This chapter will cover the most common dye stains used in forensic laboratories to date: Rhodamine 6G (R6G), Ardrox, 7-(*p*-methoxybenzylamino)-4-nitrobenzene-2-oxa-1,3-diazole (MBD), and basic yellow 40 (BY 40). Each dye stain is viewed under a specific colored light source (or a range of wavelengths). It is also possible to mix certain dyes together to cause the fingerprints to fluoresce over a wider range of wavelengths (multiple colored light sources). The most popular dye mix is *RAM*, which is a combination of R6G, Ardrox, and MBD.

Some of the preferred dye stain working solutions are made using petroleum ether. Petroleum ether is a volatile, highly flammable nonpolar solvent and should be handled with great care. It is flammable when combined with strong oxidizers or when exposed to temperatures above its flashpoint. Some dye stain formulations include methanol, which is toxic. The Royal Canadian Mounted Police (RCMP) have had success with ethanol- and methanol-based formulations of R6G, Ardrox, and BY 40 (which they refer to as brilliant yellow 40) that do not include petroleum ether.[9]

R6G, also known as basic red 1, is arguably the most popular dye stain used in the United States. It was introduced in the early 1980s and has since become part of the cyanoacrylate processing sequence.[5,10] There was some debate about whether or not the dye is carcinogenic, but research over several decades has produced mixed findings.[11] R6G is safe as long as it is handled properly.

R6G is a solid dark-green powder at room temperature. It is mixed with methanol to form a bright orange working solution (Figure 12.13) (see Appendix B). The Superglue-fumed item is dipped or sprayed and rinsed with tap water or methanol. The item is then viewed with an ALS or laser under blue-green or green illumination. If the item is viewed under blue-green light (wavelengths between 490 and 515 nm), it is viewed using an orange barrier filter. If the item is viewed under green light (wavelengths between 515 and 550 nm), it is viewed using a red barrier filter. The fluorescent prints will appear bright yellow or orange in color against a dark background (Figure 12.14).

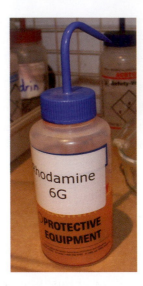

Figure 12.13 A working solution of R6G in methanol.

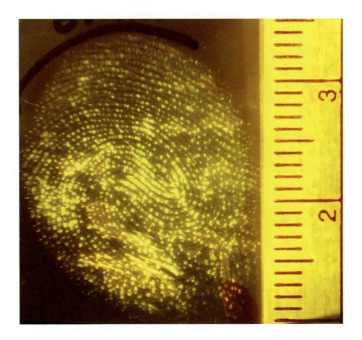

Figure 12.14 A fingerprint on a glass surface developed with cyanoacrylate fuming and dyed with R6G.

Ardrox was proposed as a strongly fluorescent alternative to R6G in the 1980s.[5] Original formulas included Freon 113 as a solvent, but research in the late 1990s demonstrated that a solvent of methyl ethyl ketone (MEK) was more economical.[12] The RCMP use a simplified formula of aqueous Ardrox solution in methanol (see Appendix B).[9] Cyanoacrylate-fumed prints treated with this dye stain vary in appearance from whitish-yellow to yellow to green when viewed under UV and blue light, depending on the solvent and light source used. Ardrox in MEK will appear green. Ardrox in methanol will appear yellow. Ardrox-dyed prints are viewed under long-wave UV radiation (in the 365–380 nm range) with

UV protective or yellow barrier filters. Like sunglasses, the UV protective glasses filter out harmful UV radiation that may damage the eyes. All exposed skin surfaces should be protected from both short- and long-wave UV radiation by wearing proper personal protective equipment at all times.

BY 40 is a nontoxic alternative reported by Kent et al. to be more effective than R6G and equivalent to Ardrox.[5] There are several suggested formulations of BY 40. The nontoxic ethanol formulation is presented in Appendix B. As its name suggests, fingerprints treated with BY 40 fluoresce yellow. Fluorescence is viewed under long-wave UV radiation around 365 nm using a UV protective or yellow barrier filter. It can also be viewed under blue-green light (450 nm) using an orange barrier filter.

RAM is a mixture of several dye stains that can be viewed under a wide spectrum of colored illumination. It is a mixture of R6G, Ardrox, and a third dye stain called MBD. *MBD* is viewed under blue-green (~450 nm) or green light (515 nm) with an orange barrier filter. This dye stain mixture allows the examiner to view the item under UV, blue, and green light ranging from 365 to 550 nm. The proper UV, yellow, orange, and red barrier filters must be used with each range of wavelengths.

Researchers are in the process of experimenting with a cyanoacrylate dye complex that is a mixture of dye and cyanoacrylate. The goal is to develop a one-step fuming process that both fumes the print and dye stains it. The dye molecules would be deposited during polymerization and could be immediately viewed with a forensic light source. Research into this process, as well as into novel dye stains, continues. Some of these dye complexes are now available through commercial suppliers.

Regardless of the dye stain used, it cannot be used on the porous areas of semiporous items because the substrate absorbs the reagent causing the background to fluoresce along with the print. Dye stains are also not effective on objects that have fluorescent surfaces. There will be no contrast observed between the fingerprint and the background if the background is also "glowing." Instead, fingerprint powder such as black magnetic powder is used on these surfaces. The powder is applied and lifted onto a latent lift card. Even if the item is nonporous, black magnetic fingerprint powder may be used after dye staining any fumed item (Figure 12.15).

12.5   Vacuum Metal Deposition

The process of *VMD* is similar to the process of Superglue fuming in a vacuum. When small amounts of metals are vaporized in a vacuum chamber, the vapors adhere to the surface of the object everywhere but along the friction ridges (Figure 12.16).[6] In this way, it is the opposite reaction of Superglue fuming in a vacuum. In the cyanoacrylate process, the vapors adhere to the friction ridges. The VMD process creates what Champod calls "negative marks," though VMD can actually produce positive development depending on a number of factors.[7] The friction ridges are visible on the object because the background is coated with vaporized metal while the fingerprints remain transparent. VMD has been utilized in the United Kingdom and other countries since 1976 but has not been routinely employed in North America.[13]

VMD has successfully developed fingerprints on all types of surfaces including plastic, cloth, glass, and paper currency. It can be used alone or in sequence after cyanoacrylate fuming and dye staining. It is a sensitive process that may be superior to cyanoacrylate

Figure 12.15 Fingerprints developed with black magnetic fingerprint powder after cyanoacrylate fuming and dye staining.

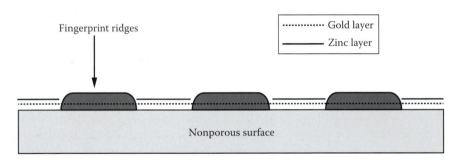

Figure 12.16 A schematic representation of how gold and zinc are deposited on a nonporous surface during VMD. (Reprinted from Champod, C., *Fingerprints and Other Ridge Skin Impressions*, Boca Raton, FL, Taylor & Francis, 2004, Figure 4.24. With permission.)

fuming aged prints. Masters and DeHaan found that VMD is significantly superior to cyanoacrylate fuming when processing latent prints older than 2 years.[14] For fresh prints, cyanoacrylate fuming was equivalent to VMD.[13,14] It is often the only technique to successfully develop prints when other techniques have failed.

The process involves alternately heating minute amounts of gold and zinc in a steel vacuum chamber (Figure 12.17). Like the cyanoacrylate vacuum chamber, the vacuum evacuates the air so the metal vapors do not have to compete with the air molecules. The item of evidence is placed in the chamber. Small amounts of gold (4–20 mg) and zinc (200 mg^{-3} g) are loaded into metal "boats."[13,14] The chamber is then sealed and evacuated to around 1×10^{-4} torr, depending on the manufacturer's specifications.[14] The gold is heated to 1000°C for 15 s.[13,14] The vaporization occurs very quickly in a vacuum. Then the zinc is heated to 1000°C. The zinc, which adheres to the gold, is allowed to vaporize until the surface is coated and the ridges become visible (Figure 12.18).

Figure 12.17 A VMD chamber. (Reprinted with permission from GoEvidence Forensic Laboratories. http://www.goevidence.com/vmd-vacuum-deposition/vmd-processing.php. Accessed June 4, 2014.)

Figure 12.18 Fingerprints on fabric developed in a VMD chamber. (Reprinted with permission from GoEvidence Forensic Laboratories. http://www.goevidence.com/services/details. php?pageid=39. Accessed June 4, 2014.)

While this method is extremely successful, it is not routinely used in most laboratories. VMD chambers are prohibitively expensive. The equipment is therefore not readily available in a majority of agencies and private laboratories. Consequently, cyanoacrylate fuming coupled with dye staining is the most common method for processing latent prints on nonporous items.

12.6 Semiporous Substrates

Paper, cardboard, and wood are porous items. Plastic, glass, and metal are nonporous items. Some items are difficult to categorize as either porous or nonporous. These items are referred to as *semiporous*. Semiporous surfaces may absorb some of the water-soluble components of latent residues, but some may remain on the surface. The sebaceous (oily and waxy) components of fingerprints may stick to the semiporous surface better than smoother, nonporous surfaces.[1]

Examples of semiporous items include magazines, waxy-coated paper products, photographs, glossy wall paints and wallpapers, latex gloves, and varnished woods. The best way to process these items is to use a combination of porous and nonporous processing techniques. For example, cyanoacrylate fuming can be followed by indanedione and/or DFO, ninhydrin, dye staining, and VMD. No matter what combination is used, it should first be tested on a similar surface before it is used on an item of evidence.

12.7 Chapter Summary

Metal, plastic, and glass are all examples of nonporous items. Powders can be used to process large, immovable objects at crime scenes but are not a sensitive processing technique. Cyanoacrylate fuming fixes latent prints to a surface and develops 3D friction ridges. In a fuming chamber, heat and humidity cause the glue to vaporize and coat the fingerprints in white polymer. In a vacuum chamber, the glue vaporizes in a vacuum, resulting in transparent cyanoacrylate prints. After visual examination, cyanoacrylate vaporization is the first process in the sequence. The resulting prints are viewed and photographed.

The next step in the sequence is dye staining. Dye stains selectively adhere to the cyanoacrylate deposited on the friction ridges. Most dye stains are fluorescent and provide excellent contrast on most substrates. Dye stains are applied by spraying or dipping the item. The item is dried and viewed with an ALS. The color light and filter used to view the item depend on the dye stain chosen. R6G, Ardrox, MBD, and BY 40 are the most common cyanoacrylate dye stains. Following dye staining, the item can be processed with fingerprint powder.

The final step in the sequence is VMD, though it is not routinely used in forensic laboratories, especially those in the United States. Small amounts of gold and zinc are vaporized in a vacuum chamber. The metal vapor coats the surface of the item everywhere but where the latent print residues are deposited. VMD can be used on all types of semiporous and nonporous surfaces and has been successful in developing aged prints.

Semiporous items such as magazines, photographs, or varnished woods do not easily fit into either the porous or nonporous processing sequences. A combination of processes can be used, such as the following sequence: cyanoacrylate processing, 1,2-indanedione or DFO, ninhydrin, dye staining and VMD.

Review Questions

1. List 10 nonporous items you see around you.
2. Put the following reagents in order of how they should be used in sequence.
   a. Magnetic powders
   b. Dye staining
   c. Cyanoacrylate fuming
   d. VMD
3. How is a latent print on a nonporous surface different from a latent print deposited on a porous surface?
4. How are latent prints on a nonporous surface similar to those deposited on porous surfaces?
5. What is the chemical name for Superglue?
6. How do cyanoacrylate vapors develop latent fingerprints?
7. How is cyanoacrylate vaporization in a vacuum chamber different from cyanoacrylate vaporization in a fuming chamber?

8. How are latent fingerprints processed in a cyanoacrylate vacuum chamber different from latent fingerprints processed in a cyanoacrylate fuming chamber?
9. Why is it necessary to dye stain cyanoacrylate prints?
10. What color/wavelength of light and barrier filters are used to view objects coated with R6G dye?
11. What color/wavelength of light and barrier filters are used to view objects coated with Ardrox dye?
12. What color barrier filters are used for each of the following colors of light:
    a. UV radiation
    b. Purple (long-wave UV) and blue light (365–445 nm)
    c. Blue-green light (445–515 nm)
    d. Green light (515–550 nm)
13. Why are the fingerprints developed with VMD referred to as "negative prints"?
14. List four semiporous substrates you see around you.
15. What would be a logical sequence for developing latent fingerprints on a photograph?

References

1. Lee, H. and Gaensslen, R.E. 2001. Methods of latent fingerprint development. In Lee, H.C. and Gaensslen, R.E. (eds.), *Fingerprint Technology*, 2nd edn. Boca Raton, FL: Taylor & Francis.
2. Lewis, L.A. et al. 2001. Processes involved in the development of latent fingerprints using the cyanoacrylate fuming method. *J. Forensic Sci.* 46(2): 241–246.
3. Yamashita, B. and French, M. 2011. Latent print development. In The Scientific Working Group on Friction Ridge Analysis, Study and Technology (SWGFAST) et al. *The Fingerprint Sourcebook*. Washington, DC: National Institute of Justice, U.S. Department of Justice, Office of Justice Programs.
4. Czekanski, P., Fasola, M., and Allison, J. 2006. A mechanistic model for the superglue fuming of latent fingerprints. *J. Forensic Sci.* 51(6): 1323–1328.
5. Kent, T. (ed.) (2004) *Manual of Fingerprint Development Techniques*. Sandridge, U.K.: Home Office Police Scientific Development Branch.
6. Wargacki, S., Dadmun, M.D., and Lewis, L. 2005. Identifying the true initiator in the cyanoacrylate fuming method. *Paper Presented at the International Association for Identification Conference*, Dallas, TX.
7. Champod, C. et al. 2004. *Fingerprints and Other Ridge Skin Impressions*. Boca Raton, FL: Taylor & Francis.
8. Watkin, J.E. et al. 1994. Cyanoacrylate fuming of latent prints: Vacuum versus heat/humidity. *J. Forensic Identif.* 44(5): 545–556.
9. Royal Canadian Mounted Police. Fingerprint development techniques. Last modified April 12, 2003. http://www.rcmp-grc.gc.ca/fsis-ssji/firs-srij/recipe-recette-eng.htm.
10. Ramotowski, R. 2012. Vapor/fuming methods. In Ramotowski, R. (ed.), *Advances in Fingerprint Technology*, 3rd edn. Boca Raton, FL: Taylor & Francis.
11. Masters, N.E. 1990. Rhodamine 6G: Taming the beast. *J. Forensic Identif.* 40(5): 265–269.
12. Gamboe, M. and O'Daniel, L. 1999. Substitute ardrox formula. *J. Forensic Identif.* 49(2): 134–141.
13. Misner, A.H. 1992. Latent fingerprint detection on low density polyethylene comparing vacuum metal deposition to cyanoacrylate fuming and fluorescence. *J. Forensic Identif.* 42(1): 26–32.
14. Masters, N.E. and DeHaan, J.D. 1996. Vacuum metal deposition and cyanoacrylate detection of older latent prints. *J. Forensic Identif.* 46(1): 32–45.

Chemical Processing Methods
Other Substrates and Matrices

13

Key Terms

- Powder suspension
- Natural yellow 3
- Sudan black
- Solvent black 3
- Physical developer
- Oil red O
- Vacuum metal deposition (VMD)
- Hemoglobin
- Pathogens
- Chemiluminescent
- Amido black
- Acid black 1
- Ninhydrin
- DFO
- Acid violet 17
- Acid yellow 7
- Gun blueing
- Crystal violet
- Sticky-Side Powder

Learning Objectives

- Define the key terms.
- Describe the various methods for processing greasy fingerprints, bloody fingerprints, fingerprints on adhesive surfaces, fingerprints on skin, and fingerprints on metallic surfaces.
- Understand the challenges inherent in processing each type of matrix.
- List which chemical reagents are most effective on each substrate color and type.
- Understand the safety concerns inherent in processing bloody fingerprints, fingerprints on skin, and fingerprints on weapons.

13.1   Other Surfaces

Fingerprint examiners frequently encounter fingerprints on challenging surfaces and in matrices other than eccrine and sebaceous material. It is not uncommon to come across a greasy or bloody fingerprint. Metallic surfaces like cartridge cases can be problematic.

177

Some of the best latent prints are found on the adhesive sides of tapes, stamps, and labels. It is also possible to visualize fingerprints on human skin, though this has been much more successful in a laboratory than in practice. When these challenging surfaces and matrices are encountered, specific chemical reagents and processes must be used in order to successfully visualize the fingerprint.

As with common porous and nonporous surfaces, the chemicals used to develop the items of interest depend on the surface the fingerprint is deposited on as well as the latent print composition. The surface may be porous, nonporous, or semiporous and dark, patterned or light in color. The fingerprints may be fresh or aged. This chapter will cover some of the miscellaneous processes not covered in previous chapters, including methods for processing greasy fingerprints, bloody fingerprints, fingerprints on adhesive surfaces, fingerprints on skin, and fingerprints on metallic surfaces. All chemical processes should be completed in the laboratory under controlled conditions. During the chemical development process, the fingerprint examiner should wear personal protective equipment such as a laboratory coat, laboratory goggles or safety glasses, and gloves. See Appendix B for all formulations and processing procedures.

13.2   Oily Fingerprints and Greasy Surfaces

Greasy or oily fingerprints may be found on any surface. They are often patent or visible (Figure 13.1). The fingerprint analyst may encounter surfaces that are contaminated with grease and therefore cannot be processed using common porous and nonporous chemical reagents. A perpetrator may have touched a greasy surface or eaten greasy food prior to touching the surface of interest. If an individual touches his or her face, then an object, and that object gets wet, the water-soluble components will be washed away and the oily residue is left behind. Oils, unlike water, do not evaporate and are not water soluble.

Figure 13.1 Greasy fingerprints on a computer tablet screen.

Oils are used in cooking, cosmetics, vehicle lubrication, and fuels. Oily fingerprints are commonly found on fast-food wrappers, bags, and cups; vehicles and garages; kitchen surfaces where greasy foods and cooking oils are used; and bathrooms, where cosmetics and lotions are often used. Fingerprint analysts cannot use standard fingerprint brush and black powder for these surfaces since the powder may clump on the greasy surface. The fingerprint brush will be ruined if it is contaminated with grease.

Oils are viscous, nonpolar substances composed of lipids or petroleum-based products such as grease, oil, or gasoline.[1] Therefore, it is common to use chemical reagents that react with or attach to these substances. These reagents form either a colored or fluorescent product. There are several processes to choose from when processing greasy fingerprints on nonporous surfaces: powder suspensions, cyanoacrylate fuming, natural yellow 3, Sudan black, and/or vacuum metal deposition.

The simplest process is to use a *powder suspension*. A powder of contrasting color (black for a light surface and white or fluorescent for a dark surface) is mixed with equal parts Kodak Photo-Flo® (or another detergent) and water. Spraying the surface or painting the surface with a camel hair or other delicate brush applies the powder suspension to the surface. The surface is then rinsed and the visible fingerprints are photographed. The process is repeated until the fingerprints are visible against the background.

There are also chemical reagents available for processing greasy or oily fingerprints. *Natural yellow 3* is a fluorescent dye synthesized from the roots of the turmeric plant (*Curcuma longa*), a spice native to India and Indonesia.[2] It is also known as curcumin.[2] The dye is a natural plant derivative and a good choice of nontoxic reagent. Because it is fluorescent, it is the best choice for processing oily fingerprints on dark surfaces or fingerprints on dark surfaces that are contaminated with grease.[3] The process involves dipping the item in the solution and rinsing with water (see Appendix B). The fluorescent fingerprints are then viewed and photographed under blue and blue-green light with yellow goggles. Natural yellow is most effective on nonporous substrates.

Sudan black is the most commonly used fingerprint reagent worldwide for developing fingerprints on greasy nonporous or porous surfaces. It is also known as *solvent black 3*. Sudan black solution dyes oily fingerprints a dark blue or black color (Figure 13.2). It is therefore useful on light surfaces where the blue/black prints will be easily visible. Sudan black can also be used to process prints on semiporous substrates such as latex gloves.[4] Items can be cyanoacrylate fumed prior to processing with Sudan black. The procedure involves dipping the item in the prepared solution for 2 min, followed by a water rinse (see Appendix B).

Porous surfaces contaminated with grease or containing oily fingerprints may be processed with *physical developer*. *Oil red O* is another chemical reagent specifically formulated for greasy or oily substrates or fingerprints on porous surfaces (see Appendix B).[5] It is a fat-soluble dye that was first used to develop lip prints in 2002.[1] Oil red O is similar to Sudan black. Sudan black is preferable because it is both more effective and it can be used on both porous and nonporous surfaces. Items processed with oil red O will develop red fingerprints on a light pink background.

Oil red O, similar to physical developer, can develop fingerprints on porous items that have been wetted or exposed to a humid environment.[1,5] Oil red O develops more fingerprints on porous items than physical developer, except on brown paper bags and fingerprint older than 4 weeks.[1,6] Oil red O is also less damaging to the item than physical developer.[1,7] Oil red O can be used in sequence with the previously mentioned techniques in the following order: indanedione or DFO, ninhydrin, oil red O, physical developer.

Figure 13.2 A fingerprint treated with Sudan black. (Reprinted with permission from Bureau voor Dactyloscopische Artikelen, BVDA America, Inc. http://www.bvda.com/EN/sect1/en_1_10a.html. Accessed June 4, 2014.)

Table 13.1 Reagents Effective for Processing Oily Fingerprints and Fingerprints on Greasy Surfaces by Substrate Type

Substrate	Reagent(s)
Nonporous, dark, or patterned	Natural yellow 3, white powder suspension, VMD
Nonporous, light	Sudan black, VMD
Porous, dark, or patterned	1,2-Indanedione, DFO
Porous, light	Oil red O, Sudan black

The final technique that may be used to develop oily fingerprints or fingerprints on greasy surfaces is *vacuum metal deposition* (*VMD*). As was mentioned previously, VMD is a technique that is extremely effective for use on almost every surface and for aged fingerprints. It is, however, cost prohibitive and most forensic laboratories do not have the capability to perform this technique. See Table 13.1 for a summary of these techniques.

13.3 Bloody Fingerprints

The human body contains a volume of blood that may fill one or two gallon jugs, depending on the individual's gender and size. Blood is composed mainly of plasma, white blood cells (leukocytes), and red blood cells (erythrocytes). Plasma is mostly water. White blood cells perform immune functions. Red blood cells contain hemoglobin bound to iron. The iron molecule binds to oxygen, which is circulated throughout the body to oxygenate the body's cells. *Hemoglobin* makes up 95% of red blood cell's protein content and can be processed by chemicals that dye proteins, making them visible.[8]

Fingerprints in blood will almost certainly be encountered when processing violent crime scenes. The safety of the fingerprint analyst and other personnel must be addressed before attempting any of the processing methods described below. Blood can contain harmful *pathogens*, or diseases, such as hepatitis or HIV. Wear gloves at all times and label evidence bags with evidence contaminated with blood, including bloody fingerprints. Wear a particulate mask to avoid inhalation of airborne blood particles. Protect clothing with a lab coat. If a crime scene has a significant amount of blood present, one may choose to wear a Tyvek™ suit, booties, and safety glasses or goggles. Avoid accidental skin punctures and exposure by handling and packaging sharp items such as knives, broken glass, or hypodermic needles with great care. Always wash skin surfaces immediately after handling contaminated items, regardless of whether the skin came into contact with the items. Wash your hands immediately after removing gloves. Use biohazard disposal bags for gloves, bags, disposable equipment, protective clothing, and any other item that may have been contaminated. When the proper safety measures have been employed, you may start the processing procedures summarized below.

Bloody fingerprints can be used to identify the source of the fingerprint. But blood also has investigative value. When one thinks of blood at a crime scene, one may initially think of its value as a source of DNA. However, DNA is not always a potent investigative tool. If the blood at the crime scene belongs to the victim, the source of the blood has little investigative value. Likewise, if the blood belongs to the suspect, but the suspect is both unknown and not found in the DNA database (known as the Combined DNA Index System, or CODIS), the DNA profile obtained is not probative.

Another issue to consider is the size of the fingerprint database versus the size of the DNA database. There are more than 10 times as many fingerprints in Automated Fingerprint Identification Systems (AFIS) than there are DNA profiles. There are many reasons for this discrepancy. Fingerprints have been used as evidence for decades longer than DNA. Fingerprints were automated more than 10 years before DNA. Perhaps the most significant difference is that DNA profiles, unlike fingerprint records, are not collected from all arrestees. Thus, there may be a higher probability of identifying a suspect if the fingerprint can be enhanced and identified. One can never assume a bloodstain or fingerprint belong to a victim, however. The investigator must decide whether it is important to know the source of the fingerprint, the source of the blood, or both. Since techniques for modern DNA extraction, amplification, and analysis require very little blood, it is entirely possible to successfully examine both the fingerprint and the DNA.

Blood is visualized at crime scenes and in the laboratory for several different reasons. Presumptive tests are used to determine whether or not a substance is blood. These presumptive tests are mixtures of reagents that change color in the presence of blood, though false-positive results may occur. Chemical reagents may also be used to enhance latent, or invisible, bloodstains at a crime scene if the scene has been cleaned up or the bloodstains have been degraded. Insects such as blowflies, house flies, and flesh flies may degrade blood at crime scenes, removing any visible trace. Some common blood reagents result in either fluorescent or *chemiluminescent* products that glow under specific lighting conditions (Figure 13.3) (see Chapter 9). These reagents may demonstrate the locations of the suspect and victim during an assault via an analysis of the origin and directionality of the bloodstains.

Protein dyes are another class of chemicals that are used to visualize faint or latent bloodstains, including bloody fingerprints. As was mentioned earlier, fingerprints in blood may be visible, difficult to see, or latent. It is often necessary to enhance the fingerprints and photograph them. The fingerprints may then be compared to a known suspect or searched in AFIS. Items suspected to have bloody fingerprints should never be cyanoacrylate fumed. The cyanoacrylate polymerization reaction will inhibit the blood reagents discussed in this

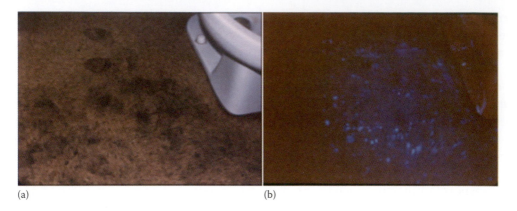

(a)   (b)

Figure 13.3 A bathroom floor at a crime scene before (a) and after (b) treatment with luminol. (Photographs courtesy of Wilson Sullivan.)

chapter. Bloody fingerprints can, however, be processed with fingerprint powder, though a disposable fingerprint brush must be used to avoid contamination or the inadvertent transmission of disease or DNA.

The most common protein dye used to enhance bloody fingerprints is *amido black*. It is also known as *acid black 1*. Amido black stains proteins a bluish-black color (Figure 13.4).[9] It has been used since the 1920s as a protein stain.[9] The original formulation of amido black working solution uses methanol as a solvent. Because methanol is highly flammable and toxic, water- and ethanol-based formulations were developed. This nontoxic formulation is well suited for use at crime scenes and is an inexpensive alternative to the traditional formulation (see Appendix B). The methanol formulation works well on nonporous substrates. The water-based formulation can be used on both nonporous and porous substrates. The water-based formulation is not as effective as the methanol formulation, as the resulting fingerprints are lighter in color.[9]

Other blood reagents have been developed to visualize latent bloodstains or enhance visible bloodstains. As previously discussed, ninhydrin, 1,2-indanedione, and DFO react

Figure 13.4 A fingerprint in blood developed with amido black.

Table 13.2 Reagents Effective for Processing Blood Contaminated Fingerprints by Substrate Type

Substrate	Reagent(s)
Nonporous, dark, or patterned	Acid yellow 7, VMD
Nonporous, light	Amido black, VMD
Porous, dark, or patterned	1,2-Indanedione, DFO
Porous, light	Acid violet 17, amido black

with proteins in porous surfaces. *Acid violet 17* is a protein dye that results in visible prints. The process for developing bloody fingerprints with acid violet is identical to amido black (see Appendix B). The fingerprint is "fixed" on the surface, stained, and rinsed. The formulations are almost identical, though it may take longer for the acid violet prints to develop. Acid violet can be used on porous items and is as effective as amido black on those substrates.[10]

Dark backgrounds pose a problem when attempting to visualize latent or patent fingerprints. Staining a bloody fingerprint black or purple would not be advantageous on a black or other dark background. *Acid yellow 7* is a reagent that causes bloody fingerprints to fluoresce, or glow, under blue-green light (385–509 nm) (see Appendix B).[11] Resulting fingerprints glow a yellow or green color. It is more useful on light fingerprints in blood than on heavy deposits.[11] Because this chemical is fluorescent, it can be used on dark or patterned backgrounds. The suggested sequence for processing bloody fingerprints on porous items is 1,2-indanedione and/or DFO, ninhydrin, amido black or acid violet, and physical developer. The suggested sequence for processing bloody fingerprints on nonporous items is VMD, fingerprint powder, acid yellow, acid violet, or amido black (depending on the color and pattern of the substrate). See Table 13.2 for a summary of these techniques.

13.4 Fingerprints on Metallic Surfaces

Metallic surfaces have posed a challenge for fingerprint analysts: specifically guns and ammunition. According to the U.S. Department of Justice, National Institute of Justice's statistics, guns were used in 68% of murders, 41% of robberies, and 21% of violent assaults in 2011.[12] As guns are common items of evidence found at crime scenes, it is imperative they be successfully processed for fingerprints. There is a low success rate for fingerprint recovery on metallic surfaces, especially on cartridge casings. The Bureau of Alcohol, Tobacco and Firearms and Explosives reported a 10% rate of recovery for useable fingerprints.[13]

There are two main classes of guns: long guns and handguns. Long guns are either shotguns, which fire a cartridge full of small projectiles, or rifles, which fire a single projectile. Handguns include pistols and revolvers, both of which fire single projectiles, known as cartridges or rounds. What is commonly known as a bullet is actually a cartridge that contains not only the projectile fired from the gun (the bullet) but also the cartridge casing that houses the bullet, the primer that initiates the burning of the gun powder, and the gun powder that creates an explosion of pressure, which causes the projectile to be fired from the gun (Figure 13.5).

All guns have similar structures. The barrel of the gun is the steel "tube" of the firearm that directs the path of the projectile when it is fired. A barrel has a caliber, or size, based on the diameter of its opening. The size of the projectile that is used in that weapon is also known as its caliber. For example, a 9 mm pistol has a barrel whose opening is 9 mm in

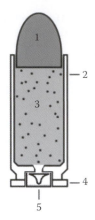

Figure 13.5 A schematic of a cartridge containing a bullet (1), cartridge case (2), gunpowder (3), rim (4), and primer (5). The cartridge case is the most viable surface for developing fingerprints on cartridges.

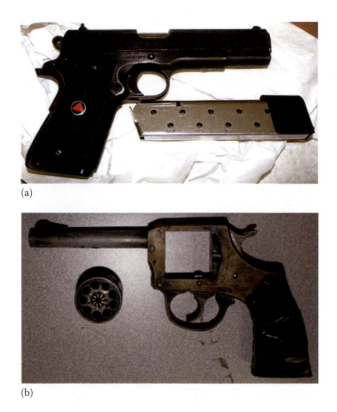

(a)

(b)

Figure 13.6 A semiautomatic pistol and pistol magazine (a) and a revolver with a cylinder (b).

diameter. It fires 9 mm (or slightly smaller) cartridges. The chamber is the part of the gun in which the cartridge is held before firing. A gun may have a magazine to hold multiple cartridges; or, in the case of a revolver, it has a revolving cylinder into which the cartridges are loaded (Figure 13.6). When a bullet is fired from a pistol or some rifles, the gunpowder is burned and consumed, and the empty cartridge casing is ejected. When a revolver is fired, the empty cartridge casing is left in the cylinder. Regardless of the weapon used, it is possible to develop fingerprints on those surfaces.

When an individual loads a gun, his or her fingerprints may be left on the exterior surfaces of the gun itself, on the magazine, or on the cartridges. Cartridge casings are especially difficult surfaces for fingerprint analysts. The Israel National Police found that the heat of the explosion that forces the bullet down the barrel also expands the cartridge casing, causing friction between the steel chamber and the casing, which may obliterate any latent fingerprints present.[13] The process of ejecting the casing also results in friction. And finally, when the ejected casing falls to the ground, it may roll and may be acted upon by physical and environmental forces. Any or all of these processes may obliterate latent fingerprints.

The weapon itself poses a problem for fingerprint analysts. Many guns have "fingerprint-resistant" coatings. Most guns have textured surfaces where one handles the weapon when firing it. These textured surfaces help the individual keep a firm grip on the gun. They are not suitable for fingerprint development. A fingerprint that may be present on a trigger cannot be processed if that trigger is ribbed or textured. A palm print cannot be processed on the grip of a gun if it is highly textured. There are, however, smooth surfaces on a firearm. These are the areas of interest when processing a gun for fingerprints.

Guns are generally made of steel. Cartridge casings may be made of any number of metals and alloys (mixtures of metals), including brass, copper, nickel, steel, or aluminum. Perspiration is acidic and may cause fingerprints to be etched on the cartridge surface without using any chemical development techniques. These fingerprints are patent and can be photographed in situ.

The most common method for developing latent fingerprints on metallic surfaces is cyanoacrylate fuming. The fingerprints developed using this cyanoacrylate method are not often visible to the human eye. Cartridge casings and guns developed in a cyanoacrylate vacuum chamber must be dye stained or powdered to see the fingerprints.

Gun blueing is another process used to develop fingerprints on metallic surfaces, especially cartridge casings. Gun blueing is an oxidation process used commercially to rustproof guns. It creates a blue/black finish that is rust resistant. The process involves depositing selenium and copper on the surface.[4] The gun must be wiped clean before the process is used for commercial purposes. If there are latent fingerprints on the surface, the reaction will occur everywhere but where fingerprints are deposited. It therefore produces light-colored fingerprints on a blue/black background. Fingerprint analysts can use this to their advantage when it is necessary to process cartridge casings for fingerprints.

Fingerprint analysts use various gun blueing formulations depending on the metal composition of the cartridge casings. Different formulations work better on specific metals and alloys. Regardless of the formulation, it can be used in sequence after the cyanoacrylate vacuum process. Leben and Ramotowski examined the effects of commercially available gun blueing formulations and dilutions on common types of cartridge cases.[14] The processes tabulated in Table 13.3 were completed after cyanoacrylate development.

Prior to processing any type of weapon for fingerprints, it is imperative that the fingerprint examiner removes any live rounds of ammunition that may be in the chamber, if this has not been done already. This renders the gun safe to handle. If the gun is not cleared, it may fire and injure or kill the analyst or any surrounding personnel. Your safety and the safety of those around you should always be the first priority when handling dangerous items or substances. It is also recommended to consult a firearms examiner prior to processing firearms for fingerprints.

Table 13.3 Gun Blueing Reagents and Dilutions for Cartridge Casings

Cartridge Type	Treatment	Gun Blue (GB) Dilution GB (mL) to Water (mL)
Nickel-plated brass	Brass Black®	1:40
Brass	Formula 44/40®	0.5:40
Lacquered steel	Cyanoacrylate fuming	N/A
Aluminum	Aluminum Black®	0.5:40

13.5   Fingerprints on Skin

Useable, identifiable fingerprints from human skin are exceedingly rare. While there has been some success in developing fingerprints on human skin in the research literature, in practice, it is not as common. Research is done in a laboratory environment where most variables can be controlled. Both indoor and outdoor crime scenes are generally not controlled environments and there are many variables that affect fingerprint deposition on skin such as temperature and humidity fluctuations, exposure, insect activity, human intervention, and weather. Live victims may wipe off prints with their hands, soap and water, or clothing. Each variable presents another challenge that decreases the probability of finding a fingerprint on human skin.

The skin itself poses challenges to the fingerprint recovery effort. Until death, skin is a regenerating organ that is part of a living, metabolizing organism. Skin cells are constantly being produced deep in the epidermis and pushed up to the surface where dead skin cells are sloughed off. Skin transfers sweat to the surface. It responds to temperature changes. It has variable surface textures and hair follicles. There is a vascular network just beneath the surface; blood pumped through veins, arteries, and capillaries is constantly in motion. The environment acts upon the skin. There may be lotions, oils, cosmetics, or other contaminants on the skin. A fingerprint on skin is composed of the same eccrine and sebaceous deposits as the substrate it is deposited on. These are just some of the processes that contribute to the diverse range of conditions and variables that cannot be controlled in a living organism in the environment.

After death, metabolism stops and the skin dries and cools. If the suspect touched the victim after death, there is a greater chance of obtaining useable fingerprints. The fingerprints, like fingerprints on any substrate, may be smeared, distorted, or obliterated. And, as was mentioned earlier, there are many variables that would affect whether or not a useable fingerprint is developed. In a review of methods and a survey of forensic scientists working in the field, Sampson and Sampson found that the following variables influence whether or not a fingerprint will be deposited and will persist on human skin: surface temperature of the skin, relative temperature of the environment, humidity, the condition of the skin surface (decomposition), and exposure.[15] The exposure will depend on the location of the scene, whether it is indoors or outdoors, the weather, or the presence or absence of clothing.

Working with a deceased victim is challenging. There are legal and safety considerations when handling a dead body. A body at a crime scene may not be handled or manipulated in any way by any personnel other than the coroner, medical examiner, or their personnel. The fingerprint analyst may ask for permission to attempt to process the body for fingerprints at a crime scene or during an autopsy, but permission may not be granted.

If permission is granted, there are safety issues to consider. The body may harbor dangerous pathogens. Suitable personal protective equipment must be worn at all times. It is recommended to use disposable supplies wherever possible to limit the chance of exposure or cross contamination.

The first known murder conviction from an identification of fingerprints from human skin was in 1978 in Florida.[15] The case was dubbed "the spa murders" as the three homicide victims were shot to death in a health spa. Three fingerprints were developed with Kromekote® cards (see below) and black magnetic powder. The fingerprints were recovered from the ankle of one of the victims, a nude female who may have been sexually assaulted. One of the fingerprints was identified to the suspect. The fingerprint had investigative value because it proved physical contact.

Since the 1970s, more than 70 methods for recovering latent fingerprints from skin have been reported.[15] The first step in any recovery attempt is to identify what Sampson and Sampson call a "target area." They report on the likely areas of fingerprint recovery on bodies:

A target area is defined for these purposes as an area of exposed surface skin that is suspected of having been touched by the perpetrator. The establishment of target areas is based on certain indicators. Indicators are the position of the body; evidence that the body was moved; partially clad remains; nude body; redressed, posed or displayed body; eye witness account(s); and in the case of a living person, information provided by the victim. Case histories report that victims' bodies were frequently handled by the extremities with prints being recovered from the ankles, wrist, and under the armpits. Other areas where prints have been found are the neck, abdomen, small of the back, buttocks, and inner thighs.[15]

Bruising, reddened skin, bindings, and ligatures can also provide target areas.

They also suggest the ideal conditions for recovering fingerprints on skin. The ambient humidity should be between 40% and 60%.[15] This is a normal, comfortable level for most people. The ambient temperature should be between 68°C and 20°C–25.5°C.[15] The body temperature of a deceased subject should also be between 20°C and 25.5°C.[15] The skin of a live victim should be between 29°C and 30°C.[15] The skin of a live victim can be cooled with a fan prior to using any of the following development techniques.

There are three categories of techniques for developing fingerprints on human skin: the direct transfer method, fingerprint powdering, and chemical reagents. These chemical reagents include amido black and cyanoacrylate fuming. All of the processes mentioned are limited to relatively fresh prints, are infrequently successful, and are best used when the fingerprints are patent and when the matrix is blood. The direct transfer method has been shown to be the most successful technique both in the laboratory and in the field. To use this process, a substrate (one of various transfer media) is pressed to the skin to transfer the fingerprint onto the substrate. Then the transferred print is processed on the chosen medium.

After a target area has been identified, a transfer medium is pressed to the skin to transfer the latent fingerprint. The most widely used and successful transfer medium is a Kromekote card. Kromekote cards are widely available from printing companies. They are white, ultraglossy cards similar in texture to photo paper. In 1978, Reichardt et al. found this technique to be successful even when the body has been submerged in water.[16]

The direct transfer process is simple. A transfer medium is pressed, glossy side down, onto the target area with firm and even pressure. The card is carefully lifted from the

Figure 13.7 A fingerprint developed on human skin using the direct transfer method. The glossy side of a fingerprint card pressed to a target area of skin on a live victim was developed with black magnetic fingerprint powder.

surface, taking care not to smear the fingerprints in the process. The fingerprint is then developed on the card with black magnetic powder (although regular black powder can be used) (Figure 13.7). The resulting fingerprint is a reversal, or mirror image, of the original fingerprint. It can easily be photographed or scanned into an image-processing program and reversed.

The powder method is somewhat less successful than the direct transfer method. The skin is simply dusted with black magnetic fingerprint powder (Figure 13.8). The resulting fingerprint may be lifted with tape. It may also be "lifted" with Mikrosil®, ForensicSil®, or another silicone lifting material.

Regardless of the method used, it may also be possible to extract DNA from the fingerprint residue. Because the fingerprint residue (containing touch DNA) is placed on the skin of another individual, it is more likely the DNA of the victim will be amplified. Färber et al.

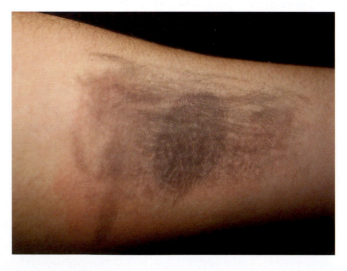

Figure 13.8 Black magnetic fingerprint powder dusted onto a target area of skin reveals a fingerprint.

found that 2% of fingerprints lifted from human skin were identified to the donor.[17] This study was, however, completed in a controlled laboratory environment. The percentage might be lower if the fingerprints were collected at a crime scene or during an autopsy. Just because the success rate is low does not mean it should not be attempted. If fingerprints recovered from human skin are not of good enough quality for comparison purposes, they may be swabbed for touch DNA.

13.6 Fingerprints on Adhesive Surfaces

Adhesive substrates include tapes, stamps, and labels. Any item with a sticky surface may contain not only fingerprint residue but also skin cells stuck to the surface. Adhesive substrates therefore hold fingerprints well. When someone pulls a piece of tape from a roll, it is necessary to touch the sticky side of the tape. When the tape is ripped from the roll and applied to another surface, the ends of the tape must be handled. It is therefore the edges and ends of adhesive substrates that are most successful for developing fingerprints. The most successful methods for processing the adhesive sides of tape include the use of liquid powder suspensions or a chemical reagent called *crystal violet*.

The first issue to address when processing the sticky side of the tape is how to expose the sticky side. Tape, labels, and stamps are often stuck to other objects and must be removed without damaging the adhesive side. There are several methods for loosening tape from another substrate. If possible, gently peel the adhesive loose with gloved fingers and forceps. If the tape is stuck to itself or another nonporous item, it may be frozen to reduce the tackiness of the adhesive. Adhesive can also be loosened with a hair dryer or heat gun, but this may cause the substrate to melt and stretch, resulting in poor quality or distorted fingerprints. If the adhesive is stuck to a porous substrate, such as a stamp or address label on an envelope, a chemical adhesive remover such as Un-du® may be used. Un-du® adhesive remover is found in the scrapbooking section of craft stores or purchased from any major forensic supplier. These solvents should be used very sparingly so as not to affect the integrity of the substrate or obliterate the fingerprint.

As with any other substrate, it is important to consider the color of the adhesive before picking a development method. Clear and light-colored tapes can be processed with crystal violet. Crystal violet is a fat-soluble stain that is especially useful on clear tapes such as Scotch® tape or packing tape (see Appendix B).[18] This process will result in purple ridges on a light purple background (Figure 13.9).

Light-colored adhesives can then be processed with a black powder suspension. Commercially available powder suspensions such as Sticky-Side Powder™ and Wetwop™ may be purchased from any forensic supplier. Fingerprint powders are mixed with a 50:50 blend of water and Photo-Flo® (or another detergent), as described in earlier chapters. Powder suspensions are painted onto the adhesive surface with a camelhair brush (Figure 13.10). The solutions are left on the surface for 10–60 s and rinsed with tap water. All of these solutions utilize a detergent component, which allows the colored powder to bind to the lipids in the fingerprint residue. Powder suspensions are also available in white, gray, and fluorescent for processing dark-colored tapes such as black electrical (vinyl) tape (Figure 13.11). Most adhesive surfaces also have a nonporous or semiporous, nonadhesive side. The nonadhesive side of tape also has forensic value. Traditional nonporous processing methods are used prior to processing the adhesive side of the tape.

Figure 13.9 A fingerprint developed with crystal violet.

Figure 13.10 A camel hair fingerprint brush.

13.7   I Had a Case: The Janitor in the Drum

A 55-gallon steel drum that had been dumped in a park drew the attention of passersby when it began to emit a strong odor. Police were called and soon suspected that something was decomposing inside. The drum was sealed with concrete and wrapped with duct tape. The drum was removed to the coroner's office for examination, where two bodies were found sealed in the drum: a female victim and a male victim later identified as a local janitor.

The first task in opening the drum was to remove the duct tape. A fingerprint examiner prepared a large batch of crystal violet in an improvised dishpan. Layer by layer, the tape was slowly unwound, passed through the solution, rinsed, and inspected for latent prints. Results were discouraging until the very end of 100 feet of tape, where a high-quality right thumb print was found. The fingerprint was later identified to the murder suspect.

It is not uncommon in processing strips of tape that the last piece removed for testing had been the first piece applied by the criminal. Why do you think this is so?

Figure 13.11 A fingerprint on black electrical tape developed with white powder suspension.

13.8   Chapter Summary

There are various methods for processing greasy fingerprints, bloody fingerprints, finger-prints on metallic surfaces, fingerprints on skin, and fingerprints on adhesive surfaces. The technique employed depends on the type, color, and condition of the substrate in question. For greasy substrates or oily fingerprints, natural yellow 3 and white powder suspensions are used on nonporous dark or patterned substrates; Sudan black is used on both nonpo-rous and porous, light-colored substrates (though background staining reduces contrast on porous items); and oil red O is used on porous, light-colored substrates. For bloody fingerprints, acid yellow is used on nonporous dark or patterned substrates; amido black is used on both nonporous and porous light-colored substrates; and acid violet is used on porous, light-colored substrates.

Metallic surfaces, such as firearms and their components, are processed in a cyanoac-rylate chamber followed by dye staining. Cartridge cases are processed with a gun blueing reagent, taking into consideration the composition of the metal. Skin can be processed for fingerprints using the direct transfer method. This method utilizes a Kromekote card pressed against the target area to transfer a latent print that is then visualized with black powder. Adhesive substrates can be processed with colored powder suspensions that contrast with the substrate. Light-colored adhesives can be processed with crystal violet. Regardless of the technique or substrate, safety must always be the fingerprint analyst's chief concern.

Review Questions

1. List five common surfaces or areas where greasy or oily fingerprints may be found.
2. What chemical reagent(s) would be used to develop an oily fingerprint on a navy blue colored envelope?

3. What chemical reagent(s) would be used to develop an oily fingerprint on a mirror?
4. What chemical reagent(s) would be used to develop an oily fingerprint on a white sheet of paper?
5. Acid yellow 7 is used to develop bloody fingerprints on what type of surface, and why?
6. Which chemical reagent(s) would be used to develop a bloody fingerprint on any type of light-colored surface?
7. Acid violet is a chemical reagent that enhances what type of fingerprint matrix? Give an example of a type of surface on which one would use this reagent.
8. What is the oxidation process called by which a gun is coated with selenium and copper to make it rust resistant?
9. Describe the direct transfer method of developing a fingerprint on human skin.
10. How is a strip of black electrical tape processed for fingerprints?
11. What is crystal violet, and what is it used for?

References

1. Ramotowski, R. 2012. Lipid reagents. In Ramotowski, R. (ed.), *Advances in Fingerprint Technology*, 3rd edn. Boca Raton, FL: Taylor & Francis.
2. Gaskell, C., Bleay, S.S., and Ramadani, J. 2012. Natural yellow 3: A novel fluorescent reagent for use on grease-contaminated, nonporous surfaces. *J. Forensic Identif.* 63(3): 274–285.
3. Gaskell, C. et al. 2012. The enhancement of fingermarks on grease-contaminated, nonporous surfaces: A comparative assessment of processes for light and dark surfaces. *J. Forensic Identif.* 63(3): 286–319.
4. Yamashita, B. and French, M. 2011. Latent print development. In The Scientific Working Group on Friction Ridge Analysis, Study and Technology (SWGFAST) et al. *The Fingerprint Sourcebook*. Washington, DC: National Institute of Justice, U.S. Department of Justice, Office of Justice Programs.
5. Beaudoin, A. 2004. New technique for revealing latent fingerprints on wet, porous surfaces: Oil red O. *J. Forensic Identif.* 54(4): 413–419.
6. Rawji, A. and Beaudoin, A. 2006. Oil red O versus physical developer on wet papers: A comparative study. *J. Forensic Identif.* 56(1): 33–50.
7. Guigui, K. and Beaudoin, A. 2007. The use of oil red O in sequence with other methods of fingerprint development. *J. Forensic Identif.* 57(4): 550–573.
8. Sears, V. 2012. Enhancement techniques for fingerprints in blood. In Ramotowski, R. (ed.), *Advances in Fingerprint Technology*, 3rd edn. Boca Raton, FL: Taylor & Francis.
9. Sears, V. and Prizeman, T. 2000. Enhancement of fingerprints in blood—Part 1: The optimization of amino black. *J. Forensic Identif.* 50(5): 470–480.
10. Sears, V., Butcher, C., and Prizeman, T. 2001. Enhancement of fingerprints in blood—Part 2: protein dyes. *J. Forensic Identif.* 51(1): 28–38.
11. Sears, V., Butcher, C., and Fitzgerald, L. 2005. Enhancement of fingerprints in blood—Part 3: reactive techniques, acid yellow 7 and process sequences. *J. Forensic Identif.* 55(6): 741.
12. National Institute of Justice. United States Department of Justice. Gun violence. http://www.nij.gov/topics/crime/gun-violence. Updated April 4, 2013. Accessed June 23, 2013.
13. Ramotowski, R. 2012. Miscellaneous methods and challenging surfaces. In Ramotowski, R. (ed.), *Advances in Fingerprint Technology*, 3rd edn. Boca Raton, FL: Taylor & Francis.
14. Leben, D. and Ramotowski, R. 1997. Evaluation of gun blueing solutions and their ability to develop latent fingerprints on cartridge casings. *FDIAI News*. January–March: pp. 10–11.
15. Sampson, W. and Sampson, K. 2005. Recovery of latent prints from human skin. *J. Forensic Identif.* 55(3): 362–385.

16. Reichardt, G.T., Carr, J.C., and Stone, E.G. 1978. Conventional method for lifting latent finger-prints from human skin surfaces. *J. Forensic Sci.* 23(1): 135–141.
17. Färber, D. et al. 2010. Recovery of latent fingerprints and DNA on human skin. *J. Forensic Sci.* 55(6): 1457–1461.
18. Champod, C. et al. 2004. Fingerprints and other ridge skin impressions. Boca Raton, FL: Taylor & Francis.

Fingerprint Analysis III

Documentation

14

Key Terms

- Documentation
- Standard operating procedures (SOPs)
- Bench notes
- Chain of custody
- Digital SLR camera
- Standard lens
- Multipurpose lens
- Macro lens
- Detachable flash
- Ring flash
- UV filter
- Polarizing filter
- Infrared filter
- Colored filter
- Latent print adapter (1:1 lens adapter)
- Close-up photo
- Direct lighting
- Front directional lighting
- Backlighting
- Oblique lighting
- Evidence-establishing (midrange) photo
- Discovery
- Objective
- Bias
- Concise
- Narrative

Learning Objectives

- Define the key terms.
- Describe the types of documentation completed by the fingerprint analyst.
- Describe the importance of maintaining a chain of custody.
- Name the types of lenses and filters used by fingerprint analysts.
- Explain the four most common photographic techniques for recording fingerprints on evidentiary items, and which fingerprint development technique is best captured by each method.

- Describe how to digitally store and manipulate fingerprint photographs.
- Explain the most important aspects of writing a final report.

14.1 Documentation

Documentation is a process that involves recording important details. It may be pictorial or narrative. Every science requires thorough documentation to record hypotheses, processes, results, and conclusions. This is integral to the scientific method. The forensic sciences rely on these processes not only to record the scientific methodology but also to have a thorough record of unbiased facts and observations for courtroom testimony (see Chapter 18). Documentation of forensic processes includes extensive note-taking at the crime scene, in the laboratory, and during the analysis phase; photography before, during, and after each process; the completion of forms and agency-prepared documents; and the preparation of visual aids such as charts or enhanced photos to use during courtroom testimony.

A fingerprint analyst may complete the following documentation: photography, sketches, chain of custody, forms required by the agency or department, notes, reports, and courtroom visual aids. Each analyst, agency, or department may have a specific set of guidelines or *standard operating procedures (SOPs)* for documenting evidence and fingerprints. Regardless of the methods or forms used, the fingerprint analyst must be as thorough as possible, recording every detail with integrity and without bias. Documentation must include every detail of processing, analysis, and interpretation from the time evidence is received until the evidence is signed over to someone else or until the case is closed. This chapter will cover common methods of documentation including laboratory notes and forms, photography, and final reports.

14.2 Laboratory Notes and Forms

Laboratory notes, often called *bench notes*, may be free form. A department or agency may have designated forms for typing or writing notes by hand. Forensic scientists generally write any of three types of notes: crime scene notes, laboratory processing notes, and notes detailing analyses and conclusions. A fingerprint examiner writes detailed notes about fingerprint processing, analysis, comparisons, and conclusions. Notes may include the following:

- A detailed description of the evidence and/or crime scene
- Steps taken to process the evidence
- Dates/times steps were performed in sequence
- Results of each step

The following is an example of laboratory processing notes written in outline form:

- Case #2013-01487 was received from Anywhere Police Department's evidence storage facility on July 11, 2013, at 0830 h.

- Item #17—gray Motorola Verizon wireless cell phone ("flip phone") with a 1.3 megapixel camera (disassembled for processing).
  - Visual examination with oblique lighting—no fingerprints of value observed.
  - Superglue fuming—25 min at 60% humidity in superglue fuming chamber yielded one fingerprint of value, labeled L001.
  - Fingerprint L001, L002, and L003 were photographed with a digital single-lens reflex (SLR) camera using oblique lighting.
  - Fluorescent orange powder—viewed with an alternate light source (ALS) at 525 nm wavelength, yielded no new fingerprints of value other than L001–L003.
  - L001, L002, and L003 were photographed under ALS with a digital SLR camera and orange filter.
  - Photographs were downloaded and saved:
    - 201301487_L001A
    - 201301487_L001B
    - 201301487_L002A
    - 201301487_L002B
    - 201301487_L003A
    - 201301487_L003B
  - No further processing was required.
  - Item #17 was repackaged and sealed on July 11, 2013, at 1450 h.
  - Item #17 was submitted to the evidence storage facility on July 11, 2013, at 1700 h.

Each step in the process is recorded in detail, along with a detailed description of the item itself. Any authorized personnel involved with the case should be able to understand exactly what was done and how the photographs can be accessed. The following is an example of fingerprint comparison notes written in outline form:

- Case #2013-01487 was received on July 13, 2013, at 0800 h from the evidence storage facility. Fingerprint comparisons were completed on the same date.
  - Latent fingerprint L001 is sufficient for comparison purposes.
  - Latent fingerprints L002 and L003 are of poor quality and are not sufficient for comparison purposes.
  - L001 was compared to the victim (Jane Doe, dob July 06, 1994) with negative results.
  - L001 was compared to the suspect (John Smith, dob September 01, 1990).
  - L001 was identified as originating from the #1 finger of the suspect.
  - The identification (ID) was verified by Francis Galton on July 15, 2013.

Your employer may also require one or more supplemental forms or other documents. Figures 14.1 and 14.2 are generic blank fingerprint processing and fingerprint comparison forms (Figures 14.1 and 14.2). Figure 14.3 is an example of a fingerprint comparison form used by the City of Pomona Police Department in California (Figure 14.3). Figure 14.4 is

Anywhere Police Department
Fingerprint Processing Worksheet

Date: _____   Time: _____   Fingerprint Examiner: _____

Case #: _____   Classification: _____

Item #	Process 1	# Prints visible	Date/time	Process 2	# Prints visible	Date/time	Process 3	# Prints visible	Date/time

Figure 14.1 Generic blank fingerprint processing form to be filled out by the fingerprint analyst.

an example of a form fingerprint analysts at the Pomona Police Department use to visually demonstrate the fingerprint comparison process (Figure 14.4).

The chain of custody form is another form used in every subdiscipline of the forensic sciences. The *chain of custody* is a form that records the dates, times, and explanations for evidence transfers. The chain of custody accounts for an item of evidence from the time it is collected until it is destroyed or stored at the conclusion of a case. When an item of evidence is collected, a chain of custody form is attached to the evidence packaging. The individual collecting or taking custody of the item fills out the form and signs his or her name, recording the date and time the item was collected. As long as the item is in that individual's possession, the chain of custody remains unchanged. When the item changes hands—for example, if it is submitted to a DNA laboratory for DNA testing—an individual at the DNA laboratory will sign his or her name on the form, thereby officially taking custody of the item (Figure 14.5).

The individual with custody of the evidence is responsible for the condition and integrity of that evidence until it is signed over to someone else. Every transfer, no matter how brief, is documented on the chain of custody form. If the evidence must be left unattended, it should be stored in a secure evidence storage area or evidence locker. The evidence must be accounted for at all times, and it is the responsibility of each individual handling the evidence to ensure that the chain is maintained. If the chain is broken, and evidence is unaccounted for during any time period, the integrity of that evidence is compromised. Questions may arise, such as the following: "How do we know the evidence was not tampered with, forged, or altered during the time it was unaccounted for?" "Was the evidence lost during that time period?" "Do the notes, forms, photos, and final report match up with the timeline documented on the chain of custody, or are there inconsistencies?" The chain of custody is a critical document that must remain with the evidence at all times.

Latent Print Comparisons

Case #: _____ Classification: _____

Date: _____ Time: _____

Latents (lab):_____ # Lift Cards: _____

[ ] Victim/Witness: _____DOB: _____ ID No ID
[ ] Victim/Witness: _____DOB: _____ ID No ID
[ ] Victim/Witness: _____DOB: _____ ID No ID

[ ] Suspect 1: _____DOB: _____ ID No ID
[ ] Suspect 2: _____DOB: _____ ID No ID
[ ] Suspect 3: _____DOB: _____ ID No ID
[ ] Other: _____DOB: _____ ID No ID
[ ] Other: _____DOB: _____ ID No ID

Latent	AFIS?	Results of Comparison (ID, No ID, Insufficient)

Notes:

Examiner: _____ Date: _____
Verified by: _____ Date: _____

Figure 14.2 Generic blank fingerprint comparison form to be filled out by the fingerprint analyst.

14.3 Photography

The word photography comes from the Greek root words *phos* (light) and *graphos* (write).[1] Photography can be thought of, in the simplest terms, as writing with light. Aristotle was the first individual in recorded history to explore how light could be manipulated to project images onto a surface.[1] Photography has been used for documentation in the criminal justice community since the rogues' galleries and portraits parlé of the 1800s (Figure 14.6). These photographs were used to document the physical appearance of criminals for future ID.

The first fingerprint cameras were large format cameras (Figure 14.7). "Large format" refers to the size of the film used in the camera. Large format film is any recording medium 4 × 5 in. (10.2 × 12.7 cm) or larger. An example of large format film is Polaroid© instant film.

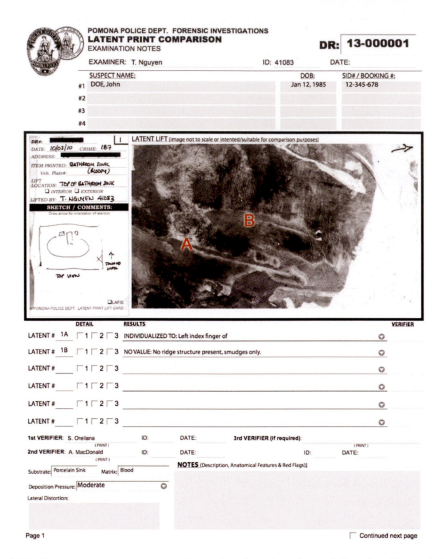

Figure 14.3 Fingerprint comparison form developed and used by the City of Pomona, California Police Department. (Courtesy of Tony Nguyen, Crime Scene Examiner with the City of Pomona Police Department.)

Film photography, most commonly 35 mm film, replaced most large format film cameras. The most common cameras used today are *digital SLR* cameras of varying resolutions and models. With a digital camera, there is no such thing as too many photographs because there are no development costs as there are with film.

Most individuals either own a digital camera or have used one. Most mobile phones contain digital cameras. There are many advantages of digital cameras versus film cameras for forensic documentation. Photos taken with a digital camera can be viewed immediately, unlike film cameras, which require the film to be processed and printed before it can be viewed. Digital photos are easily inserted into slide presentation software that can be used for courtroom presentations. Digital photos can be enhanced on a computer. The photographer can share information quickly and easily with investigators, attorneys,

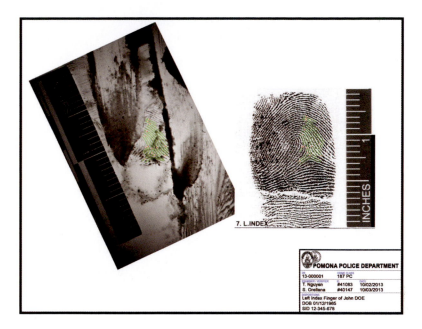

Figure 14.4 A fingerprint comparison form developed and used by the City of Pomona, California Police Department demonstrating the fingerprint comparison process. (Courtesy of Tony Nguyen, Crime Scene Examiner with the City of Pomona Police Department.)

and others involved with the case. Once the initial camera purchase is made, it is efficient and cost effective to use, store, and copy photos.

Digital cameras have interchangeable lenses, several of which are used in forensic photography. The 50–55 mm *standard lens* or 28–70 mm *multipurpose lens* is often sold with the camera (Figure 14.8). These lenses are good for photographing evidence and crime scenes. *Macro lenses* are used to photograph very small forensic evidence, such as trace evidence, serial numbers, toolmarks, and fingerprints.

Flashes are also important components of the camera. In Chapter 9, lighting was introduced as an important tool for visualizing fingerprints. Fingerprint analysts must convey what they see as accurately as possible through the camera's lens. Therefore, it is important to use different lighting techniques and camera settings to capture the best image possible. A *detachable flash* can be held at any angle to provide oblique or direct lighting (Figure 14.9). A *ring flash* mounted on the camera lens gives an even distribution of light for 360° around the fingerprint (Figure 14.9). The camera should be mounted on a tripod or camera stand to keep it steady while the analyst manipulates the light and composes the picture.

There are several filters commonly used in forensic subdisciplines. A filter is a thin, disk-shaped glass or Plexiglass camera accessory that can be screwed onto the end of the camera lens. A filter controls which wavelengths of light enter the lens, just like the colored laboratory glasses worn while using the laser or ALS. The most common filters used by crime scene technicians are *UV filters* and *polarizing filters*. UV filters block UV rays and protect the camera lens from scratches and dirt. Polarizing filters act like polarizing sunglasses. They remove glare in bright sunlight or when photographing reflective surfaces. *Infrared filters* and UV filters are used when photographing wounds on victims such as bite marks and bruising.

Anywhere Police Department
Chain of Custody

Case #   ___2013-445___   Classification: ___187___

Item #(s)   ___17___   Date: 09-14-2013

Description of evidence:

Grey Motorola Verizon wireless cell phone ("flip phone") with a 1.3 megapixel
camera

Location collected:

Front passenger seat of 1994 Volkswagon Passat, gray, license plate #BALR77, VIN
#JTHBPQ1357901349

Item #(s)	Released By	Received By	Date/Time	Reason
#17	Hillary Daly Anywhere P.D.	John Smith, Anywhere DNA Laboratory	09-14-2013 @ 1530	DNA Analysis
#17	John Smith, Anywhere DNA Laboratory	Hillary Daly Anywhere P.D.	10-07-2013 @ 0925	Fingerprint Analysis
#17	Hillary Daly Anywhere P.D.	Jane Doe, Anywhere P.D	10-07-13 0955	evidence storage

Figure 14.5 An example of a chain of custody demonstrating the transfer of evidence from
the police department to the DNA laboratory and back again to the police department for
secured storage.

The most common filters used in fingerprint analysis are *colored filters*. A filter of a certain color blocks—or cancels out—that color in an image. This is especially helpful when a
fingerprint is developed on patterned or colored backgrounds that make it difficult to see.
More often, a colored filter is used to view luminescence when a fingerprint is developed
with chemical reagents or fluorescent powders (Figure 14.10). The most common filter used
in the fingerprint laboratory is the orange filter, since it is used to photograph indanedione,
DFO, Rhodamine 6G, RAM, and several other fingerprint reagents.

Regardless of the type of camera, equipment, or accessories used, the photographs
must be accurate representations of the evidence. They will serve as your memory when
writing a final report and testifying in court. They will illustrate your processes and results
for jurors, investigators, attorneys, and any other individuals who must understand or analyze the case at hand.

Figure 14.6 A photograph of a French portrait parlé class, ca. 1910–1915. (Reprinted from the Library of Congress, Prints and Photographs Division, Washington, D.C. hdl.loc.gov/loc.pnp/pp.print. Accessed on June 4, 2014.)

Figure 14.7 The first fingerprint camera. (Reprinted with permission from the People's Collection Wales and the South Wales Police Museum. http://www.peoplescollectionwales.co.uk/items/7348. Accessed June 4, 2014.)

Another accessory for fingerprint photography is the *latent print adapter (1:1 lens adapter)* (Figure 14.11). The adapter is a Plexiglas tube that screws onto the lens just like a filter. The tube is placed over a latent fingerprint of interest. The camera autofocuses on the image and takes the photo (Figure 14.12). This is a fast and easy way to take quality photographs of latent fingerprints either after visible fingerprint processing techniques or at crime scenes. It also keeps the lens at 90°, negating distortion.

Figure 14.8 55 mm camera lens.

Figure 14.9 A digital SLR camera with a detachable flash and ring flash.

Figure 14.10 Green-, yellow-, and red-colored filters.

Figure 14.11 A 1:1 latent print adapter attached to the lens of a digital SLR camera.

Figure 14.12 A photograph of a latent fingerprint taken with a 1:1 latent print adapter attached to a digital SLR camera.

14.4 Evidence Photography

Photographic documentation of fingerprint analysis begins when the evidence is received for processing. Each agency or department has its own SOPs for photographing evidence. What is presented here is a very thorough documentation process. When the evidence is received, the sealed package is photographed (Figure 14.13). Any label or identifying marks are documented and photographed. The seal is then broken and the package opened. The evidence packaging may be a box, bag, or envelope.

When the evidence is removed from the package, it is photographed with a scale (a small ruler or other graduated measuring device). This is known as a *close-up photo*. If there are multiple items present, the items can be photographed together, and then

Figure 14.13 Photograph of a sealed evidence package containing several items of evidence. A chain of custody is attached.

individually, with identifying information included in the photograph. Identifying information can be printed or handwritten on a card and should include the following information: case number, item number(s), fingerprint analyst's name or initials and ID number (if applicable), and the date (Figure 14.14). The scale is used to determine the approximate size of the object. The photos will not be 1:1 renderings of the item. Many items are common objects that are of a known size: a pillow, a fork, or a sheet of paper. However, every item photographed must contain a scale.

Figure 14.14 Close-up evidentiary photograph of an AK-47 with an ID card that includes the case number, item number, date, and photographer's initials.

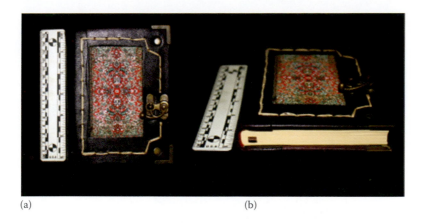

(a)   (b)

Figure 14.15 An object photographed at a 90° angle (a) and an oblique angle (b).

The item is photographed close-up with the lens of the camera held parallel to the object to minimize distortion. A line drawn from your eye through the camera to the object must form a 90° angle to the plane of the evidence. This is best accomplished with a tripod. Distortion occurs in photographs when an object is photographed at an angle (Figure 14.15). This is not a true rendering of the evidence.

If the item can be disassembled into its component parts—such as a flashlight with batteries—it should be photographed after disassembly with a scale and identifying information. It is preferable to process any item of evidence that can be disassembled prior to disassembly, especially if fingerprints on the exterior of the item may be damaged or obliterated during the disassembly process. For example, a fingerprint analyst may encounter a cell phone with a removable battery. The battery cover must be removed in order to access the battery. If a latent fingerprint has been deposited on the back of the cell phone, it may span both the frame of the phone and the battery cover. If the cover is removed prior to processing, the fingerprint may be cut in half, smeared, or otherwise obliterated. Processing an item that must be disassembled can be accomplished in two "rounds." The first round of processing should be performed on the entire object, prior to its disassembly. Then, the item can be disassembled and processed again.

Once items of evidence are photographed, they may be processed. After each step in the processing sequence, all resulting fingerprints will be photographed. Fingerprints, whether visible or fluorescent, must be photographed with scale and identifying information, just as the evidence was photographed prior to processing. It is important to photograph the item parallel to the plane of the evidence, with a scale and identifying information. It is also preferable to fill the frame of the camera's viewer with the fingerprint to capture as much detail as possible. How the fingerprint is photographed depends on how it was processed and how it appears after each processing technique.

14.5   Photographic Lighting Techniques

There are four common lighting techniques used to document fingerprints: *direct lighting, front directional lighting, backlighting,* and *oblique lighting.* There is no one right way to photograph a fingerprint. The type of photographic technique selected depends on the processing technique, extent of development, background substrate, and amount of distortion.

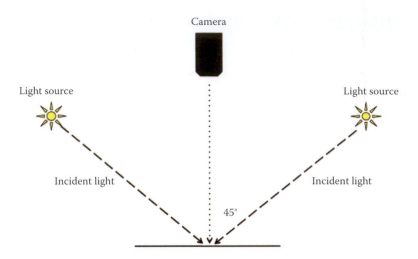

Figure 14.16 A schematic demonstrating the direct lighting photographic technique.

For the *direct lighting* technique, the camera is mounted on a camera stand (copy stand) (Figure 14.16). The item with the fingerprint is placed on the stand, and the camera is focused on the fingerprint, filling the frame with the visible friction ridge detail. Two lights on arms mounted to either side of the camera stand shine light on the evidence at a 45° angle. This provides even illumination from both sides of the evidence. Direct lighting is best used when the fingerprints are visible on the surface. This includes patent fingerprints, fingerprints developed with ninhydrin or indanedione, or powdered prints. Another method of capturing a high-resolution image of the visible friction ridges developed with ninhydrin or indanedione is to scan the paper on a flatbed scanner set to 1000 ppi (pixels per square inch).

The direct lighting method is not useful on highly reflective substrates or on fluorescent fingerprints. Reflective objects, such as mirrors or CDs, cause the light to reflect off the surface and enter the lens. The resulting photograph is too bright to capture friction ridge details. Fluorescent fingerprints must be photographed under a forensic light source with the appropriate colored filter attached to the camera lens.

Visible fingerprints on reflective or concave objects—objects that curve inward, such as cups or sunglass lenses—are best photographed with *front directional lighting* (Figure 14.17). For this lighting technique, the camera is mounted and the object placed on a camera stand as with direct lighting. A sheet of Plexiglas is held at an angle between the camera lens and the object. A single light source is used to shine incident light at an angle parallel to the plane of the lens and the fingerprint substrate. Some of the light passes through the Plexiglas and some reflects off of the transparent sheet. This technique spreads out the light to indirectly shine it onto the object, limiting the bright reflection caused by direct lighting.

Fingerprints on transparent objects such as glass, plastic, or clear tape are viewed and photographed most effectively with *backlighting* (Figure 14.18). The object is placed on a light box, which shines light through the transparent object from underneath. The use of a light box is often the most effective way to view visible friction ridges, regardless of whether or not they will be photographed.

One of the most effective lighting techniques in fingerprint analysis (and throughout the forensic sciences) is *oblique lighting* (Figure 14.19). Oblique lighting can be used to view

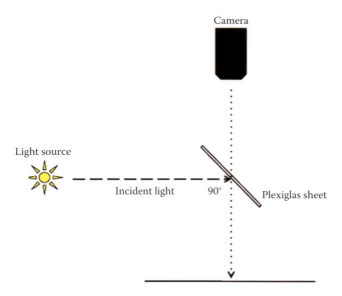

Figure 14.17 A schematic demonstrating the front directional lighting photographic technique.

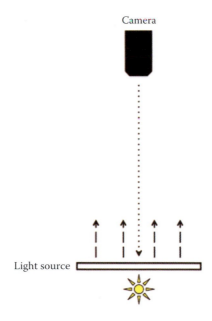

Figure 14.18 A schematic demonstrating the backlighting photographic technique.

latent fingerprints on objects. It can also be used to enhance details in shoeprints and tire tracks, as well as toolmarks and wounds such as bite marks. When photographing plastic prints or 3D prints, oblique lighting reveals details when light passes across the surface creating contrast with light and shadow. This can be accomplished on a camera stand by either lowering the arms holding the lights to the level of the camera stand table or holding a flashlight at various acute angles. Superglue fuming results in slightly 3D fingerprints as the cyanoacrylate polymer builds up on the friction ridge residue. Therefore, oblique lighting is often the best technique to use for capturing superglue-fumed prints.

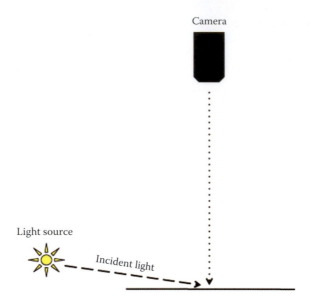

Figure 14.19 A schematic demonstrating the oblique lighting photographic technique.

It is necessary to record fingerprints in context. The location and direction of fingerprints on an object may be important investigative data. When photographing fingerprints in context, an *evidence-establishing*, or *midrange*, photo of the area must be taken. The object is photographed from farther away to show the fingerprint in context and then zoomed in to fill the frame with the fingerprint and capture the detail.

14.6   Common Problems with Photography

Just like photographing your family vacation, photographing evidence and latent prints may be susceptible to several common problems. These problems include photos lacking ID, photos lacking orientation, incomplete documentation, lack of camera control, and incorrect use of lighting. A photo lacks ID when it is taken out of context or without a label. For example, a cartridge casing with a fingerprint may be one of many cartridge casings collected as evidence in a particular case. If the cartridge casing is not labeled in the photograph, it is unclear on which casing the fingerprint was found.

In a photo that lacks orientation, it may be difficult to determine which way is the up direction or where the print is located on the item. For example, consider a palm print found on a window during a burglary investigation. The window may have been opened either from the inside by the homeowner or from the outside by the burglar. If the photograph only shows the palm print, and not where it is located or its direction, the investigative value of that palm print is lost.

Lack of camera control can result in blurry or distorted photos. Always use a tripod if possible to limit camera control problems. Lighting problems occur when there is either too much light, causing overexposed, bright photos, or too little light, causing underexposed, dark photos. Both overexposed and underexposed photos make it difficult to observe and analyze detail.

14.7   Uploading and Storing Photos

Every photograph you take is evidence. Photographic evidence is a record of the crime scene, evidentiary items, and fingerprints. They are admissible in court and as such are subject to analysis and scrutiny by a judge, attorneys, jurors, and opposing experts. Photographs are subject to *discovery*, meaning they must be made available to both the prosecution and defense. For this reason, no photo should ever be deleted, including those determined to be of no value. The sequence of photos, from the first photo of a case to the last photo of a case, should be unbroken. If a photo is blurry, it should be retaken, not deleted. Deleting photos results in a break in the sequence. A defense attorney, judge, or jury might question why the photograph is missing, what the photograph represented, and whether or not the photograph was deleted because it may have exonerated the defendant.

Always take digital photos and save those photos in a lossless file format such as TIFF, RAW, or JPEG2000. Lossy file formats, such as JPEG, should never be used. These file formats compress the image, resulting in some loss of detail. When photos are saved, they must be stored as "read-only" files so the originals cannot be manipulated. Regardless of whether the photographs are stored electronically or on DVDs, those photographs are evidence, and the chain of custody must be maintained.

Lastly, some photos may need to be enhanced in order to analyze them. Original images must never be manipulated. It is acceptable to make a copy of the original image and enhance that copy. The copy should be clearly saved and named as a copy. There are several reasons to enhance a photograph. If it is under- or overexposed, simple corrections can be made using image-enhancing software. If a fingerprint is the subject of the photograph, it may be enhanced in order to use it for comparison. For example, if a fingerprint developed with ninhydrin is photographed on a patterned background, it may be difficult to see and therefore difficult to analyze. The photo can be manipulated using Adobe Photoshop or other image enhancement software. The color information can be deleted so the image is in black and white. The pattern may be diminished or removed, the contrast increased, and the image sharpened. When an image is enhanced in order to see the details for analysis, a detailed record or history of every step in the enhancement process is maintained. Anyone should be able to duplicate exactly what you did and get the same result.

14.8   Final Reports

Just as a book report is a summary of the plot and underlying theme of a book, a final report is a summary of all the work done on a case and the implications of forensic analyses. A final report is written as a narrative, like an essay. It is the last step in the documentation process, unless court demonstrations are created at a later date. Photos and notes can be used to write a detailed, thorough final report. In order to write an unbiased, scientific narrative of a case, the report must be

- Objective
- Clear and concise
- Organized
- Thorough
- Written in accordance with your agency/department SOPs

A narrative is *objective* when it is not influenced by one's personal feelings or *biases*. Everyone has inherent biases, or influences. Our biases are based on our life experiences, education, and values. A negative bias might be a prejudice against a certain ethnic group or an assumption about an individual's personality based on that person's appearance or age.

In law enforcement, you may think an individual who was arrested for burglary is most likely guilty, especially if that person was arrested for burglary in the past. Or perhaps a detective assures you of an arrestee's guilt prior to the forensic analysis of the evidence. As scientists, we must push those biases aside and examine the facts as objectively as possible. Remember that in a court of law, an individual is innocent until proven guilty.

A final report should be clear and concise. When the content of your report is clear, any individual not associated with the case should be able to read it, understand it, and fully grasp the details of the case and your involvement with the investigation. While there may be many details to cover in a final report, it must always be concise. Writing that is *concise* is as brief as possible without sacrificing content. If something can be described in either 100 words or 50 words, it is always preferable to cut the description down to 50 words. According to Strunk and White's *The Elements of Style*, an authoritative text on English composition and grammar, "Vigorous writing is concise. A sentence should contain no unnecessary words, a paragraph no unnecessary sentences, for the same reason that a drawing should have no unnecessary lines and a machine no unnecessary parts."[2] This is how you should approach your final report.

Your final report is organized in a way that any investigator, lawyer, or juror who picks up your report should be able to understand the details of the case, your actions, and the result of any analyses you did. Your department or agency may have a specific format for you to follow as a part of its SOPs. Or you may type your report into special report-writing software. Regardless of the format you use, you should introduce the details of the case first, then describe your actions in chronological order, and conclude with your opinion based on your analysis. One way to organize your narrative is to write about what you did in chronological order. If you went to the crime scene, then processed evidence at the laboratory, and then compared the resulting fingerprints to the suspects, your report should be written in that order.

While your report must be concise, it must also be thorough. It must describe in detail everything you did pertinent to the case. No detail, no matter how trivial it may seem, should be left out of the narrative. You never know what will become important, or even critical, to the case as the investigation unfolds. An item of evidence you may have thought was insignificant may in fact be the pivot point if the case goes to court.

And finally, your report should be written in accordance with your agency or department SOPs. They may require a specific format or syntax. Agencies benefit from standardizing their reports so anyone who reads a report originating from that agency will know where to find certain relevant pieces of information. If the reports all look the same and contain similar wording or content, an investigator, police officer, attorney, or jury member can efficiently find the specific information he is looking for.

A final report should be in *narrative* form. It is not meant to be a story, but a sequence of events related in paragraph form. The following are excerpts from actual final reports:

Excerpt: Fingerprints at Crime Scenes

Black fingerprint powder was used to examine the point of entry, point of exit, areas where items were disturbed, and items of evidence at the scene. Three (3) latent fingerprints (labeled L01, L02 and L03) were lifted from the door handle on the door leading from the main hallway of the home into the second bedroom at the northeast corner of the house. These latent prints were lifted onto standard latent fingerprint lift cards. Elimination fingerprints were collected from the victim….

Excerpt: Laboratory Processing

Item #3, a serrated hunting knife with a black rubber grip and an 8 in. blade, was removed from secure evidence storage at the Police Department Crime Laboratory in order to process it for fingerprint evidence. The item was documented comprehensively with photographs and notes. The item was then processed in the superglue fuming chamber, with positive results. The resulting latent fingerprints, labeled L034 and L035, were photographed with a Canon D-10 digital SLR camera….

On 09-09-2013, the evidence associated with case number 2013-00525 was transported to the Crime Laboratory for the purpose of fingerprint processing and comparison to the named subjects (see above). Following documentation of the initial condition of the evidence, the packaging was un-sealed. Items #1 through #12, and #14 through #16, were processed for fingerprints using cyanoacrylate fuming, Rhodamine 6G and magnetic fingerprint powder. All resulting fingerprints were photographed for further analysis and comparison. Items #13 and #16 were processed for fingerprints using Indanedione and ninhydrin. All resulting fingerprints were photographed for further analysis and comparison. (See the attached 'Fingerprint Processing Worksheet' for details.)

Excerpt: Fingerprint ID

The fingerprints corresponding to case #2013-12345 were removed from secure storage at the Police Department Crime Laboratory Fingerprint Analysis Division for comparison with the suspects, victims and witnesses named above. The comparisons were completed, utilizing ACE-V methodology, with the following results:

- L001: ID to #2 finger of (s) Smith, John Q. (dob 01-02-1984)
- L002: No ID
- L003: No ID
- L004: Insufficient for comparison purposes

14.9   I Had a Case: Missiles in the Israeli Desert

In some cases, it is not possible to transport evidence to a laboratory to process it for fingerprints. This was the case for Israeli investigators when they discovered Dragon anti-tank missiles—stolen from an ammunitions depot—hidden in the desert (Figure 14.20). Moving the missiles to the laboratory for processing was ruled out for safety reasons. So investigators built a mobile laboratory to process the missiles for fingerprints in the field (Figure 14.21).

Prior to processing the surface of the missiles for fingerprints, a visual examination was conducted and one fingerprint in dust and sand was visible with oblique white light. The fingerprint was photographed extensively (Figure 14.22). Forensic investigators then carried out sequential processing methods, using white light, an ALS, superglue fuming, dye staining, and a powder suspension. The original fingerprint was destroyed in the subsequent processes and no other fingerprints were developed. The dust fingerprint was

Figure 14.20 Dragon antitank missiles discovered under shrubbery in the Israeli desert.

Figure 14.21 An improvised superglue fuming chamber was constructed to process the missiles at the site where they were discovered.

entered into the Automated Fingerprint Identification System (AFIS) and was identified to a suspect. The suspect was arrested and implicated an additional accomplice to the crime. Had the fingerprint not been found and thoroughly documented during a visual examination of the evidence, there would have been no forensic evidence linking the potential terrorists to the stolen missile.

14.10   Chapter Summary

Documentation of forensic processes includes extensive note-taking at the crime scene, in the laboratory, and during the analysis of evidence; photography before, during, and after each process; the completion of forms and agency-prepared documents; and the

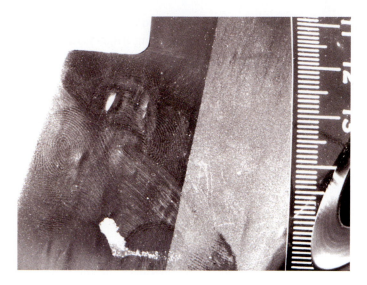

Figure 14.22 A photograph depicting the dusty/sandy fingerprints visualized on the missile prior to sequential processing.

preparation of visual aids such as charts or enhanced photos to use during courtroom testimony. Laboratory notes should include a detailed description of the evidence, steps taken to process the evidence, dates and times procedures were performed, and the results of each process. A chain of custody form accounts for all evidence transfers.

Digital SLR cameras are most often used to photograph fingerprints, evidence, and crime scenes. They may be used with a standard, multipurpose, or macro lens and a UV, infrared, polarizing, or colored filter. Direct lighting is best used with patent prints, ninhydrin and indanedione prints, and powdered prints. Front directional lighting is best used with fingerprints on concave items or reflective substrates. Backlighting is used for transparent items. Oblique lighting is used for photographing superglue prints or plastic prints. Digital photographs must be saved in a lossless format and can only be manipulated if a copy is made. Photographs are evidence. A final report is an objective, clear, and concise summary of all the work done on a case and the implications of forensic analyses.

Review Questions

1. What are SOPs?
2. What details should be included in laboratory notes?
3. What is a chain of custody form?
4. What type of camera is most often used to photograph crime scenes and evidentiary items?
5. What are the three types of lenses?
6. What is a filter? What are the four most common filters used by forensic scientists?
7. What is a 1:1 lens adapter used for?
8. Describe the direct lighting photographic technique. What fingerprint development techniques can be photographed using the direct lighting technique?

9. On what substrates is the direct lighting method unsuitable?
10. What photographic method is best for capturing fingerprints on transparent objects such as glass, plastic, or clear tape?
11. What fingerprint development techniques are best photographed using oblique lighting?
12. What digital formats are unacceptable for recording and storing fingerprint images?
13. True or false. Photographs are evidence and are subject to discovery.
14. True or false. You should never make a digital copy of a fingerprint image. Explain your answer.
15. What does "objective" mean in the context of final narrative fingerprint reports?
16. A final report should be _____ and _____.

References

1. Hutchins, L. 2011. The preservation of friction ridges. In *The Fingerprint Sourcebook*. The Scientific Working Group on Friction Ridge Analysis, Study and Technology (SWGFAST), et al. Washington, DC: National Institute of Justice, U.S. Department of Justice, Office of Justice Programs.
2. Strunk, W. and White, E.B. 1972. *The Elements of Style*. New York: Macmillan.

Crime Scene Processing 15

Key Terms

- Crime scene investigation
- Evidence
- Crime scene
- Evidence linkage triangle
- Elimination fingerprints
- Crime scene kit
- Point of entry
- Point of exit
- In situ
- Dusting for prints
- Orientation
- Burglary
- Robbery
- Casement
- Contraband
- Contamination
- Cross contamination
- Degradation

Learning Objectives

- Define the key terms.
- Understand the peculiarities of crime scene processing.
- Recognize areas of interest for fingerprint processing in burglary, commercial, and vehicle scenes.
- Describe how DNA analysis and fingerprint analysis can both aid in the investigation of both violent and nonviolent crimes.

15.1   Crime Scene Investigation

Crime scene investigation (CSI) is a forensic analysis of the location and circumstances surrounding a crime. It comprises gathering investigative, forensic, and physical evidence to link a sequence of events to reconstruct the crime scene. *Evidence* can be anything associated with a crime scene that may determine innocence or guilt in a court of law. Evidence can determine whether or not a crime occurred.

A *crime scene* is the location where a crime took place. The primary crime scene is the location where the initial criminal act took place. There may also be secondary or tertiary crime scenes. For example, if someone is killed at a residence, transported, and dumped in a ditch by the side of a road, the primary crime scene is the residence. The secondary crime scene is the ditch where the body was dumped. If the vehicle is recovered, it becomes the tertiary crime scene.

A crime scene can be an unsafe environment. There are many unknown factors. It is important, first and foremost, to protect yourself from harm. Safety precautions should be taken when handling sharp items (broken glass, syringes, knives, etc.) or working around biological substances such as blood or semen. Gloves should be worn at all times. At scenes contaminated with blood, it is beneficial to double glove (wear two pairs of nitrile or latex gloves at the same time). A mask and eye protection (laboratory glasses or goggles) can also be worn, along with disposable plastic coveralls and boot covers.

Regardless of the nature of the scene—whether it is a burglary, robbery, or homicide—fingerprints serve an important function in crime scene investigation and reconstruction. Fingerprint examiners can establish identity and associate an individual with the scene or evidence. Recall the *evidence linkage triangle* (Figure 15.1). Fingerprints can link a suspect to a crime scene, a suspect to a victim, and a victim to a crime scene. Most often, the crime scene investigator is interested in linking the suspect to the crime scene either directly by identifying fingerprints on furniture or stationary structural elements or indirectly by identifying fingerprints on evidentiary items.

Latent fingerprints are compared with known fingerprints. Latent prints at crime scenes may not belong only to the suspect or victim. They also may belong to witnesses, family members, bystanders, and normal commercial foot traffic in the vicinity. For example, if a bank is robbed, the *point of entry* (POE) is the front door of the bank. A crime scene investigator processes the glass doors and recovers 10 fingerprints and 15 palm prints. What are the chances the fingerprints belong to the suspect versus the hundreds of patrons who frequent that bank? It is not possible to collect known fingerprints from every bank patron. In the case of a residential burglary, however, it is possible to collect exemplars from everyone who lives in the home and anyone with legitimate access to the residence.

Exemplars from victims and witnesses are needed to eliminate the latent prints that do not belong to the suspect. These are known as *elimination fingerprints*. Elimination

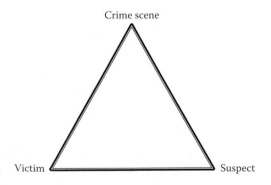

Figure 15.1 The evidence linkage triangle demonstrating the relationships between the crime scene, victim, and suspect. Fingerprint evidence can link the victim to the crime scene, the suspect to the crime scene, and/or the suspect to the victim.

fingerprints can be taken by using the ink or powder methods described in Chapter 5 of this book. The types of latent prints recovered at the scene determine the types of exemplars it is necessary to collect at the scene. If latent palm prints are recovered, the crime scene investigator collects palm print exemplars as well as fingerprints from the victims and witnesses.

There are myriad situational factors that determine whether or not latents of value are found at a scene. If the scene is indoors, how clean are the surfaces? Are they dirty or dusty? Are the surfaces suitable for developing fingerprints of value? If the scene is outdoors, environmental factors influence whether latents of value are preserved. Dry conditions, wind, rain, sun, and other weather factors may obliterate or deteriorate fingerprints. Fingerprints may be preserved longer in humid conditions and in protected areas. The perpetrator may have worn gloves or touched surfaces with dry hands.

Victims and witnesses watch crime dramas and often have unrealistic expectations of forensic practitioners. This is known as the "CSI effect." The victim may want to know why you are not using a forensic light source, why you did not find fingerprints at the POE, or why you are not collecting DNA evidence. The crime scene investigator can address these questions by politely explaining the actions taken. This is a good time to educate a layperson about the science of fingerprints just as the forensic expert will educate the jury in court, as described in Chapter 18 of this book.

15.2   Crime Scene Kit

A fingerprint analyst working in a laboratory has chemical storage cabinets, laboratory glassware, benchtop workspace, and large equipment stored in a controlled environment. The crime scene is an uncontrolled environment. All the equipment and supplies you will need must be brought to the scene in a crime scene vehicle and carried into the scene by hand (Figure 15.2). The crime scene investigator utilizes tools of the trade that are particular

Figure 15.2 Crime scene kit.

to crime scene processing. The basic items can be carried in a *crime scene kit*. The following is a list of equipment and supplies necessary for a thorough CSI for fingerprint evidence:

- Gloves
- Writing implements
- Scales
- Magnifier
- Rubber/gel lifters
- Fingerprint powders (black, bichromatic, magnetic, and fluorescent)
- Fingerprint brushes (fiberglass, feather duster, and magnetic)
- Fingerprint lift tape (various widths)
- Latent print backing cards (black and white)
- Silicone-based casting material
- Light sources (flashlight and forensic light sources)
- Camera equipment (camera body, lenses, filters, flashes, tripod, and 1:1 latent print adapter)
- Ink pad
- Tenprint cards or elimination print packet
- Handiprint System®
- Evidence packaging (paper bags, boxes, envelopes, etc.)
- Evidence packaging tape

15.3   Processing the Crime Scene

The first step to process a crime scene for fingerprints is to conduct a thorough search of the surfaces of interest. The crime scene investigator will concentrate efforts on areas and surfaces the suspect is likely to have interacted with. It is not necessary to fingerprint every smooth, clean surface at the scene. Energy should be expended on surfaces relevant to the context of the scene, location, and type of crime. The following is a list of areas to focus on at the crime scene and will be discussed in detail later in the chapter:

- Point of entry (POE)
- Point of exit
- Areas of disturbance or items described by the victim or witness as out of place or moved
- Area where the crime took place, if known
- Ancillary areas such as bathrooms and kitchens
- The path the perpetrator may have taken through the scene (from the POE to disturbed areas to the point of exit)

Once the area of interest has been identified, a visual examination of the surface is the first step in fingerprint processing. Oblique lighting can be used to visualize fingerprints that may not be clearly visible in daylight or direct white light. The best tool for visual examination is a flashlight. A flashlight held at oblique (and even parallel) angles to the surface may reveal friction ridge detail (Figure 15.3). If fingerprints are observed, they are photographed in situ (in place). Midrange photos are taken to show context. Close-up

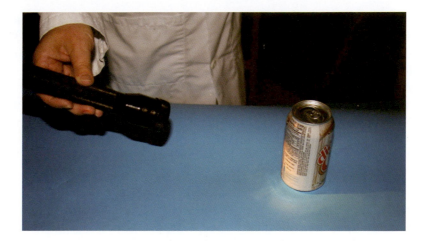

Figure 15.3 A forensic scientist examines an item of evidence using oblique lighting.

photographs can be taken with a 1:1 adapter or a macro lens. Plastic fingerprints are also photographed. If the plastic print is durable, it can be cast with silicone casting material.

When all visible fingerprints are recorded, the surface is processed for fingerprints using the appropriate processing technique. It is often preferable to transport portable items of evidence to the forensics laboratory for processing and analysis. The fingerprint analyst uses chemicals and specialized equipment to visualize latent fingerprints on evidence. Many texts suggest attempting chemical processing methods such as superglue fuming at the scene (Figure 15.4). This is not recommended for several reasons. First, chemicals and fumes present a hazard to health and property. Second, the laboratory is a more controlled environment, leading to better quality results. In order to assure the best quality fingerprints are developed, evidentiary items must be packaged carefully so as not to damage latent fingerprints.

The powder and brush method of fingerprint processing is the workhorse of crime scene fingerprint development. The technique, known colloquially as *dusting for prints*, seems simple. However, it takes practice to utilize this method effectively to develop fingerprints of value. Because the fingerprint powder is brushed over the surface, it is possible to

Figure 15.4 A cyanoacrylate fuming wand for superglue fuming surfaces at a crime scene. (Reprinted with permission from Safariland, Inc. http://forensicssource.com/CategoryDetail. aspx?CategoryName=Cyanoacrylate-Fuming-Supplies. Accessed June 5, 2014.)

wipe away the latent prints rather than develop them. A gentle touch and attention to detail are required. The following methodology is suggested.

First, select a fingerprint powder. The color of the fingerprint powder should contrast with the color of the surface. Black fingerprint powder is often the color of choice because it provides the best contrast on glass surfaces, light-colored glossy painted surfaces, metal, plastic, and finished wood surfaces. Bichromatic powder is effective on dark surfaces where the black powder is not easily visible. Magnetic powder is best suited for smaller areas where a gentler touch is warranted. Fluorescent powder is useful on patterned or multicolored surfaces as well as electronics but can only be visualized with a forensic light source in a darkened room.

After selecting the appropriate fingerprint powder, pour a small amount onto a clean sheet of paper (Figure 15.5). This is a preferable method to repeatedly dipping the brush into the container of powder. This method keeps the powder in the jar from getting contaminated, dirty, or wet. Contamination is especially relevant since the advent of DNA technology and the emergence of new methods for examining touch DNA.

Remove a fiberglass brush from its protective tube. The brush fibers should not be entangled or contaminated with dirt other than fingerprint powder. A wet or dirty brush should be discarded in favor of a clean, dry brush. Twirl the brush to loosen the fibers. Gently tap the brush into the powder to pick up a small amount of powder. Shake or twirl the brush to remove excess powder from the bristles (Figure 15.6).

Gently pass the brush over the surface using a twirling motion. Be careful to only touch the surface with the tips of the bristles. A very small amount of powder is all that is needed to identify areas with latent prints. When friction ridges begin to appear, concentrate your efforts on that area (Figure 15.7). Gently pass the brush over the area until you see good contrast and friction ridge detail. Overprocessing may result in accidentally obliterating the print. Work slowly and methodically. When the fingerprint is developed, it is photographed in situ with a scale.

Figure 15.5 A small amount of black fingerprint powder is deposited on a sheet of white paper.

Figure 15.6 A fiberglass fingerprint brush is shaken to remove excess powder from the bristles.

Figure 15.7 Latent fingerprints are revealed as the fingerprint brush is gently passed over the surface of interest.

After the fingerprint is documented, it is lifted onto a latent print backing card. Choose a roll of latent lift tape of suitable size. If the impression is a palm print or a set of simultaneous impressions, a wider tape is used. Two-inch lift tape is commonly used for a fingerprint. Pull enough tape from the roll to cover the area surrounding the latent print. Place the end of the tape on the surface next to the latent print. Sweep a finger down the

Figure 15.8 Latent lift tape is placed over the developed fingerprint.

Figure 15.9 The fingerprint is lifted onto a latent print backing card.

length of the tape over the latent impression with a smooth, even motion (Figure 15.8). Rub the tape to remove any air bubbles and to make sure the adhesive sticks to the entire area of the impression. In a smooth motion, holding both the roll and the loose end of the tape, pull the tape off the surface. Place the tape onto a latent print backing card in the same way the tape was placed onto the substrate (Figure 15.9). Rub the tape to remove any air bubbles.

Document the location and orientation of the fingerprint after it is mounted on the latent lift card. Indicate the up direction with an arrow on the front of the lift card (Figure 15.10). The latent is given a unique identifier, such as L001 or #1. Sketch the location of the fingerprint in its original location on the back of the latent lift card

Figure 15.10 Directionality is indicated by an arrow on the front of the latent lift card.

Figure 15.11 The date, crime type, case number, victim, address, location, examiner, examiner's ID number, sketch, latent print identifier, and directionality information are recorded on the back of the latent lift card.

(Figure 15.11). On many fingerprint lift cards, there are preprinted spaces to fill in the following information:

- Sketch/diagram
- Case number
- Date
- Latent lift number
- Type of offense
- Victim/suspect
- Address/location
- Where the prints were lifted from
- Who lifted the prints (name, initials, and/or ID#)

Whether or not the information is printed on the card, it should be included for reference.

Documentation is important not only to record the case number and parties involved but also to provide context. The sketch and arrows provide context and orientation. It is often the *orientation*—the location and direction of the fingerprints—that is a crucial piece of investigative evidence. Details of the examiner's actions at the crime scene are also documented in narrative form as described in Chapter 14.

There are several common errors made by inexperienced practitioners dusting a crime scene. The inexperienced crime scene investigator may load the brush with excess powder coating the surface and the latent print residue with powder. Recall that fingerprint powder adheres to the oils and moisture in the matrix. If there is too much powder on the surface, there will be excessive background "noise." The goal is to develop a fingerprint that has contrast between the ridges and the furrows. Using too much fingerprint powder causes granules to be deposited between, as well as on, the ridges.

Another common error is when the practitioner is "heavy handed" with the fingerprint brush. Inexperience or impatience may cause the crime scene investigator to wipe the surface with the brush in long strokes, similar to painting a wall. This may wipe away latent prints or develop prints with drag marks through them. Skillful fingerprint development is gained through training, practice, and experience. All types of crimes, from autorelated offenses to homicides, may require the crime scene investigator to dust for fingerprints. The offenses in the following are some of the most commonly encountered crimes.

15.4   Modus Operandi

The successful identification of a latent print is only the beginning of an investigation. A fingerprint identification provides an answer to "who," but not to "what, when, or how." In the investigation of a crime scene, knowledge and understanding of human behavior are invaluable as clues to where to find the best physical evidence, including latent prints. The more an investigator understands about the how and why of a suspect's criminal actions, the easier it is to concentrate on those areas that will be most productive in the hunt for evidence. Like the rest of us, much of a criminal's behavior is habitual. Certain burglars prefer certain entry points and particular methods of entering and searching. These habits become a criminal's *modus operandi* (MO).

An experienced scene investigator can often propose a suspect or link multiple crimes to the same person simply by recognizing the MO. For example, suppose a series of residential burglaries in apartment buildings involves entry by use of pliers to twist open the doorknob on the front door. Once inside the apartments, the suspect goes directly to the master bedroom and cleans out the jewelry from the top dresser drawers. If and when a suspect is apprehended, knowledge of the burglar's MO can lead to solving similar burglaries.

Behavioral peculiarities may also lend a particular signature to the criminal's behavior. The burglar may go to the refrigerator and make a sandwich or open a beer and leave it on the counter (Figure 15.12). The burglar may use the bathroom or defecate on the living room floor; write a message on the wall; or pick up and look at family pictures. Peculiarities become habits that can assist in identification and prosecution (Figure 15.13).

Figure 15.12 At this burglary crime scene, the burglar put down his screwdriver and made himself a sandwich. His fingerprints were identified from the plate.

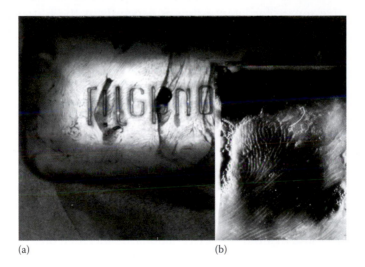

(a)   (b)

Figure 15.13 Enlargement (b) of a patent print on a bar of soap (a) identified to the suspect in a homicide.

15.5 Categories of Crime Settings: Burglaries

Regardless of the type of crime, the setting or location will most often be one of the following: a residential scene, a commercial scene, or a vehicle. As mentioned earlier, a crime may involve multiple scenes. Each of these three settings presents challenges. A crime scene investigator must learn to master all.

The most common felony in a residential setting is a burglary. *Burglary* is the illegal entry of an individual into a building or vehicle with the intent to commit larceny or another crime. This is in contrast to a *robbery*, which is committed in the presence of the occupant and is a more serious crime. No other crime has been more fruitful in terms of numbers of suspects identified by fingerprints than the burglary. As such, residential burglary is the primary and most important training ground for scene investigators. Residential burglary is also commonly the lesser-included offense in more serious but far less common offenses like home invasion robberies, rapes, and homicides. The more experience scene investigators have with common residential burglaries, the more qualified they become investigating more serious crimes in that same setting. Some of the hallmarks of a residential scene include the following:

- Normal everyday access is usually limited to residents and invitees. The presence of a foreign fingerprint is more incriminating. Elimination prints of the residents are usually easy to obtain.
- Points of entry are generally less secure and composed of house-grade double-hung or sliding windows and wooden doors.
- Since this is a crime of stealth on private property, eyewitnesses are rare.
- The environment is often rich in surfaces handled by the suspect that can yield latent prints.

The most productive source for latent prints is generally at the initial POE. Windows are far more productive than doors because doors are often kicked or forced open, wood grain on the door surface can obscure fingerprint ridge structure, and door hardware is frequently handled in the same place and tends to build up a film of residue that blocks latent prints. Very few people wash or wipe clean their door handles. This same reasoning also applies to anything with a small surface area that is handled repeatedly in the same place every time: light switches, drawer pulls, window latches, telephone buttons, keyboard keys, and garage door buttons. Keep in mind that every scene is unique and exceptions are possible.

In examining a POE window in which the glass has not been broken, search all parts of the glazing (the windowpane) using a very bright flashlight. It is helpful to circle the latents on the glass using a marker and number or letter the latents. Photograph or diagram the window overall so that the locations of latents are visible in relationship to each other. Then lift the prints making sure that the label designations are included on the lift; for example, if the latent is labeled "1" on the window, the lift of that print must be "1" on the lift cards (Figure 15.14).

Latent prints on the outside of a window can lead to the identification of a suspect; however, the crime of burglary must show entry with the intent to commit theft or another

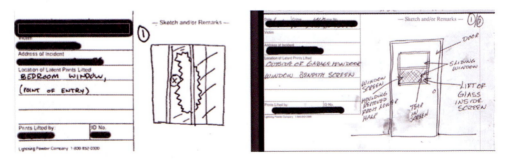

Figure 15.14 The backs of two latent lift cards with associated fingerprint designations and sketches.

Figure 15.15 At this crime scene, the suspect removed the screen to gain entry to the bedroom window. The latent fingerprint lifted from the frame was identified in Automated Fingerprint Identification System (AFIS).

crime. A print on the outside of a window does not necessarily mean it was placed there at the time the crime was committed. Latent prints have been shown to stay on window glass for months or years, surviving rain and snow. If the ridges of the hand that left the print had oily or greasy residues, even an old latent print could appear to be fresh even when it was not. For this reason, once latent prints have been discovered on the outside, it is imperative to process the inside glass and especially the inside window *casement* (the outer frame of the window). If the intruder removed a screen before entering the window, latent prints on the frame of the screen can indirectly establish the age of the print if it can be shown by its position that the latent could not have been placed while the screen was mounted (Figure 15.15).

Fortunately, the interior and exterior casements of most residential windows are painted with enamel paint that is an excellent surface for latents. Process the entire circumference of the interior window and casement. Again, use a marker to outline and diagram any prints that are found. It is these interior latents that will prove that entry, an element of the crime, was made (Figure 15.16).

A burglary in which window glass has been broken offers additional opportunities for evidentiary fingerprints. Once an intruder has broken a windowpane, the individual will often remove fragments of glass from the molding in order not to be cut when crawling or reaching in. No effort should be spared in retrieving these fragments—identified by their straight edges from the side that was held in the molding—from the ground or the interior floor. While picking out these glass fragments, the suspect will often deposit a thumbprint on one side and an index and/or middle finger on the other. The only time this could occur is after the window has been broken. Thus, from one fragment of glass, you can prove identity, entry, and time of deposit (Figure 15.17).

When processing the inside of the home, it is preferable to be accompanied by a resident who can point out exactly what items are out of place. Large appliances such as TVs or sound systems often have decorative items on top or around them that the suspect must move before stealing the equipment. Picture frames, magazines, figurines, and DVD cases can all be good sources for latents. The top dresser drawers in the master bedroom are often ransacked for valuables. Jewelry boxes and small glossy boxes are often emptied and left behind. They, too, offer rich surfaces for latents (Figure 15.18).

Figure 15.16 At this crime scene, the latent lift from the inside window casement resulted from the suspect reaching in with the right hand while climbing into the room.

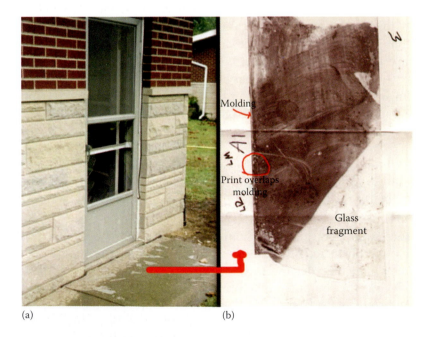

(a)   (b)

Figure 15.17 Fingerprints (b) lifted from glass fragments picked out of the molding (a).

Figure 15.18 Typical ransacked dresser in the master bedroom offering multiple surfaces for a latent print search.

15.6 Categories of Crime Settings: Commercial Scenes

Commercial settings offer their own challenges to the investigator. Some of the hallmarks of a commercial setting include the following:

- Commercial establishments are often open to the public and/or have an influx of different groups of people during operating hours. Attempting to gather elimination prints is often a daunting task.
- The criminal usually has a focus of attack, that is, money or merchandise. There is less random searching resulting in relatively fewer items to process.
- Eyewitnesses in the form of employees, customers, guards, and surveillance cameras are more common.
- The environment consists of industrial surfaces and points of entry that are dirty or dusty or otherwise not conducive to prints. Also, commercial scenes are difficult to preserve because the management is usually anxious to reopen for business.

The directed nature of attack makes it fairly easy to focus on what items need to be processed for prints, but a few observations may be helpful.

Cash registers are a challenge for latent recovery. Buttons and levers are usually too soiled because they are handled many times a day and are seldom cleaned. Unless the entire register was picked up and moved, the most productive source of latent prints is the bottom of the cash tray. Best practices require that the plastic tray be taken to the lab and fumed with cyanoacrylate to recover any latents.

Display cases in businesses opened to the public are usually cleaned frequently to better display the merchandise. Jewelry stores often clean the surfaces with glass cleaner several times a day. It is helpful if an employee or a surveillance video can point out the precise area touched by the suspect. If prints are located, they should be delineated with a marking pen, diagrammed, and photographed before lifting. The direction of the latent fingers on the display case can serve to determine where the suspect was standing at the time of the crime, for example, behind the counter reaching into the display case doors.

In robberies, the suspect often wanders the store picking up merchandise randomly before approaching the cash register. Often, the individual will bring the items to the checkout counter as if to make a purchase and then just leave them. If the item was from a cooler, it will soon be wet with condensation from the warmer store air. Latent prints can be developed if the items are allowed to dry thoroughly prior to processing.

15.7   Categories of Crime Settings: Vehicles

Vehicles are often used as either the tool or object of crime. A vehicle can be a weapon, a means of criminal transport, a container for *contraband* (illegal items), or the target of theft. Some of the hallmarks of a vehicle scene include the following:

- Vehicles are mobile and operate on public streets. Latent prints identified from a vehicle are often insufficient to support prosecution. Even an identified latent from the inside rearview mirror does not prove that the subject ever drove the car.
- Points of entry are often difficult to process because the safety glass of the windows crumbles on impact.
- Most surfaces within a vehicle are textured (dashboard, seats) or covered with a barrier of grime (gearshift, buttons, steering wheel).
- In spite of these limitations, crimes are solved every day from latent prints lifted from vehicles. The most productive sources for latents are windows, doorframes, rearview mirrors, and personal items inside the vehicle.

15.8   Fingerprints and DNA

In the United States, DNA has historically been an investigative tool in violent crime investigations such as homicides and sexual assaults. In Great Britain, however, DNA has been collected at not only violent crimes but also property crimes, since 2000.[1] The British Home Office determined that though DNA is found only about 17% of the time, it generates a higher proportion of matches to suspects than fingerprints alone.[1] A study conducted in the United States and published in 2008 found that DNA collected from property crimes resulted in twice as many suspect identifications as fingerprint evidence (16% of suspects were identified through biological analysis versus 8% by fingerprints).[1] Blood and saliva evidence yielded the most significant proportion of DNA versus touch DNA, which was not as successful.

The same considerations must be taken into account when collecting both DNA evidence and fingerprint evidence at property crimes. Roman et al. state that "By following the steps burglars take in effecting their crimes, it is possible to determine the likely locations of DNA evidence at a crime scene. Residential burglars proceed through several steps, including generating a motive, target identification, entering the dwelling, searching the house, gathering items, leaving the house, and disposing of items."[1] The POE and other areas described earlier are important targets for not only fingerprint evidence but also biological evidence.

Precautions must be taken if the scene investigator plans on recovering both biological and fingerprint evidence. DNA evidence is subject to contamination, cross contamination, and degradation. It must be collected and stored properly for future analysis. *Contamination* occurs when the biological evidence is corrupted by an outside source. For example, if a scene investigator breathes on an item of interest or touches an item with ungloved hands, the investigator's DNA may transfer to the item. *Cross contamination* may occur when two separate evidentiary items come into contact. Biological evidence from one item may be transferred to another item. For example, if a bloody knife is improperly packaged, some of the blood may transfer to other items of evidence. DNA is also subject to *degradation*, which is the breakdown of DNA in biological material over time due to exposure to chemicals such as bleach or environmental factors such as heat and sunlight.

The scene investigator can minimize contamination by wearing gloves and a particulate mask. Gloves should be changed frequently. Disposable fingerprint brushes and powders are available from forensic supply companies. Cross contamination is minimized by packaging items in the proper containers. Degradation is avoided by collecting biological evidence samples prior to fingerprint processing. The samples or items should be stored in a cool, dry area until they can be transported to a laboratory or facility for controlled evidence storage.

Most law enforcement agencies do not routinely collect biological evidence at nonviolent crime scenes. For many, the process is cost and time prohibitive. DNA analysis is an expensive, time-consuming process. Many departments have backlogs of cases awaiting analysis. Many do not have the funding to cope with expanding DNA laboratory capabilities that would require hiring more analysts, investing in equipment and supplies, and possibly expanding facilities. While not a common process to date, collecting both fingerprint and biological evidence at nonviolent crime scenes leads to many more arrests and convictions than fingerprints alone.

15.9   I Had a Case: Point of Entry

Crime scene investigators were dispatched to a burglary at a residence. The POE was the bathroom window, which had been left unlocked. The perpetrator had removed the window screen and placed a patio chair beneath the window. He then climbed through the window, over the toilet, and into the bathroom.

The interior bathroom window casement was processed with black fingerprint powder. Six fingerprints corresponding with the index, middle, and right fingers of the right and left hand were recovered on the interior of the windowpane just above the window frame. The fingerprints were oriented in the upward direction. What does the orientation of the fingerprints tell you about the crime? If you were to open a window from the outside, where would you place your hands? You would likely pull up on the window with both hands, possibly depositing your fingerprints on the inside of the window facing in the up direction. Would an individual opening the window from the inside leave fingerprints in that position? Most likely he would not. This is evidence that the burglar, not the homeowner, placed his fingerprints on the inside of the window. The fingerprints were later identified to the perpetrator who, during interrogation, admitted to several other burglaries in that neighborhood with the same MO.

15.10   Chapter Summary

CSI is a forensic analysis of the location and circumstances surrounding a crime. The crime scene is an uncontrolled environment versus the forensic laboratory, which is a controlled environment. Crime scene investigators carry basic items for crime scene processing in a crime scene kit. When an area of interest is identified at a crime scene, it is visually inspected for fingerprints, processed with fingerprint powder, and documented. Portable items of evidence should be transported to the forensic laboratory for processing in a controlled environment. MO is habitual criminal behavior.

Burglaries are common residential felonies. The POE, especially the window, is a productive source for latent prints, as are disturbed areas such as items out of place, ransacked areas, and items that are missing. Commercial scenes are challenging because they are open to the public or have an influx of different groups of people during operating hours. These scenes often have a focused goal. Most surfaces at the scene are not often conducive to developing fingerprints, though success may be possible on cash register trays, display cases, or displaced merchandise. A vehicle can be a weapon, a means of criminal transport, a container for contraband, or the target of theft. The most productive sources for latents are windows, doorframes, rearview mirrors, and personal items inside the vehicle. Used together, fingerprints and DNA can be effective weapons for solving routine cases.

Review Questions

1. Define "crime scene investigation."
2. What is the purpose of collecting evidence?
3. Why is it important to take elimination fingerprints from individuals who have legitimate access to the crime scene?
4. Are latent prints of value always found at a crime scene? Why, or why not?
5. Why is it preferable to collect items of evidence rather than processing them at the crime scene?
6. What is modus operandi (MO)?
7. Define burglary and robbery.
8. What are the hallmarks of a residential scene?
9. What is the most productive source for latent prints at a scene?
10. What are the hallmarks of the commercial scene?
11. What are the hallmarks of the vehicle scene?
12. What are the precautions that must be taken if a scene investigator is planning on recovering DNA evidence from a scene?

Reference

1. Roman, J. et al. 2008. *The DNA Field Experiment: Cost-Effectiveness Analysis of the Use of DNA in the Investigation of High-Volume Crimes*. Washington, DC: Urban Institute, Justice Policy Center.

Fingerprint Comparisons 16

The examiner makes a transition from insufficient knowledge, through doubt, to knowing and belief.

John Vanderkolk[1]

Key Terms

- Exclusion
- Identification
- Inconclusive
- Level one detail
- Level two detail
- Level three detail
- Ridgeology
- ACE-V
- Analysis
- Comparison
- Evaluation
- Verification
- Standardization
- Quantitative
- Qualitative
- Subjective
- Loupe
- Pointers
- Bias
- One dissimilarity rule
- Point standards
- Sufficiency graph

Learning Objectives

- Define the key terms.
- Understand the purpose of fingerprint comparisons.
- Explain the three possible conclusions to a fingerprint comparison.
- Explain the three levels of fingerprint detail and their role in comparisons.
- Describe ACE-V methodology.
- Explain why there is no minimum point standard for fingerprint comparisons.

16.1   Fingerprint Comparisons

The purpose of processing latent fingerprints and collecting known fingerprints is to compare one to the other to determine whether they come from a common source (i.e., whether or not the same person made both the known print and the latent). A latent print identification is possible due to the two premises of fingerprint analysis: friction ridges are both unique and permanent.

As was discussed in previous chapters, latent prints are developed using powders or chemicals. They are documented either on latent print lift cards or as digital photographs. Known fingerprints are recorded with powder or ink or as digital images in an Automated Fingerprint Identification System (AFIS) computer. How one proceeds depends on the circumstances surrounding the crime. If a suspect is identified, and the suspect's fingerprints are available, that suspect's known fingerprints can be compared to the latent fingerprints. It may also be necessary to compare elimination fingerprints to the latent fingerprints. If there is no suspect named in a crime, the latent fingerprints can be first compared to the elimination fingerprints and then searched in the AFIS database.

A latent print will not usually be an exact replica of any other latent print or known print from a single source. Even if an individual places his finger on the same surface multiple times, the latent prints will not look exactly the same. The processing method, deposition pressure, distortion, surface characteristics, amount of matrix on the friction ridges, motion, and the elasticity of the skin can all affect the way a latent print looks when it is developed. Similarly, those same factors affect the way a known print looks on a tenprint card or on a computer screen. A latent print examiner is looking for the pattern type, ridge count, ridge flow, and, most importantly, the types and locations of minutiae along those friction ridges.

Comparing fingerprints is an exercise in pattern analysis. Some people are more adept than others at pattern analysis. Some individuals can look at two seemingly identical images and pick out the differences between them. An example is shown in Figure 16.1. There are six differences between the photo on the left and the photo on the right. Can you find the differences (Figure 16.1)? Now examine Figure 16.2 (Figure 16.2). Which line is longer? In actuality, both lines are the same length. The successful latent print examiner is detail oriented and can perceive detail without succumbing to inherent biases imposed by the human mind.

16.2   Level 1, 2, and 3 Detail

A comparison of two fingerprints can lead to one of three conclusions: an *exclusion*, *identification*, or *inconclusive* result. Fingerprint examiners describe three levels of detail within a friction ridge impression. *Level one detail* refers to the overall ridge flow of the fingerprint. This includes the pattern type, shape, and the position of the core related to the delta. While the examination of level one detail is an excellent place to start, under no circumstances, can it be used to conclusively identify a latent print to a known source. For example, assume the latent print is an ulnar loop with a ridge count of 16. The #3 finger of the suspect is also an ulnar loop with a ridge count of 16. Are those prints from the same source? Due to the high percentage of loop patterns in the general population, it is not unusual to see multiple fingerprints from different sources that are the same pattern type with the same ridge count.

(a)   (b)

Figure 16.1 Find the six differences between the picture (a) and the picture (b).

Figure 16.2 Human perception may lead one to believe the line on the top line is longer than the one underneath it. The lines are, in fact, the same length.

A latent print examiner examines the level one detail to narrow down the possible source of the fingerprint. Continuing with the last example, if the suspect has 10 loops, but none of the loops have a ridge count of 16, the suspect is excluded as the source of the latent print. Alternately, the suspect may have 10 loops, but only two are ulnar loops with a ridge count of 16. Now you have narrowed down the source to 2 possible fingers instead of 10. If you were to look at every fingerprint of every suspect, witness, and victim with a magnifier without first examining the level one detail, it would take much longer than necessary to determine the source of the latent print. It is important to "see the forest for the trees" and work efficiently, not harder.

Level two detail refers to the minutiae within the pattern. An analysis of level two details includes not only the types of minutiae (e.g., ending ridges, dots, and bifurcations) but also the relative positions of the minutiae along the friction ridges (Figure 16.3). Where is the bifurcation in relation to the ending ridge? How many ridges separate the two minutiae? Is the ending ridge pointing up or down? Is the bifurcation pointing up or down? Is the ending ridge close to the bifurcation? Minutiae are examined under

Figure 16.3 The minutiae in this double loop whorl fingerprint are denoted with red dots. The types of minutiae and their relative positions along the ridges are considered when examining level two detail.

a magnifier. Unlike level one detail, level two detail may lead not only to an *exclusion* but also to an *identification*.

 Level three detail refers to the minute features and dimensions of the friction ridges. It is an examination of the shapes, sizes, and relative positions of the pores along the ridge, as well as an examination of the edge shapes and widths (Figure 16.4). The study of level three details is known as *ridgeology*. These level three details are not always visible in many

Figure 16.4 A double loop whorl fingerprint with edge shapes and pores.

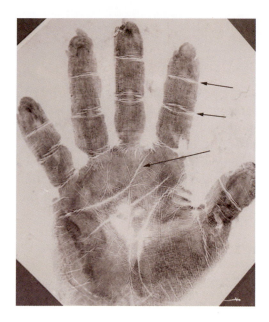

Figure 16.5 Arrows denote creases of the finger joints and palm.

latent and known prints. However, when they are visible, they are useful for forming a final conclusion. Each level of detail focuses on more and more unique features.

There are other features that augment or lend confidence to a fingerprint conclusion. Scars and creases may appear as straight, curved, or jagged white lines within a print (Figure 16.5). Blisters, cuts, or warts may also be visible in a fingerprint, but these heal and change shape over time. Level one, two, and three details are observed in a particular order based on the methodology fingerprint examiners employ to compare fingerprints. This methodology is commonly referred to as analysis, comparison, evaluation, and verification (*ACE-V*).

16.3 ACE-V

ACE-V is a scientific methodical evaluation of level one, two, and three detail in context. Regardless of the medium used to record the known fingerprints—ink, powder, or digital— latent print examiners use a process known as ACE-V to perform fingerprint comparisons. This methodology *standardizes* the comparison process to ensure that every examiner follows the same steps to identify the source of any latent fingerprint. The ACE-V process is not only used to identify the source of a fingerprint but also to exclude an individual as the source of the fingerprint. An *exclusion* conclusion is just as valuable as an *identification* conclusion.

ACE-V methodology was developed as an approximation of the scientific method. The components of the scientific method are

- Observation
- Hypothesis
- Experimentation

- Analysis
- Conclusion
- Peer review

The ACE-V method was developed to standardize fingerprint comparisons and to give the science legitimacy in the greater scientific community. It was initially standardized by the Scientific Working Group on Friction Ridge Analysis, Study and Technology (SWGFAST) in 2009 and revised in subsequent instructive documents.[2,3]

ACE-V is a systematic approach to looking at the latent print and making a determination. It follows a logical progression from an overall examination of the pattern to a more detailed examination of the minutiae and other features of the fingerprint. Vanderkolk describes the decision-making process as follows:

> *The examiner transitions through the examination by analyzing, comparing, and evaluating the details of the prints through critical and objective comparative measurements of the details of general ridge flow, specific ridge paths and ridge path lengths, the sequences and configurations of ridge paths and their terminations, and the sequences and configurations of edges or textures and pore positions along ridge paths.*
>
> *The examiner makes a transition from insufficient knowledge, through doubt, to knowing and belief. The examiner bases this knowing on the previous training, experience, understanding, and judgments of self and a belief in the legitimacy of the training, experience, understanding and judgments of the collaborated community of scientists.[1]*

The examiner's final determination—identification, exclusion, or inconclusive—is the result of a qualitative and quantitative analysis. Quantitative analysis refers to countable data such as statistics or countable observations. Qualitative analysis refers to data that are not countable but scientifically valid nonetheless. Fingerprint analysis is *quantitative* because there are aspects of fingerprint analysis that involve counting ridges, minutiae, etc. The analysis is *qualitative* because the examiner's opinion is *subjective*, meaning the conclusion is based on the personal opinion of the examiner. The examiner's opinion is based on training, experience, and education.

16.4   Analysis

Analysis is the first phase of the ACE-V process. This phase is analogous to the observation and hypothesis phases of the scientific method. The analysis involves observing the overall features of the latent and known prints and making a hypothesis as to whether or not they come from the same source. It is tempting to immediately place a fingerprint magnifier (also known as a *loupe*) on the latent print to visualize the minutiae. This puts the examiner at a disadvantage, because the examiner is unable to see the overall pattern and ridge flow. Analyzing the fingerprint at a distance allows the examiner to observe the shape and flow of the fingerprint.

The analysis phase begins with an assessment of the overall quality of the fingerprint. Is the latent print sufficient? If the print is a smudge or poor quality latent, the examiner may choose not to analyze that fingerprint. If the print is of sufficient quality to compare to the exemplar, the examiner determines the pattern type, if possible. If the latent print is of the statistically common loop pattern, any exemplar fingerprints with arches or whorls are excluded. Once the pattern is determined, the examiner looks at the overall ridge flow, shape, and, if the fingerprint is a loop, the ridge count of the loop. If the latent fingerprint and the known fingerprint have similar level one detail, the examiner moves on to the comparison phase of ACE-V.

16.5   Comparison

The comparison phase of ACE-V is analogous to the experimentation and analysis phases of the scientific method. It is the process of comparing fingerprints side by side under magnification or enlarged on a computer screen. If the comparison is being done by hand, the latent print is placed to the left of the known print. It is placed on the left to avoid potential *bias*. If one is accustomed to reading from left to right, it stands to reason the examiner will "read" the fingerprint from left to right. The examiner will look at the print on the left, identify a point of interest, and compare that point with the print on the right. If the known print is placed to the left of the latent, the examiner may see a particular minutia point of interest and believe a feature is also present in the latent. That feature may be an artifact of distortion. The examiner may become biased by what they observe in the known fingerprint.

Stand magnifiers, known as *loupes*, are well suited to fingerprint comparisons because the examiner's hands are free to use fingerprint *pointers*. Pointers are metal implements resembling pens that have pointed tips. They serve as "placeholders" while the examiner is compares minutiae in the latent print to minutiae in the known print (Figure 16.6). The examiner identifies a starting point, or target area. The target area may be a core, a delta,

Figure 16.6 A loop fingerprint viewed through a magnifier. Pointers act as "placeholders" when examining a fingerprint under magnification.

or perhaps a unique area of friction ridge detail. Where the examiner starts is arbitrary and depends on personal preference and the nature of the latent print. The pointer in the left hand is placed on a minutia point in the latent. The pointer in the right hand is then placed on the corresponding minutia point in the known print. The examiner can then move on to the next minutia in the latent and mark it with the left-hand pointer. The right-hand pointer moves to the corresponding minutia point in the known print. This process continues until the examiner is confident they can come to a conclusion about the source of the latent print.

16.6   Evaluation

The evaluation phase is analogous to the conclusion phase of the scientific method. The examiner will conclude whether or not the latent print and exemplar originate from the same source. It is during the evaluation phase that "the examiner will ultimately decide whether the unknown impression is from a different source or the same source as the compared impression, or is inconclusive."[3] This determination is based on the examiner's level of confidence with the quantity and quality of features in both the latent and known print. The evaluation is based on the qualitative and quantitative aspects of the latent print in question, as well as on the examiner's knowledge, training, and experience. The quantitative factors are the numbers and sequences of minutiae observed (the level two detail). The qualitative factors are the overall level one and three details: ridge flow, pattern type, scars, pore sizes and locations, etc.

There are three possible conclusions to a fingerprint comparison: *identification*, *exclusion*, or *inconclusive*. An identification conclusion means that both the latent fingerprint and the known fingerprint came from the same source. For example, the examiner concludes that the suspect touched the knife because the fingerprint on the knife is from the same source as the suspect's exemplar print. Identification implies that the fingerprint examiner, after analyzing all of the data, has concluded that the latent print and the known print are from the same source. SWGFAST document #10 states, "individualization of an impression to one source is the decision that the likelihood the impression was made by another (different) source is so remote that it is considered as a practical impossibility."[3]

If there are dissimilarities between the known impression and the latent print, the conclusion reached must be an exclusion. If there is one minutia point in the latent that is not present in the known print, regardless of how many points are found in common, the conclusion must be to exclude the individual as the source of the latent. This is known as the *one dissimilarity rule*.

An inconclusive decision is reached if the fingerprint examiner is unable to either identify or exclude the individual in question as the source of the latent print. There are several reasons for an inconclusive result. The latent fingerprint may not have enough information to make a conclusive determination. The latent print may be of poor quality or may have an insufficient amount of minutiae despite its clarity. The known print may not have the necessary minutiae or clarity to conduct a thorough comparison. For example, if the latent fingerprint is the left delta of a whorl, and the known fingerprint does not include the left delta, there may not be enough data to do a thorough comparison. This is why it is critical to collect comprehensive exemplars.

16.7   Verification

The verification stage is analogous to the peer review process of the scientific method. It is a way to double-check the first examiner's conclusion. A second fingerprint examiner will perform the ACE steps of ACE-V independently and reach their own conclusions. Verification is essential to prevent mistakes. If a mistake is made, an innocent person may be imprisoned, or a guilty person may go free. Either mistake is unacceptable. The verifier will either support or refute the first examiner's conclusions. The conclusion will be reported if both examiners agree to the identification, exclusion, or inconclusive result.

16.8   How Many Points?

David Ashbaugh summarizes the philosophy of latent print comparisons with the following statement: "Friction ridge identification is established through the agreement of friction ridge formations, in sequence, having sufficient uniqueness to individualize."[4] This statement can be broken down to the following elements:

- Minutiae and ridge flow must be the same in both the latent and known print.
- The minutiae must be found in the same general arrangement in both prints.
- The ridge flow, minutiae, and distribution of minutiae must be unique enough to attribute them to one source.

Figure 16.7 is an example of a fingerprint comparison resulting in a positive identification (Figure 16.7).

How many points do you have to count before you can identify a fingerprint? How many minutiae must you find in common between the latent and known print? How do you know you have enough? What number establishes sufficiency? In the past, *point*

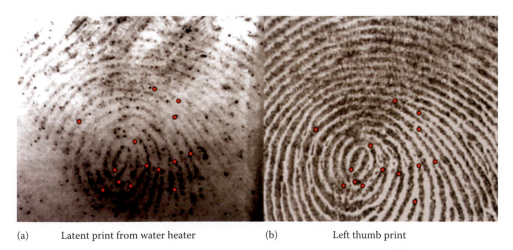

(a)   Latent print from water heater   (b)   Left thumb print

Figure 16.7 The image on the left is a latent print lifted from a water heater at a crime scene. The image on the right is the known left thumbprint of the suspect. The red dots denote minutiae in common between the two fingerprints. The latent fingerprint (a) and the known fingerprint (b) are identified as originating from the same source.

standards were imposed on the examiner. One had to count at least 12, 14, or even 16 points, depending on the agency's SOPs, in order to effect an identification.

There is inherent fallacy in this school of thought. Consider the situation where there may be a clear latent print with good contrast but only six points in common with the known print. Perhaps the latent and the known are both central pocket loop whorls with a distinctive scar through the core and a clear delta. Perhaps both the latent and the known print share a distinctive, uncommon set of minutiae. Perhaps the third level detail and crease formations are in complete agreement. There are many situations where the fingerprint examiner is confident about an identification that may not be the result of even 10 consistent minutiae.

So how many points are sufficient for an identification conclusion? Vanderkolk states, "For impressions from volar skin, as the quality of details in the print increases, the requirement for quality of details decreases. So, for clearer prints, fewer details are needed and for less clear prints, more details are needed. This follows the law of uniqueness in pattern formations in nature."[1] The fingerprint examiner bases their conclusion on a preponderance of both quantitative and qualitative data. It is up to the examiner to make an educated and thoughtful determination of sufficiency.

In 1973, the International Association for Identification (IAI) established that there is no valid basis for requiring an identification to be based on counting a certain number of points. That position was further revised in 2009 to state, "There currently exists no scientific basis for requiring a minimum amount of corresponding friction ridge detail information between two impressions to arrive at an opinion of single source attribution."[5] An international declaration was proposed and signed by 11 countries, including the United States, at the International Symposium of Fingerprint Detection and Identification in Ne'urim, Israel, in 1995.[6] This became known as the Ne'urim Declaration. The revised 2009 IAI statement closely resembles the international declaration, asserting that it is not scientifically valid to require a minimum number of points to make a fingerprint identification.

Figure 16.8 is a pictorial representation of this quantitative–qualitative threshold known as a *sufficiency graph* (Figure 16.8).[3] It represents the thought process of the latent print examiner during the analysis phase as well as the evaluation phase. A latent print that is high quality but contains few minutiae may not be deemed sufficient for comparison purposes. It is a waste of the examiner's time to evaluate a latent print that does not have enough information and would be deemed insufficient during the analysis phase.

The curves of the sufficiency graph are meant to be guidelines, not strict rules delineating what constitutes an identification or exclusion. Area "A," the red zone, is an area of low confidence. It demonstrates that a latent print with a significant number of matching minutiae does not automatically result in an identification conclusion. The latent print in question may be unclear, distorted, or otherwise poor quality and not suitable to be identified conclusively to a source without an abundance of matching minutiae. Similarly, if a latent print is of high quality, the fingerprint examiner may require fewer minutiae to come to an identification conclusion.

Area "B," the yellow zone, is a figurative gray area. This is the area where the examiner may rely on experience, knowledge, and training to come to a subjective conclusion. The less experienced examiner may come to a conclusion of inconclusive or exclusion. The more experienced examiner may call the comparison an identification. Area "C," the green zone, is an area of high confidence. It represents the evaluation of a high-quality

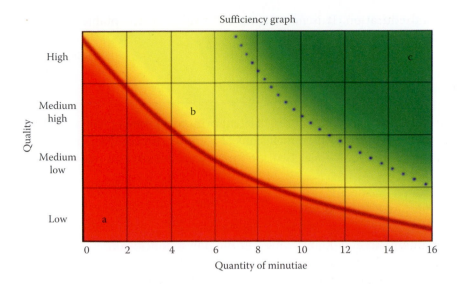

Figure 16.8 The sufficiency graph for weighing qualitative and quantitative information when comparing a latent fingerprint to a known fingerprint. The red zone (a) is an area of low confidence. In the yellow area (b), qualitative and quantitative aspects of the fingerprint must be weighed to reach a conclusion. This area may be skewed toward the red or green areas depending on the latent print examiner's experience, knowledge, and training. The green area (c) is an area of high confidence where a conclusion may be reached with a high level of confidence. (Reprinted from the Scientific Working Group on Friction Ridge Analysis, Study and Technology (SWGFAST), Document #10: Standards for Examining Friction Ridge Impressions and Resulting Conclusions (Latent/Tenprint), http://www.swgfast.org/documents/examinations-conclusions/130427_Examinations-Conclusions_2.0.pdf, last modified March 13, 2013. With permission.)

latent print with an abundance of minutiae. Regardless of where the latent print falls on the spectrum, it is up to the latent print examiner to give their opinion based on both qualitative and quantitative information in the print and their specialized knowledge, training, education, and experience as a forensic scientist.

16.9   Chapter Summary

The purpose of latent print comparisons is to determine if two fingerprints originate from a common source. A comparison of two fingerprints can lead to one of three conclusions: an *exclusion, identification,* or *inconclusive.* Level one, two, and three details are used to describe the features of fingerprints. Level one detail is the overall quality and ridge flow; for example, the pattern type, shape, core, and delta. Level two detail refers to friction ridge minutiae that are the features or characteristics used for identification. Third level detail refers to the minute features of the friction ridge, including the shape, size, and position of pores and the edge shapes of ridges.

ACE-V methodology is used to compare latent to known fingerprints. It stands for analysis, comparison, evaluation, and verification. Conclusions are based on a preponderance of qualitative and quantitative information in the latent print. The examiner effects an identification, exclusion, or inconclusive conclusion based on experience, training, and education. It is not scientifically valid or acceptable to impose a point standard for identification.

Review Questions

1. What is the purpose of comparing a latent print to a known print?
2. What are the three possible conclusions of a fingerprint comparison?
3. Which level of detail—one, two, or three—can be used to make an identification conclusion?
4. What is level one detail?
5. What does ACE-V stand for?
6. What is ACE-V?
7. Which component of ACE-V involves making a conclusion as to the source of the print?
8. Is there a minimum point standard for effecting an identification conclusion? Why, or why not?
9. Why is the verification step necessary?
10. True or false. A latent print examiner's conclusion and expert opinion are subjective.
11. True or false. Conclusions are based on a preponderance of qualitative and quantitative information in the latent print.

References

1. Vanderkolk, J. 2011. Examination process. In *The Fingerprint Sourcebook*. The Scientific Working Group on Friction Ridge Analysis, Study and Technology (SWGFAST) et al. Washington, DC: National Institute of Justice, U.S. Department of Justice, Office of Justice Programs.
2. The Scientific Working Group on Friction Ridge Analysis, Study and Technology (SWGFAST). Document #8: Standard for the Documentation of Analysis, Comparison, Evaluation, and Verification (ACE-V). http://www.swgfast.org/documents/documentation/121124_Standard-Documentation-ACE-V_2.0.pdf (last accessed on June 5, 2014).
3. The Scientific Working Group on Friction Ridge Analysis, Study and Technology (SWGFAST). Document #10: Standards for Examining Friction Ridge Impressions and Resulting Conclusions. http://www.swgfast.org/documents/examinations-conclusions/130427_Examinations-Conclusions_2.0.pdf (last accessed on June 5, 2014).
4. Ashbaugh, D. 1999. *Quantitative-Qualitative Friction Ridge Analysis: An Introduction to Basic and Advanced Ridgeology*. Boca Raton, FL: Taylor & Francis.
5. Polski, J. et al. 2011. The report of the international association for identification, standardization II committee. https://www.ncjrs.gov/pdffiles1/nij/grants/233980.pdf (accessed October 31, 2013).
6. Almog, J. and Springer, E. (eds.) (1996). *Proceedings of the International Symposium on Fingerprint Detection and Identification*, June 26–30, 1995, Ne'urim, Israel. Israeli National Police, Jerusalem, Israel.

Palm Print Comparisons

17

Once examiners are trained to understand the common physical features of the palmar surface of the hand, they soon discover that the palm is not just a large surface area of friction ridge information. Actually, it is a large number of small friction ridge areas joined together.

Ron Smith[1]

Key Terms

- Creases
- Interdigital
- Thenar
- Hypothenar
- Distal transverse crease
- Proximal transverse crease
- Radial longitudinal crease
- Finger joints
- Carpal delta
- Vestige

Learning Objectives

- Define the key terms.
- Name the three major areas of the palm.
- Name the three major creases of the palm.
- Describe the ridge flow in the palm and finger joints.
- Describe the minor creases found in each area of the palm.
- Understand how to orient a latent palm print, and determine where to look in the palm exemplars.

17.1 Palm Print Comparisons

The act of comparing latent palm prints to exemplar palm prints is no different from comparing fingerprints. A latent print examiner places the latent print beside the exemplar palm print, either on the computer screen or under a magnifier. The examiner employs ACE-V methodology to analyze, compare, and evaluate the palm print. If an identification conclusion—or possibly an exclusionary or inconclusive result—is affected, a second examiner verifies the conclusion.

Fingerprints and palm prints both contain friction ridge detail. Fingerprints and palm prints both contain the same types of minutiae: ending ridges, bifurcations, and dots. Both may contain creases, scars, and other identifying marks. Both can be found at a crime scene or on an item of evidence. Both can be used for identification or exclusionary purposes. However, many fingerprint examiners struggle with palm print identification. The reason is because it is often difficult to orient a latent palm print. Which way is "up"? Which part of the palm does the latent represent? Is this ridge detail from the left or right hand? Is it part of a palm, or is it part of a finger?

Compare the surface area of your fingertips to the surface area of your palm. How many fingerprints can fit in one palm print? 15? 20? A latent palm print may be as small as a delta or as large as an entire palm. Smaller sections are more difficult to orient, but are less daunting if you know a few tips and tricks.

This chapter addresses only some of the common features of the average palm print. There are several features that are not addressed, as the topic of palm print orientation and identification could fill an entire text.

17.2 Anatomical Areas and Major Creases of the Palm

Palm prints, like fingerprints, can be identified to a common source. It can be difficult to know where to start when confronted with a partial latent palm print. There are many patterns to look for that are common to most palms in the general population, which can narrow down the origin and orientation of the palm fragment. For example, there are four deltas in the palmar area just below the fingers. These deltas each have a distinct position, shape, and associated ridge flow. The patterns and major features discussed in the following are common in both hands and throughout most of the population of palms in the world.

A study of palm prints begins with the general anatomical regions of the palm. The palm and finger joints are unique areas of ridge flow, separated by *creases*. There are three main areas of the palm: the interdigital, the hypothenar, and the thenar. The *interdigital* area is the portion of the palm directly below the index, middle, ring, and little fingers (Figure 17.1). The *thenar* area is the portion of the palm at the base of the thumb (Figure 17.2). The *hypothenar*, also known as the "writer's palm," is the portion of the palm below the interdigital area and across from the thenar area (Figure 17.3).

Each anatomical area is associated with one of three major creases in the palm: the distal transverse crease, the proximal transverse crease, and the radial longitudinal crease (Figure 17.4). Creases are white because they are furrowed areas of skin that do not come into close contact with a substrate and are therefore not developed by powders, ink, or chemicals. Some creases are wide, but others are thin and appear as white scratches on the surface.

The major creases of the palm are recorded as curved or jagged white lines in inked or powdered palm exemplars. There are many minor creases throughout the palm that are recorded as minute straight, jagged, or curved white lines (Figure 17.5). The creases of the hand conform to the flexibility of the hand. The hand bends and flexes along these creases, just as the creases between the finger joints flex as the fingers are bent.

The *distal transverse crease* separates the interdigital area from the hypothenar. The word distal refers to anatomical parts of the body located away from the center of the body. This crease starts at the edge of the palm and ends in the interdigital between the index and middle fingers. At the edge of the hand, the crease is wider and

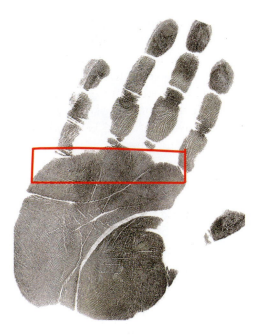

Figure 17.1 The area bounded by the red rectangle is the interdigital area of the palm.

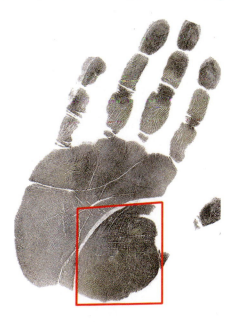

Figure 17.2 The area bounded by the red rectangle is the thenar area of the palm.

displays a "crow's-feet" pattern (Figure 17.6).[1] The crease narrows and branches where it ends in the interdigital area.

The *proximal transverse crease* separates the interdigital area from the thenar. It runs roughly parallel to the distal transverse crease. Proximal refers to anatomical parts of the body located closer to the center of the body. Therefore, the distal transverse crease is closer to the fingers than the proximal transverse crease. This crease starts at the edge of the palm between the thumb and index finger. It ends somewhere in the hypothenar.

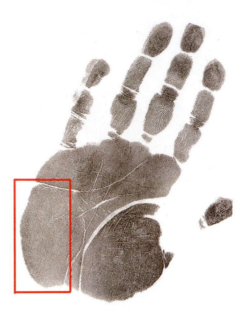

Figure 17.3 The area bounded by the red rectangle is the hypothenar area of the palm.

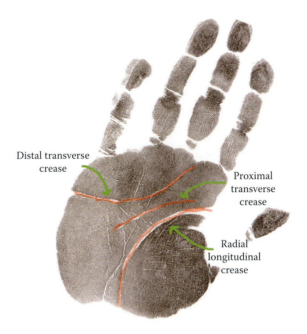

Figure 17.4 The three creases of the palm are the distal transverse crease, the proximal transverse crease, and the radial longitudinal crease.

The *radial longitudinal crease*, colloquially referred to as the "lifeline," curves along the border of the thenar area of the palm. This crease allows the opposable thumb to flex and bend across the palm. The crease begins near or at the beginning of the proximal transverse crease and curves around the thenar to the base of the hand. The length of each crease varies between individuals, just as ridge flow or patterns vary.

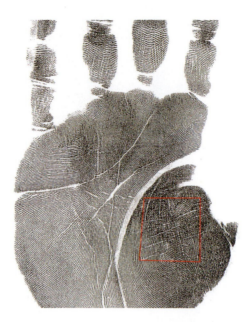

Figure 17.5 The minor creases of the palm are located throughout the hand and finger joints. The area bounded by the red rectangle shows an abundance of minor creases in the thenar area.

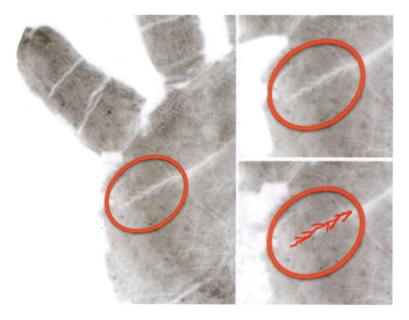

Figure 17.6 When the distal transverse crease exits the palm between the hypothenar and interdigital areas, it often displays a "crow's-feet" pattern feathering out toward the edge of the palm.

The fingers above the interdigital area of the palm are separated into sections called *finger joints*. The thumb is made up of two joints, while the fingers are made up of three joints each. Fingerprints are prints from the first joint of the fingers. The second and third joints do not display patterns such as arches, loops, and whorls. However, they all have similar ridge flow.

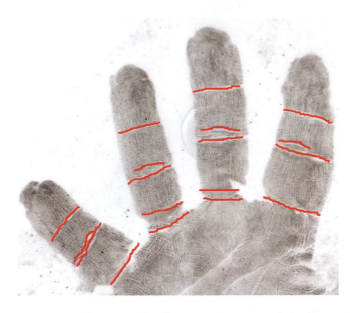

Figure 17.7 There are creases between the finger joint creases of the finger joints. One crease is found between the first and second joints, two creases between the second and third joints, one crease between the third joint and the interdigital of the index and little fingers, and two creases between the third joint and interdigital of the index and little fingers.

The creases between the joints are similar between fingers. There is generally one crease between the first and second joints of the fingers. Two creases separate the second and third joints. The index and little fingers have one crease between the third joint and the interdigital area of the palm. The middle and ring fingers are separated from the interdigital area by two creases (Figure 17.7). While most people have these major anatomical regions in common, the interdigital, hypothenar, and thenar positions, creases and minutiae are unique to each individual.

17.3   Interdigital Area

Fingerprints have a pattern type: a specific ridge flow that is dependent on the proliferation of ridges across the surface of the regressing volar pad. The center of the friction ridge area becomes the core. Wherever the ridge flow diverges, a delta is formed. There are a finite number of fingerprint patterns (arch, loop, and whorl) that can develop on the surface of the fingertip. Similarly, the ridge flow on the palmar surface of the hand develops as the volar pads on the palms recede. While it is possible to observe patterns such as loops or whorls in the hypothenar area of the palm, most of the ridge flow within the palm is common to a majority of the population (Figure 17.8).

The interdigital area has a significant amount of unique ridge detail and patterns in a small area. There are deltas and loops in configurations that may help orient a latent fingerprint. Deltas are located below the index, middle, ring, and little fingers (Figure 17.9). The delta beneath the index finger is more or less an equilateral delta. The three angles of the delta are roughly 120° each. The deltas directly under the middle and ring fingers have two obtuse angles and one acute angle forming a "Y" shape. The acute angle points upward

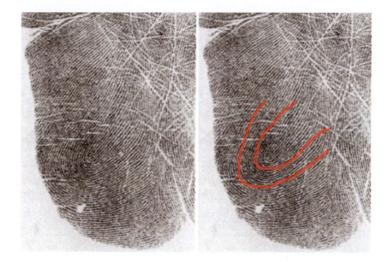

Figure 17.8 A loop pattern in the hypothenar area. (Adapted from Smith, R., Advanced palm print comparison techniques, in *Workshop Presented by Ron Smith and Associates, Inc.*, Sponsored by the International Association for Identification and the California Department of Justice Automated Latent Print Section, Rancho Cordova, CA, 2006.)

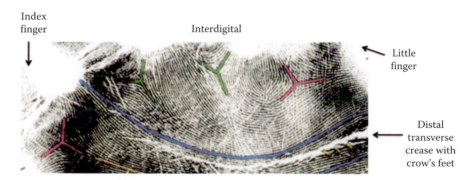

Figure 17.9 The deltas of the interdigital area of the palm (right hand) are indicated in green and purple. The delta under the index finger is equilateral and is located directly beneath the finger. The delta under the little finger, shifted slightly toward the ring finger, forms an acute angle facing the delta of the ring finger. The deltas beneath the middle and ring finger form acute angles facing upward, toward the third joints of the fingers. The ridge flow in the interdigital area is denoted in blue.

toward the third joints of the fingers. The delta under the little finger is not directly below the finger, but is instead shifted toward the ring finger. The shape is similar to the deltas below the middle and ring fingers, but unlike those deltas, the acute angle faces the delta below the ring finger.

The ridge flow in the interdigital stems from the flow of ridges from the deltas. The ridges originating from the delta under the little finger flow in a loop from that delta to the delta under the ring finger. The ridges originating from the delta under the middle finger flow along the top of the distal transverse crease in a wave pattern and out the side of the hand (on the hypothenar side). The ridges originating from the delta under the index finger flow diagonally across the entire width of the palm. These ridges pass between the distal transverse crease and the proximal transverse crease. The interdigital area is the most variable segment of the palm, with its complex concentration of deltas, looping patterns, and ridge flow. The large amount of detail also makes the interdigital area the easiest area to orient.

17.4   Hypothenar Area

The hypothenar is a fairly uniform area of ridge flow. Because of this, and because it is a large area of the palm, it can be difficult to orient these latents. The ridges of the hypothenar flow at a slight downward angle out of the side of the palm. If the ridges were canals, any water poured into the canals would flow down and out the side of the hand. The ridges closest to the center of the palm funnel inward. The funnel narrows around the proximal transverse crease. It widens until the ridges flow out the side of the hand. The ridge flow toward the base of the palm flattens out similar to a slide at a playground. Though the ridge flow is consistent, a loop or whorl may be observed. The loops and whorls are distinguishable from finger patterns due to their large size.

At the base of the palm, near the center, is the *carpal delta*. The carpal delta is the area where the ridge flow from the hypothenar meets the ridge flow of the thenar. The position of the carpal delta differs between individuals and may be either at the base of the hand near the wrist or higher in the palm. However, it will always be positioned near the center of the palm in the junction between the hypothenar and thenar. Just below the carpal delta is the wrist, which is extensively creased but has no ridge detail (Figure 17.10).

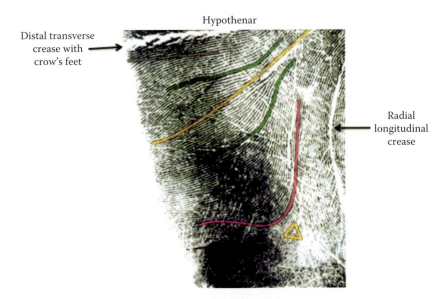

Figure 17.10 The hypothenar area of the palm (left hand). The yellow line denotes the ridge flow from the interdigital delta under the index finger along the proximal transverse crease through the hypothenar. The green curves represent the ridge flow funneling around the proximal transverse crease. The purple curve demonstrates the ridge flow as it flattens out toward the bottom of the hypothenar. The yellow triangle denotes the carpal delta.

Minor creases are visible throughout the palm, but there are creases specific to the hypothenar. Many of the minor creases of the hypothenar are located along the edge of the palm commonly known as the "writer's palm." These creases are visible as thin white lines that cut across the flow of ridges in that region.

17.5   Thenar Area

Ridge flow in the thenar is similarly straightforward. This area is bordered on one side by the radial longitudinal crease and on the other by the base of the thumb. The ridges generally flow in a half-moon pattern in concentric curves around the thumb. The curves are not uniform, however. As they approach the thumb, the half moon creases become flatter and longer at the top and more curved toward the bottom. While the ridges of the hypothenar flow out the side of the hand, the ridges of the thenar flow out the bottom of the hand (Figure 17.11). It is possible to see a pattern called a *vestige* in the thenar. This unusual pattern looks like two narrow, flattened loops that meet. Between the flattened heads of the ridges are ridges perpendicular to the flow of ridges in the thenar (Figure 17.12).

Minor creases in the thenar can help orient latent prints where the ridge flow is unclear. The creases often appear as thin white lines arranged in a basket weave pattern, or appear as deeper, horizontal *scratches* (Figure 17.13). Because the webbing between the thumb and index finger is thinner than the muscular base of the thumb, it does not often come into contact with the surface. A latent palm print may display a large "starburst" crease pattern in that area, which can assist with latent print orientation (Figure 17.14). The edge creases of the thenar are parallel with the flow of the ridges, unlike those in the hypothenar.

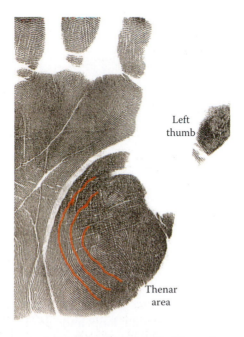

Left
thumb

Thenar
area

Figure 17.11 The thenar area of the palm (left hand). The red curves denote the half-moon-shaped ridge flow of the thenar.

Figure 17.12 A vestige in the thenar area of the palm (right hand). (Adapted from Smith, R., Advanced palm print comparison techniques, in *Workshop Presented by Ron Smith and Associates, Inc.*, Sponsored by the International Association for Identification and the California Department of Justice Automated Latent Print Section, Rancho Cordova, CA, 2006.)

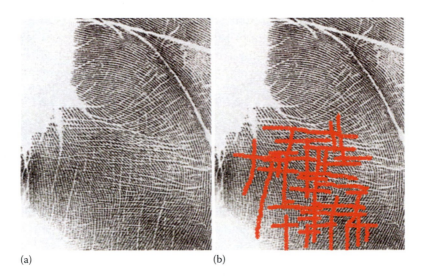

(a)   (b)

Figure 17.13 The thenar (a) often contains minor creases arranged in a basket weave pattern (b, in red). (Adapted from Smith, R., Advanced palm print comparison techniques, in *Workshop Presented by Ron Smith and Associates, Inc.*, Sponsored by the International Association for Identification and the California Department of Justice Automated Latent Print Section, Rancho Cordova, CA, 2006.)

17.6 Finger Joints

The second and third joints do not have arch, loop, and whorl patterns like the first joints. The finger joints have many thin vertical creases, and it can be difficult to see the pattern of ridge flow. The ridges of the inner finger joints—the ring and middle fingers—are generally

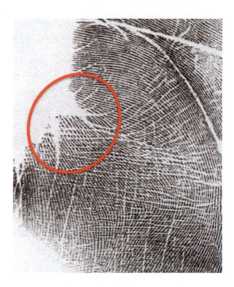

Figure 17.14 The starburst pattern of creases in the thenar. (Adapted from Smith, R., Advanced palm print comparison techniques, in *Workshop Presented by Ron Smith and Associates, Inc.*, Sponsored by the International Association for Identification and the California Department of Justice Automated Latent Print Section, Rancho Cordova, CA, 2006.)

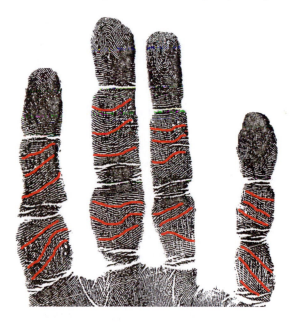

Figure 17.15 General ridge flow in the second and third finger joints. (Adapted from Smith, R., Advanced palm print comparison techniques, in *Workshop Presented by Ron Smith and Associates, Inc.*, Sponsored by the International Association for Identification and the California Department of Justice Automated Latent Print Section, Rancho Cordova, CA, 2006.)

horizontal, wavy lines. The outer finger joints—the joints of the little and index fingers— have ridges that slant downward, away from the inner fingers (Figure 17.15). The extensive creases of the joints look like vertical scratches in the pattern. These creases are thin and dense. Regardless of the ridge flow and crease pattern in the latent palm print, an identification can only be affected if the minutiae agree in type and position.

17.7   Chapter Summary

The orientation of latent palm prints can make palm print comparisons challenging. Knowledge of the anatomical parts of the palm makes these comparisons less problematic. The three parts of the hand are the interdigital, hypothenar, and thenar. The three major creases are the distal transverse crease, the proximal transverse crease, and the radial longitudinal crease.

The interdigital area of the hand is the region above the distal transverse crease and below the fingers. There are four deltas in the interdigital area, each associated with one of the four fingers. The ridge flow of this area stems from the deltas. The hypothenar area is characterized by uniform ridge flow that originates from a funnel in the center of the hand and spreads out to exit the side of the hand known as the writer's palm. The thenar area is characterized by half-moon-shaped ridge flow that curves around the thumb. Basket weave patterned creases crisscross the surface of the thenar. The inner finger joints have horizontal, wavy creases. The outer finger joints—the joints of the little and index fingers—have ridges that slant downward, away from the inner fingers.

Review Questions

1. What methodology is used to compare latent palm prints with exemplar palm prints?
2. What is the area of the palm at the base of the thumb called?
3. What is the area of the palm directly beneath the fingers called?
4. Describe the position and shape of the interdigital deltas and the ridge flow from those deltas.
5. What is the name of the crease that separates the thenar from the hypothenar area?
6. True or false. The second and third joints of the index and little finger have horizontal, wavy ridge flow.
7. Describe the flow of ridges in the hypothenar region of the palm.
8. Where is the basket weave pattern of creases observed?
9. Where are you likely to see patterns such as whorls or loops?
10. What is the name of the delta positioned near the wrist in the base of the palm?

Reference

1. Smith, R. 2006. Advanced palm print comparison techniques. *Workshop Presented by Ron Smith and Associates, Inc.* Sponsored by the International Association for Identification and the California Department of Justice Automated Latent Print Section, Rancho Cordova, CA.

Courtroom Testimony

18

The right to search for truth implies also a duty; one must not conceal any part of what one has recognized to be true.

Albert Einstein

Key Terms

- Mock court
- Expert witness
- Federal Rule of Evidence 702 (FRE 702)
- Prosecution
- Defense
- Voir dire
- Qualifying questions
- Curriculum vitae (CV)
- Perjury
- Pretrial conference
- Direct examination
- Exhibits
- Cross-examination
- Subpoena
- Demeanor
- Precedent
- Case law
- Frye standard
- Rule of general acceptance
- Daubert standard
- Daubert hearing

Learning Objectives

- Define the key terms.
- Understand the basic structure of the judicial system.
- Understand the role of the expert witness in the criminal justice system.
- Give examples of how to be an effective teacher on the witness stand.
- Explain the three main phases of expert testimony and how the fingerprint analyst prepares for each phase.

- Describe the importance of a pretrial conference.
- Describe the demeanor and dress of the successful expert witness.
- Describe the Daubert trilogy and explain how it applies to fingerprint testimony.

18.1   Expert Witness

Regardless of the type of fingerprint analysis conducted, all fingerprint examiners will, at some point in their careers, testify to an actions and conclusions in a court of law. As a forensic scientist, the fingerprint analyst must not only conduct scientific analyses but also communicate their results in a court of law. The courtroom is the final stop for any criminal investigation. Bringing a suspect to justice, or exonerating the innocent, is the goal of forensic analysis.

Most criminal cases never make it to court. The accused either takes a plea deal (admits guilt and accedes to a predetermined punishment) or is never brought to trial. Regardless of how often a fingerprint analyst testifies, it is critical that all forensic scientists receive training to prepare for their testimony. The fingerprint analyst should practice testifying by participating in *mock court* sessions. Mock testimony gives fingerprint analysts practice so they can plan out their testimony, know what to expect, and be prepared.

A forensic scientist who testifies in court may be considered an *expert witness* if accepted as an expert by a judge in a court of law. An expert witness is anyone who knows more about a particular topic than the average person. This is defined by the Federal Rules of Evidence (FRE), which govern how evidence is presented in a court of law. *Federal Rule of Evidence 702 (FRE 702)*, adopted in 1975, applies to scientific and technical experts, as follows:

> *If scientific, technical, or other specialized knowledge will assist the (judge and/or jury) to understand the evidence or to determine a fact in issue, a witness qualified as an expert by knowledge, skill, experience, training or education, may testify thereto in the form of an opinion or otherwise, if (1) the testimony is based upon sufficient facts or data, (2) the testimony is the product of reliable principles and methods, and (3) the witness has applied the principles and methods reliably to the facts of the case.[1]*

In other words, an expert in a particular field may testify to their opinion if the opinion is based on commonly accepted facts or data. Science is based on data that are rigorously tested and published. Forensic science is a branch of science and is therefore subject to rigorous testing, peer review, and publication.

The difference between a lay witness and an expert witness is an expert witness can testify to their opinion. A lay witness must only testify to what was seen, experienced, or heard. He may not give an opinion or testify to what someone else said or witnessed. The following is an example of the difference between lay witness testimony and expert witness testimony. In the following example, the expert witness is a police officer:

Lay witness: *It looked like the car was speeding.*
Police officer: *According to the radar gun, the car was traveling 85 miles/h in a 65 miles/h zone.*

The following is an example of lay witness testimony versus the testimony of a trace evidence examiner testifying to characteristics of hair:

Lay witness: *She had long brown hair.*

Trace evidence examiner: *The hair analyzed is human in origin, dark brown, and artificially treated. It shows characteristics of Asian descent. It is 36 cm long.*

18.2 Judicial System

The United States was founded on the belief that its citizenry deserve the right to live freely. The *Sixth Amendment* to the Constitution of the United States (Figure 18.1) guarantees every US citizen accused of a crime the following rights:

- The right to a public trial
- The right to a speedy trial
- The right to be judged by a jury of your peers
- The right to know what you are accused of
- The right to confront witnesses against you (including expert witnesses)
- The right to *subpoena* witnesses (compel witnesses to testify or face legal ramifications)
- The right to an attorney appointed by the court

These rights assure that anyone accused of a crime is tried fairly and equitably.

Figure 18.1 The Bill of Rights includes the first 10 amendments to the U.S. Constitution.

The three branches of government in the United States are the executive branch (president and cabinet), judicial branch (courts), and legislative branch (Senate and House of Representatives). The judicial system in the United States is both sophisticated and complicated. It can be daunting to those who may have never stepped foot inside a courtroom. The language used in the courtroom is specialized and unique to the law profession.

There are three main levels of federal courts for criminal matters: district courts, circuit courts, and the Supreme Court. There are 94 district courts in the United States, 12 circuit courts, and 1 Supreme Court.[2] District courts are trial courts, and they hear 98% of cases.[2] The circuit court is the court of appeals (appellate court). The Supreme Court is the highest court in the country and hears only about 200 cases per year. It is known as "the court of last resort" and is preceded over by nine Supreme Court justices nominated by the president and confirmed by the Senate. Most criminals are tried in state courts. Forensic scientists do not just testify in criminal cases. They may also testify in civil cases, which are disputes between two or more parties.

The main players in the courtroom are the prosecutor, defendant, judge, and jury. The justice system is an adversarial system, meaning there are two sides presenting their case to the trier of fact (judge or jury). One side is called the *prosecution* and is the side representing the state, federal government, or complainant. The other side is the *defense*. The defendant is the individual accused or the focus of a civil or criminal action. Each side presents its case to the jury by questioning witnesses and presenting evidence. The job of the attorney is to present a narrative, or theory, of the case. A narrative is, in a sense, a story about what may have happened. Assistant or deputy district attorneys are prosecutors who represent the government (county, state, or federal). Public defenders are attorneys who are appointed to the defense if the defendant either cannot afford his own attorney or would prefer not to hire a private attorney.

The judge is the referee in a courtroom (Figure 18.2). The judge makes sure both sides follow the rules and settles disputes. Judges have many other functions, but in a criminal trial, the expert witness should be aware of the judge's role as a moderator.

Figure 18.2 A judge directing proceedings in a courtroom.

Attorneys may object to portions of your testimony or to the question asked by the opposing side. When this happens, the expert must stop talking and wait for the judge to rule on the objection. He may sustain the objection, verifying that the objection has merit. Or he may overrule the objection, declaring it invalid. Either way, proceedings will continue after the judge's ruling. The judge decides questions of the law and keeps order in the courtroom.

The jury is a panel of 6–12 laypersons called to jury duty. Each potential juror is asked a series of questions during the process of *voir dire*. The purpose of voir dire is to determine which individuals are best suited to serve on the jury for the case at hand. The individuals chosen to serve on the jury have the obligation to view all the evidence presented and listen to both the attorneys' narratives of the case and the witnesses brought forth. Following the trial, the jury is responsible for determining guilt or innocence.

18.3   Testimony Is Teaching

Juries are composed of 6–12 people from a variety of backgrounds and occupations. A jury may consist of a grandmother, a nuclear physicist, a college student, a stay-at-home mom, a doctor. Because the average jury is made up of a diversity of individuals of various socio-economic and educational backgrounds, it is challenging to explain scientific analyses. The most successful fingerprint expert can successfully explain the science behind the analysis to the average person.

We have all had teachers who have made an impact in our lives. What qualities did those teachers possess? What makes them great teachers? A group of college students came up with the following list of qualities of an effective teacher:

- Uses visual aids
- Defines terms in plain language
- Uses descriptive wording
- Is relatable
- Presents information in a linear, methodical fashion
- Uses anecdotes and examples
- Uses conversational language versus jargon and scientific terms
- Does not talk down to their audience
- Relates personal stories
- Repeats information in different ways

If you can teach effectively, you will be a successful expert witness and a successful forensic scientist. Similarly, those who have experience with public speaking make great expert witnesses because they display the following qualities of an effective public speaker:

- Speak with appropriate volume to be heard and understood
- Make eye contact with members of the audience
- Act naturally
- Do not fidget or display nervous gestures
- Exude confidence and competence
- Are passionate about the topic they are presenting

How might you incorporate these qualities into courtroom testimony? Most people are not born with these qualities. It takes practice to become an effective teacher and public speaker. The fingerprint analyst should plan out courtroom testimony ahead of time and think of ways to incorporate the qualities listed earlier. If while testifying the jury looks disinterested, employ some of the tactics given earlier to maintain their interest. Encourage them to look at their own fingerprints. Show the jury visual aids. Change your tone to express your passion and interest in the topic.

It can be challenging to explain scientific concepts to the layperson. Here is an example of how a fingerprint analyst may describe friction ridge development to a jury:

Question: How is it possible to compare two fingerprints and determine whether they come from the same source?

Answer: There are two characteristics of fingerprints that enable us to compare them and determine whether they come from the same source. First, your fingerprints are unique. They develop before birth by a variety of genetic and environmental factors. We call this prenatal development: "pre" meaning before and "natal" meaning birth. We know this because of scientific research and because nature is inherently random. For example, no two zebras have the same pattern of stripes. No two snowflakes are alike. Second, your fingerprints are permanent. When prenatal fingerprint development is complete, the fingerprint structure is set for life. It will not change, though a scar or injury might change the appearance of a small portion of the fingerprint. Because every fingerprint is unique and permanent, we can compare two fingerprints and determine whether they come from the same source.

The previous example uses the following teaching techniques: defines terms ("prenatal"), is relatable ("your fingerprints are unique"), presents information in a methodical fashion ("First, your fingerprints are unique…." "Second, your fingerprints are permanent…."), uses anecdotes (zebra and snowflake examples), uses conversational language, and does not talk down to the jury.

The following is an example of fingerprint expert testimony from a fingerprint analyst describing a latent print and how to develop prints on paper using ninhydrin:

Question: Could you please describe what a latent fingerprint is and the process you used to visualize fingerprints on the document in question?

Answer: When you touch an object, sweat and other substances (such as lotion, grease, or cosmetics) that coat your friction ridges transfer the friction ridge pattern to the surface of the object. For example, when I touch this wood surface (expert touches the witness stand), the sweat and lotion coating my fingerprints are deposited onto the wood surface. This is similar to a rubber stamp, which deposits ink onto a piece of paper in the exact pattern of the stamp. Unlike a rubber stamp, our fingerprints are invisible. An invisible fingerprint is called a latent fingerprint. Latent is Latin for "hidden."

In order to compare latent fingerprints with known, or visible, fingerprints, we have to make those invisible fingerprints visible. Fingerprint powders and brushes are used at crime scenes, as you may have seen on the television or in movies. However, fingerprint analysts also use chemicals to make fingerprints visible. Sweat is made up of water and excretory products from the human body. It is composed of 98%–99% water and 1% other components such as salts, fats, proteins, and amino acids. Amino acids are the building blocks of proteins. Because the document is paper, it is porous, meaning it absorbs water. When you touch a piece of paper, your fingerprint is absorbed by the surface and stays there. We can use a chemical called ninhydrin to develop the fingerprints. Ninhydrin is a chemical that turns purple when it comes into contact with amino acids. In this case, when I treated the evidentiary documents with ninhydrin, the chemical reacted with the fingerprints in the paper and turned the latent fingerprints purple, as you can see in the photographs (shows photographs of evidence before and after processing).

This testimony reflects the aforementioned teaching tools, along with visual aids: both the photographs and the physical demonstration of touching the witness stand in order to demonstrate latent print deposition. It also uses minimal jargon.

18.4 Qualifying Questions

There are three main phases of expert witness testimony: voir dire, direct examination, and cross-examination. During every phase of testimony, the expert witness makes eye contact with the attorney asking the question and directs the answer to the jury. A successful expert witness makes eye contact with every juror during testimony.

The first phase of testimony is *voir dire*, during which time the attorney asks the expert *qualifying questions*. This is similar to the voir dire process that occurs during jury selection when the potential jurors are asked questions to determine their eligibility to be jurors. During the voir dire process for an expert witness, the attorney asks questions to determine whether the fingerprint examiner is qualified as an expert in a court of law. Qualifying questions for a fingerprint expert may include questions about the expert's employment, level of experience, education, training, professional knowledge of fingerprint history and science, and professional affiliations. All of this information, other than fingerprint history and scientific concepts, should be included in your *curriculum vitae* (CV), your professional resume.

Forensic scientists' education is not limited to their college majors, degrees received, and courses taken. Education is a lifelong process. A professional fingerprint analyst continually attends professional training courses and conferences to learn new techniques and keep up with current research. Science is constantly changing and advancing, and fingerprint science is no different. A successful fingerprint analyst is amenable to change, growth, and professional development.

During qualifying questioning, you will be asked about your work experience, the positions and titles you have held, your employer, and how long you have worked in each position. You may be asked about how many crime scenes you have examined, how many fingerprint comparisons you have performed, how many times you have testified in a court of law, how many presentations you have given, or how many articles you have published. You may be asked whether you are a member of a professional organization such as the International Association for Identification (Figure 18.3), have received any awards or honors for your work, or are certified in your field of expertise.

As a recent college graduate or new hire at a police department, you may not have much experience in these areas. Regardless of your experience, you are qualified to testify as an expert witness because of your knowledge, skills, and abilities above and beyond those of the layperson. It is unethical, and unlawful, to embellish your accomplishments or CV. If you exaggerate or blatantly lie about your level of experience or background on

Figure 18.3 The logo of the International Association for Identification. (Reprinted with permission from the International Association for Identification. http://www.theiai.org. Accessed June 5, 2014.)

the witness stand, it is considered *perjury*. Perjury is the act of falsifying information while under oath and is a criminal act.

During this phase of testimony, you will also explain the science behind your analyses. If you compared a latent fingerprint to a known fingerprint, you will explain to the jury what a latent fingerprint is. You will also explain what known fingerprints are. Finally, you will explain how you compare fingerprints to determine if they come from the same source. You should only explain the basic, relevant information required for the jurors to understand what you specifically did for the case at hand and why.

The best way to prepare for the voir dire phase is to prepare your own qualifying questions for the attorney. You are the expert. You know best which questions are relevant and which questions highlight your expertise to the judge and jury. If you know what will be asked, you can prepare your answers prior to testifying. This not only gives you the opportunity to practice but also gives you the confidence to know there will be few, if any, surprises during your testimony. The following is a sample list of qualifying questions (and answers) for a fingerprint expert:

1. Please state and spell your name.
   My name is John Smith. J-O-H-N S-M-I-T-H
2. What is your official job title?
   I am a fingerprint examiner.
3. By whom are you currently employed?
   I am currently employed by the Anywhere Police Department.
4. What are your duties as a fingerprint examiner?
   As a fingerprint examiner, I examine fingerprints from items of evidence associated with various crimes. I perform laboratory examinations using fingerprint powders and chemicals to develop fingerprints on evidentiary items. I then determine if the fingerprints are sufficient in quality to compare with known, or exemplar, finger-

prints. I compare those fingerprints and form an opinion based on my conclusions and write a final report to explain my analyses and conclusions.

5. How long have you been employed as a fingerprint analyst?
I have been employed as a fingerprint analyst for approximately 2 years.

6. How many examinations have you done during your career?
I have examined over a hundred cases, resulting in thousands of fingerprint comparisons.

7. What is your educational background?
I have a Bachelor of Science degree in biology and a Master of Science degree in forensic science.

8. Have you received any other training in fingerprint analysis?
Yes. I have attended two professional training conferences. I also attended a 40 h course entitled "Fingerprint Comparisons" and a 24 h course entitled "Comparing Palm Prints."

9. Do you belong to any professional organizations?
Yes. I belong to the International Association for Identification.

10. Have you published any articles or books on the subject?
Yes. I published a Master's thesis entitled "Novel approaches to fingerprint development on unfinished wood surfaces" in 2011.

11. Have you testified as an expert in a court of law?
Yes.

12. How many times?
Three times.

13. What is a latent fingerprint?
If you look closely at your fingers, you notice there are patterns made up of ridges, which we call friction ridges. Along each friction ridge are pores. These pores excrete sweat, which coats the friction ridges. When you touch a surface, the pattern of your fingerprint may be transferred to that surface. This is similar to a rubber stamp coated in ink, which deposits its pattern onto a surface. Unlike the ink on a rubber stamp, the pattern formed by the transfer of sweat to a surface is invisible. Latent fingerprints are fingerprints that cannot be seen by the human eye. They require some type of development technique, such as fingerprint powder or chemicals, to make them visible. Latent fingerprints are from an unknown source and must therefore be compared with known fingerprints.

14. What are known fingerprints?
Known fingerprints, or exemplars, are fingerprint records from a known source. They are intentional reproductions. For example, when someone is arrested, their fingerprints are taken to verify their identity. A thin layer of ink is applied to the friction ridges and then rolled onto a special card called a tenprint card. The individual's name and identifying information are on that card. A computerized record is often acquired.

15. How do you go about comparing latent fingerprints to known fingerprints?
The friction ridges on your hands and feet are not continuous. Some ridges diverge into two ridges, similar to a fork in a road. These are called bifurcations. Some ridges abruptly stop. These are called ending ridges. There are also very short ridges; some so short they appear to be dots. The places where the ridges diverge or abruptly stop

are called minutiae, or points. Each fingerprint has an assortment of these minutiae throughout the pattern. Each person has a unique assortment of minutiae throughout his or her fingerprint. Fingerprint analysts compare the placement and type of minutiae in the latent fingerprint with the placement and type of minutiae in the known fingerprint. If the minutiae are present in both prints in the same configuration, we can determine as a result of our training and experience that those two fingerprints likely come from the same source.

16. "What are the basic factors in the use of fingerprints as a means of identification? (Alternative: Why are fingerprints used as a means of identification?)"[3]
    Fingerprint identification is based on two premises: one, that fingerprints are unique and two, that fingerprints are permanent. Your fingerprints develop before birth. Fingerprint development is a randomized, natural process that is dependent on both genetic and environmental factors. This makes them unique. No two people have the same fingerprints. Even identical twins have different fingerprints.

    Your fingerprints are also permanent, which means they will not change over time. The fingerprints you are born with are the fingerprints you have as an adult. Fingerprints are formed in a deep layer of skin called the basal layer, which forms the blueprint for the arrangement of friction ridges and minutiae you see on the surface of the skin. That blueprint is changed only if the basal layer is damaged. For example, if you cut your finger deep enough to penetrate the basal layer, it will form a scar. Because fingerprints are unique and permanent, we can use them to identify the source of a latent fingerprint by comparing it with a known fingerprint.

At this point in the voir dire process, after your qualifications and knowledge of the subject matter have been evaluated, the judge will accept or reject the fingerprint examiner as an expert in the field of fingerprint analysis.

The qualifying questions should be presented to the attorney during a *pretrial conference*. A pretrial conference is a meeting with the attorney during which you explain your qualifications, analyses, results, conclusions, and any other information relevant to the case. It accords you the ability to explain your results and why they are relevant to the case at hand. You can also address any problems with the analysis, challenges, or possible cross-examination issues.

The attorney is an expert in the law, not in fingerprint analysis. It is therefore important to educate the attorney just as you would the jury. Do not assume the attorney speaks your language: the language of science. Attorneys juggle multiple cases at one time and may not initially want to schedule a meeting. Insist on a pretrial conference. This will ensure there are no surprises or confusion at trial. Both you and the attorney will be prepared.

18.5   Direct Examination

The next phase of expert witness testimony is the *direct examination* of the expert witness. During direct examination, the attorney who subpoenaed the expert will ask questions. These questions are related specifically to the examiner's actions and conclusions. During the pretrial conference, you will discuss your analyses and conclusions and help the attorney formulate a line of questioning for the direct examination phase of your testimony. The following are examples of questions asked during the direct examination phase as a continuation of the earlier examples of questions asked during voir dire:

17. Do you recognize exhibit #1?
    Yes.
18. Did you examine exhibit #1 for fingerprints?
    Yes.
19. How did you analyze exhibit #1?
    I developed one latent fingerprint using a chemical called ninhydrin. This chemical reacts with the amino acids in sweat and turns fingerprints purple. After I processed the paper, I photographed the resulting latent fingerprint, which is labeled L001 in the photograph.
20. Is this the photograph to which you are referring?
    Yes.
21. Did you perform any fingerprint comparisons in this case?
    Yes.
22. Which fingerprints did you compare?
    I compared the unknown latent fingerprint, L001, with the known fingerprints of the suspect, Jim Daniels.
23. How were these known fingerprints recorded?
    The known fingerprints were recorded on a tenprint card in ink.
24. And how did you perform your comparison?
    I compared the minutiae in the latent fingerprint with the minutiae in the known fingerprint using ACE-V methodology.
25. What is ACE-V methodology?
    ACE-V is the standardized, methodical process fingerprint examiners use to compare unknown latent prints with known prints. ACE-V stands for analysis, comparison, evaluation, and verification. During the analysis phase, I look at the overall pattern and quality of the fingerprint image and determine if it is suitable for comparison. During the comparison phase, I compare the minutiae of the latent fingerprint to the minutiae in the known fingerprint. During the evaluation phase, I make a determination of whether or not the fingerprints are from the same source. The verification phase is a peer review process by which another qualified fingerprint analyst repeats the analysis, comparison, and evaluation phases and comes to his own conclusion. This is the methodology I followed in this case. I brought a charted enlargement of the fingerprint comparison to court today as a demonstration.
26. Is this chart a true and accurate representation of the latent and known fingerprints you used for your comparison?
    Yes. This is an enlarged copy of the photograph of the latent print. And this is the known print of the right index finger of the suspect.
27. Can you please walk us through the comparison process?
    (Expert demonstrates the comparison process by pointing out corresponding minutiae between the latent and known fingerprints on the court chart.)
28. What was your conclusion in this case, regarding the fingerprint you developed on exhibit #1?
    Utilizing ACE-V methodology, I concluded that fingerprint L001 is consistent with the right index finger of the suspect, Jim Daniels.

When a question is asked, take a moment to think about the question. Take a deep breath. Formulate your answer. And answer only the question asked. (Note that questions 17–21 are strictly yes or no questions. The expert answered them correctly without needless elaboration.) It takes only a few seconds to pause, though it may seem longer when you are on the witness stand. When expert witnesses rush into answering questions, whether out of nervousness or habit, they may end up not answering the question at all, explaining beyond the scope of what was asked, forgetting a crucial detail, or confusing the jury. Taking a minute to pause and think about the answer makes the fingerprint examiner a better, and more effective, expert witness.

As the attorney asks questions, there may be a need to address legal matters. There may be objections to questions asked. The attorney may need to ask the court whether a particular item or document be admitted as evidence. Evidentiary items admitted as evidence in court are known as *exhibits*. Regardless of the interruption, you must immediately stop speaking and wait for the judge to indicate that you may continue. At that time, you can ask the attorney to repeat the question if necessary.

18.6   Cross Examination

When the attorney is finished with the direct examination, the opposing attorney has an opportunity to ask questions of the expert witness. This is the *cross-examination* phase of testimony. More often than not, the prosecuting attorney will conduct the direct examination and the defense attorney will conduct the cross-examination. Unlike voir dire and direct examination, you will not know what questions will be asked. You can anticipate certain questions because they logically follow up on the questions asked during direct examination.

Consider the following example. A car is burglarized outside an apartment. During the crime scene investigation, a fingerprint is developed on the exterior of the car's trunk. The latent fingerprint is identified to the suspect. What questions may arise that are relevant to the case? The defense attorney may ask, "Isn't it possible that my client, who lives in the adjacent apartment building, could have touched the car while walking by?" Yes, this scenario is possible. Or the attorney may ask, "Just because his fingerprint is on the car, does that mean he is responsible for burglarizing the car?" No, it does not necessarily mean he is responsible for burglarizing the car. As an unbiased scientist, you do not have a stake in whether the prosecutor "wins" or "loses." Your job is to present the facts and answer the questions truthfully and to the best of your ability.

The defense attorney's role is to ensure the accused gets a fair trial. This is a right guaranteed by the Sixth Amendment to the Constitution of the United States. The role of defense attorneys is to ensure the facts are accurately stated. They ensure every applicable forensic analysis was completed accurately and thoroughly. They may attempt to find inconsistencies in your testimony. They may try to discern whether you are biased or have committed ethical violations. If you have done your job as a scientist, you have nothing to fear from cross-examination. The defense attorney should be treated with the same respect the forensic scientist gives to the prosecuting attorney. Always be polite, make eye contact, and address the attorney as sir or ma'am.

The defense attorney is trained to use tactics to challenge the expert witness. The attorney may ask questions at a rapid pace. The simple solution is to pause after every question and answer truthfully, just as you would during direct examination. Another tactic the attorney may employ is asking multiple questions at once. This can be mitigated by politely asking the attorney to ask one question at a time. The attorney may use a loud voice, stand between the expert and the jury, or use other tactics to pull attention away from the expert.

The defense attorney may ask questions in the form of statements to further divert the jury's focus. "You were working several cases at that time, weren't you?" "And you investigated several burglaries." "And your cousin lives in the apartment building where the car was burglarized." Do not be intimidated. If the defense attorney becomes aggressive, the jury will sympathize with the expert witness. After all, they would not want to be sitting up there in the expert's place. When the cross-examination is complete, and if there are no more questions from either attorney, the expert witness will be dismissed and can leave the courtroom.

18.7 Preparing for Court

Prior to the trial, the expert witness receives a *subpoena*. A subpoena is an order to appear to testify as a witness on a particular date and time (Figure 18.4). Once the subpoena is received, alert the attorney to schedule a pretrial conference. Gather the documentation to review the details of the case. This includes photographs, diagrams, case notes, laboratory worksheets, final reports, and anything else relevant to the examiner's involvement with the case. Is the documentation complete? Has the case been reviewed? Is everything in order so you can reference it quickly? Is the CV up to date and complete? Has it been provided to the attorney?

When the documentation is in order, the examiner prepares for testimony. The examiner may choose to prepare a short slideshow or presentation to assist with jury education. Some fingerprint analysts prefer to draw as they teach. For example, one can draw a simple diagram of a bifurcation, dot, and ending ridge, fingerprint pattern types, or the layers of the skin. If fingerprint comparisons were done, a clear, enlarged court chart is desirable so the jury can follow along as you describe your process step by step, point by point (Figure 18.5).

It is natural to be nervous on the day of trial; however, there are things the examiner can do to minimize nervousness and maximize preparedness. Familiarizing themselves with the case, gathering the documentation, and preparing teaching aids will alleviate some of the tension. Another way to minimize nervousness is to visit the courtroom (Figure 18.6). Familiarization with the location of the courtroom, the layout, and the path to the witness stand is recommended. Is there a witness waiting room outside the courtroom? Do the doors swing outward or inward? Is the witness stand behind a podium (Figure 18.7)? Is there a microphone? The examiner may be able to attend a case in progress. If visual aids requiring audiovisual equipment will be used, where are the hookups and plugs? Where should the expert stand so as not to impede the jury's view? It may even be possible to test out the equipment ahead of time. Knowing the environment will take away many unknown factors that lead to nervousness.

The expert must dress professionally for court. For men, this means a suit and tie. For women, a pants suit or knee-length skirted suit is acceptable. Clean, polished, conservative shoes are best. For women, heels should be low and neutral in color. In his book *Dress for Success*, John Molloy explores the impact of appearance on the perceptions of others.[5] Molloy notes that jurors respond more positively to professionals dressed in a conservative

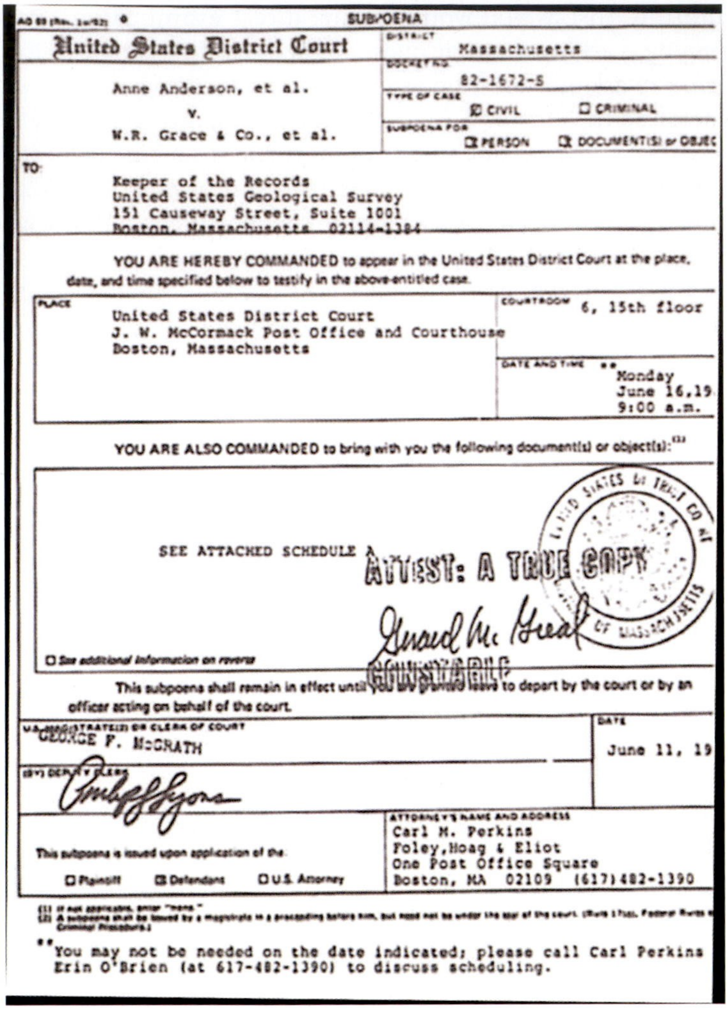

SUBPOENA

United States District Court

DISTRICT: Massachusetts

Anne Anderson, et al.
v.
W.R. Grace & Co., et al.

DOCKET NO.: 82-1672-S

TYPE OF CASE: ☒ CIVIL ☐ CRIMINAL

SUBPOENA FOR: ☒ PERSON ☒ DOCUMENT(S) or OBJEC

TO:
Keeper of the Records
United States Geological Survey
151 Causeway Street, Suite 1001
Boston, Massachusetts 02114-1384

YOU ARE HEREBY COMMANDED to appear in the United States District Court at the place, date, and time specified below to testify in the above-entitled case.

PLACE:
United States District Court
J. W. McCormack Post Office and Courthouse
Boston, Massachusetts

COURTROOM: 6, 15th floor

DATE AND TIME **: Monday June 16,19 9:00 a.m.

YOU ARE ALSO COMMANDED to bring with you the following document(s) or object(s):[1]

SEE ATTACHED SCHEDULE A

ATTEST: A TRUE COPY

CONSTABLE

☐ See additional information on reverse

This subpoena shall remain in effect until you are granted leave to depart by the court or by an officer acting on behalf of the court.

U.S. MAGISTRATE[2] OR CLERK OF COURT: GEORGE F. McGRATH

DATE: June 11, 19

(BY) DEPUTY CLERK

This subpoena is issued upon application of the:
☐ Plaintiff ☒ Defendant ☐ U.S. Attorney

ATTORNEY'S NAME AND ADDRESS:
Carl M. Perkins
Foley,Hoag & Eliot
One Post Office Square
Boston, MA 02109 (617)482-1390

**You may not be needed on the date indicated; please call Carl Perkins Erin O'Brien (at 617-482-1390) to discuss scheduling.

Figure 18.4 A copy of subpoena from a federal court case. (Reprinted from the Science Education Resource Center (SERC), an office of Carleton College, Northfield, MN, Retrieved December 10, 2013, from http://serc.carleton.edu/files/woburn/resources/subpoena_usgs.jpg.)

blue or gray business suit who carry a light briefcase. The expert should wear nothing to distract the jury such as a colorful tie, large jewelry, or heavy makeup. Jingling keys or coins also distract jurors.

Looking like an expert does not stop at appearance. It is also in the expert's *demeanor*. Demeanor refers to how one carries oneself: the way the expert stands, moves, and conducts himself or herself. It is the expert's behavior and manner. Even if the expert is nervous, they must stand up tall with their shoulders back and exude an air of self-confidence. Jurors do not respect or respond to experts who act nervous, slouch, and fidget. They also open themselves up to aggressive cross-examination. Articulate, confident experts will hold the jury's attention. Remember that public speaking is

10% what you say
20% how you say it
70% how you look

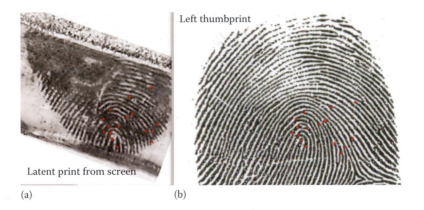

Left thumbprint

Latent print from screen

(a)   (b)

Figure 18.5 A court chart illustrates the comparison of a latent fingerprint (a) to a known fingerprint (b).

Figure 18.6 The layout of a typical courtroom.

Figure 18.7 Witness stand.

The following are criteria for the ideal expert witness, according to attorney and forensic science consultant Gil Sapir: "knowledge, reputation for honesty, objectivity, personal appearance, dignity, voice, modesty, even temperament, memory for facts without references, communication skills, integrity, trustworthy, and ability to teach and educate."[5]

In *Advances in Fingerprint Technology*, Robert Hazen and Clarence Phillips offer the following suggestions for becoming a successful expert witness:[6]

1. Conduct mock court sessions and obtain feedback.
2. Test answers to the basic qualifying questions on nonfingerprint persons and obtain feedback.
3. Dress the part.
4. Listen.
5. Think positively.
6. Remember at all times to be objective.
7. Watch the jury for nonverbal communication feedback.
8. Learn to effectively use silence.

18.8   The Day of Court

Be sure to get a good night's sleep and eat breakfast the day of trial. Bring all documentation. Arrive at the courtroom early. A confident demeanor should enter with the expert when they enter the courthouse. Allow some time to check in with the attorney and find the courtroom. The subpoena may contain instructions for where to go upon arrival. The expert may have to wait in a witness waiting room or hallway. Anyone encountered upon entering the courthouse may have some role in the proceedings. Be polite and professional when addressing people, but never discuss the case at hand with anyone.

The expert is called into the courtroom when it is his or her turn to testify. When the expert enters the courtroom, he or she walks confidently to the witness stand with head held up and shoulders back. After the court officer administers the oath, the expert sits. The officer asks if the expert swears to tell the truth. The proper response is, "I do." Take the oath with a clear voice that can be heard by the entire courtroom. When the expert has taken the oath, they are instructed to sit. Take a seat and get comfortable. Arrange the documentation on the podium. Remember, the jury will not respond to a robot. It is desirable to be "likeable." Smile and nod at the jurors, and make eye contact with every juror during testimony.

18.9   Daubert Trilogy

Several court cases involving forensic testimony have resulted in a *precedent*, which is a rule developed as a result of court case. The court's ruling becomes *case law*, and all similar court cases to follow are subject to the precedent. The first judicial decision to effect how fingerprint examiners testify was a result of *Frye v. United States* in 1923.[7] The question that arose in court was whether the polygraph test was reliable enough to be admitted as evidence in court. The polygraph testimony was not admitted into court because it had not gained general acceptance in its scientific field and was therefore not considered reliable evidence. A precedent was established, and all scientific testimony to follow was held to the *Frye standard*. The following is an excerpt from this decision:

> *Just when a scientific principle or discovery crosses the line between the experimental and demonstrable stages is difficult to define. Somewhere in this twilight zone the evidential force of the principle must be recognized, and while the courts will go a long way in admitting expert testimony deduced from a well-recognized scientific principle or discovery, the thing from which the deduction is made must be sufficiently established to have gained general acceptance in the particular field in which it belongs.[7]*

The Frye standard is also known as the *rule of general acceptance*. It states that scientific testimony is admissible in a court of law only if it is generally accepted by the relevant scientific community.

Until 1993, fingerprint testimony was accepted according to the Frye standard. Fingerprint analysis had been around since the early 1900s and was accepted by the relevant forensic science community. One court decision changed the course of forensic fingerprint analysis. In 1993, the Daubert family sued Merrell Dow Pharmaceuticals, Inc. alleging that the company's pregnancy antinausea drug caused birth defects.[8] Testimony from various doctors and medical researchers brought into question whether the Frye standard was adequate to determine admissibility of scientific methodology.

The court's decision became known as the *Daubert standard*, which is a standard for determining the validity of scientific processes prior to the jury trial. The Daubert standard expands the Frye test of general acceptance. It concludes that scientific testimony should be judged on more rigorous criteria. Those criteria are the following:[8]

1. The science must be generally accepted in the relevant scientific community.
2. The science must demonstrate a calculable error rate.
3. The science must be testable.
4. The science must be subject to peer review and publication.
5. The science must have existing controls and standards.

These criteria are reminiscent of the scientific method. The scientific method is a systematic process for doing research and testing theories and observations. It involves the following steps:

1. Making an observation
2. Creating a hypothesis
3. Testing the hypothesis through experimentation with standards and controls
4. Analyzing the results (which may lead to calculable error rates)
5. Forming a conclusion that either confirms or refutes your hypothesis
6. Publishing your research, which is subject to peer review and testing

If the admissibility of a type of science is in question, there may be a *Daubert hearing*: a short proceeding in court outside of a jury trial to determine whether or not the expert will be allowed to testify to their conclusions. Several experts may be called to testify as to the reliability or fallibility of the science. The judge serves as the "gatekeeper." The judge is solely responsible for making the final determination of admissibility. Forty states have adopted the Daubert standard as of October 2013.

Fingerprint analysis has been subjected to Daubert hearings since Daubert's inception. This is because there is no known error rate for the science. There are several reasons why a standard calculation of error rate is not feasible. It is near impossible to create two latent fingerprints that are identical. Friction ridges are positioned along the 3D, elastic surface of the skin. Latent prints are deposited on substrates of different textures, shapes, and materials, and are processed with various powders and chemicals. Many forensic scientists are working on developing a statistical model for fingerprint analysis. Sir Francis Galton was the first to develop a statistical model in the late 1800s. As of 2013, there is no standardized statistical model with which to analyze the error rate of fingerprint identifications. What can be calculated is the practitioner error rate: how often an individual fingerprint examiner makes an error. To date, every Daubert hearing addressing the admissibility of fingerprint evidence has resulted in the evidence being allowed at trial.

Two more court cases expanded on the Daubert standard. In the case of *General Electric Co. v. Joiner*, the court reiterated that the judge would be the "gatekeeper" for admissibility of scientific evidence.[9] In the case of *Kumho Tire Company v. Carmichael*, the Daubert standard was extended to include not only scientific evidence but also technical evidence from nonscientists.[10] In this case, the technical evidence in question was the testimony of an engineer. FRE 702 indicates expert testimony applies not only to science but also to technical expertise, such as that of an engineer, mechanic, or plumber. The Kumho Tire decision applies FRE 702 to the Daubert standard. These three cases—Daubert, Joiner, and Kumho Tire—are collectively known as the "Daubert trilogy."

18.10   I Had a Case: The Assassination of President John F. Kennedy

(See Appendix C for historical fingerprint expert testimony from the Warren Commission Hearings held to investigate the 1963 assassination of President John F. Kennedy.)[11]

18.11   Chapter Summary

An expert witness is anyone who knows more about a particular topic than the average person due to experience, training, and education. According to FRE 702, an expert in a particular field may testify to an opinion based on commonly accepted facts or data. Testimony requires the expert witness to teach the jury about his or her science. An effective expert witness speaks with appropriate volume, makes eye contact with jurors, acts naturally, does not display nervous gestures, exudes confidence and competence, and is passionate about the topic presented.

A pretrial conference is a meeting with an attorney during which the expert explains qualifications, analyses, results, conclusions, the scientific basis for conclusions, and any other information relevant to the case. The three main phases of testimony are the qualifying questions (voir dire), direct examination, and cross-examination.

The Frye standard, known as the rule of general acceptance, states that a science is admissible in a court of law if it is generally accepted by the relevant scientific community. The Daubert standard revised Frye to also require scientific testimony to have a calculable error rate, be testable, be subject to publication and peer review, and maintain controls and standards. The Joiner decision states that the judge is the "gatekeeper" for admissibility of scientific testimony. The Kumho Tire decision revised Daubert to include not only scientific testimony but also technical testimony.

Review Questions

1. Define "expert witness."
2. Describe FRE 702 and explain how it relates to fingerprint testimony.
3. What are the rights guaranteed by the Sixth Amendment?
4. List five qualities of an effective teacher.
5. List five qualities of an effective expert witness.
6. Define a latent fingerprint as you would in court.
7. Write your own qualifying questions and answers. Assume you have been working as a fingerprint analyst for the Anywhere Police Department for 1 year.
8. What is a pretrial conference, and why is it important?
9. What are the three main phases of testimony?
10. Define demeanor.
11. What is the Frye standard?
12. What is the Daubert standard, and how does it impact the forensic scientist?

References

1. Federal Rule of Evidence 702. *Testimony by Expert Witnesses*. Fed. R. Crim. P. 702. Pub. L. 93–595, §1. Jan. 2, 1975.
2. Feder, H. and Houck, M. 2008. *Succeeding as an Expert Witness*, 4th edn. Boca Raton, FL: CRC Press.
3. Hazen, R. and Philips, C. 2012. The expert fingerprint witness. In Ramotowski, R. (ed.), *Advances in Fingerprint Technology*, 3rd edn. Boca Raton, FL: Taylor & Francis.
4. Molloy, J. 1988. *John T. Molloy's New Dress for Success*. New York: Warner Books, Inc.
5. Sapir, G. 2008. Forensic science, ethics and the expert witness. *Paper Presented at the Bioinformatics 6th Annual Conference*, Dayton, OH.
6. Hazen, R. and Phillips, C. 2001. The expert fingerprint witness. In Lee, H. and Gaensslen, R.E. (eds.), *Advances in Fingerprint Technology*, 2nd edn. Boca Raton, FL: Taylor & Francis.
7. Frye v. United States. 293 F. 1013 (D.C. Cir 1923).
8. Daubert v. Merrell Dow Pharmaceuticals, Inc. 1993. 509 U.S. 579.
9. General Electric Co. v. Joiner. 1997. 522 U.S. 136, 138–139, 118 S. Ct. 512, 517.
10. Kumho Tire Co., Ltd. v. Carmichael. 1999. 526 U.S. 137,119 S. Ct. 1167, 1171, 1174.
11. John F. Kennedy Assassination Homepage. Warren Commission Hearings: Vol. IV. 1964. http://www.jfk-assassination.de/warren/wch/vol4/page1.php (last modified December 5, 2004, accessed September 11, 2013).
12. Science Education Resource Center (SERC). An office of Carleton College, Northfield, MN. 1986. *Trial Documents*. http://serc.carleton.edu/files/woburn/resources/subpoena_usgs.jpg (retrieved December 10, 2013).

Appendix A Sequential Processing

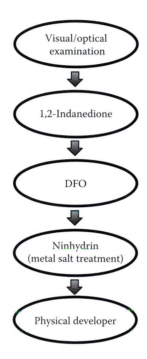

Figure A.1 Porous items (dry).

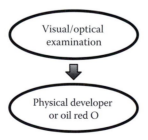

Figure A.2 Porous items (wet).

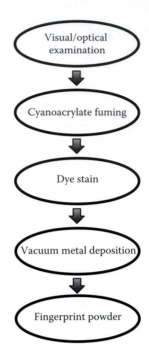

Figure A.3 Nonporous items (dry).

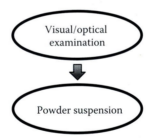

Figure A.4 Nonporous items (wet).

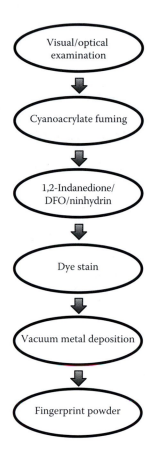

Figure A.5 Semiporous items (dry).

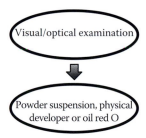

Figure A.6 Semiporous items (wet).

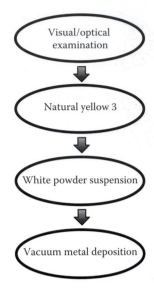

Figure A.7 Greasy fingerprints (nonporous dark/patterned surfaces).

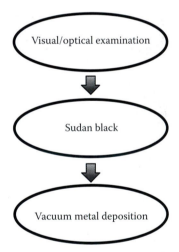

Figure A.8 Greasy fingerprints (nonporous light surfaces).

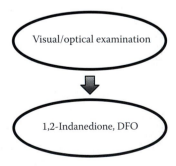

Figure A.9 Greasy fingerprints (porous dark/patterned surfaces).

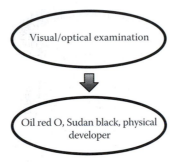

Figure A.10 Greasy fingerprints (porous light surfaces).

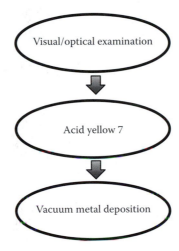

Figure A.11 Bloody fingerprints (nonporous dark/patterned surfaces).

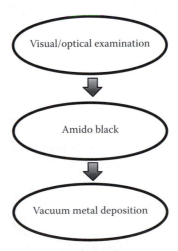

Figure A.12 Bloody fingerprints (nonporous light surfaces).

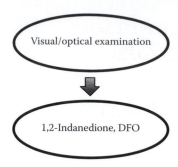

Figure A.13 Bloody fingerprints (porous dark/patterned surfaces).

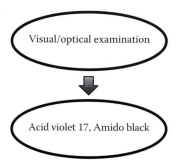

Figure A.14 Bloody fingerprints (porous light surfaces).

Appendix B Latent Print Reagent Formulations and Processes (In Alphabetical Order)

All reagents should be stored in clearly labeled glass containers away from direct sunlight. Wherever possible, the least toxic and/or flammable solution is presented. Personal protective equipment should be worn at all times when working with chemical reagents regardless of toxicity or flammability.

Acid Violet 17[1]

Fixing solution

20 g	5-sulfosalicylic acid
1 L	Distilled water

1. Mix 5-sulfosalicylic acid with distilled water in a beaker over a magnetic stirrer.
2. Immerse the evidentiary item in the fixing solution for five or more minutes.

Working solution

1 g	Acid violet 17
250 mL	Ethanol
50 mL	Acetic acid
700 mL	Distilled water

3. Mix the working solution in a beaker over a magnetic stirrer for 5 min.
4. Immerse the evidentiary item in the working solution for three or more minutes.
5. Rinse with distilled water.
6. Dry at room temperature.

Destaining solution

250 mL	Ethanol
50 mL	Acetic acid
700 mL	Distilled water

7. Immerse the item in a destaining solution (given earlier) to lessen background staining.

Acid Yellow 7[1]

Fixing solution

20 g	5-sulfosalicylic acid
1 L	Distilled water

1. Mix 5-sulfosalicylic acid and distilled water in a beaker over a magnetic stirrer.
2. Immerse the evidentiary item in the fixing solution for five or more minutes.

Working solution

1 g	Acid yellow 7
250 mL	Ethanol
50 mL	Acetic acid
700 mL	Distilled water

3. Mix the working solution in a beaker over a magnetic stirrer for 1 min.
4. Immerse the evidentiary item in the working solution for 5 min.
5. Rinse in distilled water.
6. Dry at room temperature.

Destaining solution

250 mL	Ethanol
50 mL	Acetic acid
700 mL	Distilled water

7. Immerse in a destaining solution of either 10% bleach or the destaining solution (given earlier) to lessen background staining.

Amido Black[1]

Fixing solution

20 g	5-sulfosalicylic acid
1 L	Distilled water

1. Mix 5-sulfosalicylic acid and distilled water in a beaker over a magnetic stirrer.
2. Immerse the evidentiary item in the fixing solution for 5–6 min.

Working solution

1 g	Amido black
250 mL	Ethanol
50 mL	Acetic acid
700 mL	Distilled water

3. Mix the working solution in a beaker over a magnetic stirrer for 5 min.
4. Immerse the evidentiary item in the working solution for 3–4 min, or spray the item and let it run over the fixed fingerprints.
5. Rinse in distilled water.
6. Dry at room temperature.

Destaining solution

250 mL	Ethanol
50 mL	Acetic acid
700 mL	Distilled water

7. Immerse the item in a destaining solution (given earlier) to lessen background staining.

Ardrox[2]

Working solution

10 mL	Ardrox
1 L	Methanol

1. Mix the aqueous Ardrox solution with methanol in a beaker over a magnetic stirrer.
2. Dip or spray the superglue-processed evidentiary item with the working solution.
3. Rinse gently under running tap water.
4. Hang to dry in a fume hood.
5. Observe the fluorescence under UV illumination (365–380 nm) using UV protective goggles, violet/blue illumination (435–445 nm) with yellow goggles, and/or blue illumination (445–480 nm) with orange goggles.

Basic Yellow 40/Brilliant Yellow 40 (BY 40)[3]

Working solution

2 g	BY 40
1 L	Ethanol

1. Mix the BY 40 in ethanol in a beaker over a magnetic stirrer.
2. Dip or spray the superglue-processed evidentiary item with the working solution.
3. Rinse gently under running tap water.
4. Hang to dry in a fume hood.
5. Observe the fluorescence under UV illumination (~365 nm) using UV protective goggles.

DFO[4]

Stock solution

0.25 g	DFO (1,8-Diazafluoren-9-one)
40 mL	Methanol
20 mL	Acetic acid

1. Dissolve the DFO in methanol and acetic acid in a beaker over a magnetic stirrer for approximately 20 min until completely dissolved.

Working solution

60 mL	DFO stock solution
940 mL	HFE7100™

2. Slowly add the HFE7100™ solvent to the stock solution.
3. Dip or spray the evidentiary item until it is saturated.
4. Hang the item to dry in a fume hood.
5. When dry, heat the item in an incubator at 100°C for 20 min.
6. View the item through a red filter or using red goggles under green light (530–570 nm) using an alternate light source or laser.

1,2 Indanedione[5]

Zinc chloride stock solution

0.4 g	Zinc chloride
10 mL	Ethanol
1 mL	Ethyl acetate
190 mL	HFE 7100™

Working solution

0.8 g	1,2-indanedione
79 mL	Ethyl acetate
10 mL	Glacial acetic acid
80 mL	Zinc chloride stock solution
930 mL	HFE 7100™

1. Dissolve the indanedione completely in ethyl acetate and glacial acetic acid in a beaker over a magnetic stirrer.
2. When the indanedione is completely dissolved, add the zinc chloride stock solution.
3. Slowly add the HFE7100™.
4. Dip or spray the evidentiary item with the working solution until it is saturated.
5. Dry in a fume hood.

6. Heat in an incubator at 100°C for 20 min.
7. Document visible fingerprints.
8. View the item through a red filter or using red goggles under green light (530–570 nm) using an alternate light source or laser.

Natural Yellow 3[6]

Working solution

1.0 g	Natural yellow 3
100 mL	Ethanol
50 mL	Distilled water

1. Dissolve the natural yellow 3 in ethanol in a beaker over a magnetic stirrer.
2. Add the distilled water and stir vigorously for 5 min until a clear solution is produced.
3. Dip the evidentiary item into the working solution for approximately 10 s.
4. Rinse gently under running tap water.
5. Hang to dry in a fume hood.
6. Observe the fluorescence under blue to blue-green illumination (420–540 nm) using yellow/orange goggles.

Ninhydrin[5]

5 g	Ninhydrin crystals
45 mL	Ethanol
2 mL	Ethyl acetate
5 mL	Acetic acid
1 L	HFE 7100™

1. Dissolve the ninhydrin crystals in ethanol, ethyl acetate, and acetic acid in a beaker over a magnetic stirrer.
2. When the ninhydrin is completely dissolved, slowly add the HFE7100™ solvent.
3. Dip or spray the evidentiary item until it is saturated.
4. Hang to dry in a fume hood.
5. Label and photograph the visible fingerprints.

Oil Red O[5]

Working solution

1.54 g	Oil red O
770 mL	Methanol
9.2 g	Sodium hydroxide (NaOH)
230 mL	Distilled water

1. Dissolve the oil red O in methanol in a beaker over a magnetic stirrer.
2. Dissolve the sodium hydroxide in distilled water.
3. Mix the resulting oil red O and sodium hydroxide solutions thoroughly.
4. Filter the resulting working solution to remove undissolved solids.

Buffer solution

101.55 g	Sodium phosphate monobasic monohydrate
338.79 g	Sodium phosphate dibasic heptahydrate
6 L	Distilled water

5. Dissolve the sodium phosphate monobasic monohydrate in 1 L of distilled water.
6. Dissolve the sodium phosphate dibasic heptahydrate in 1 L of distilled water.
7. Mix the two resulting solutions in a beaker over a magnetic stirrer and add distilled water to a total final volume of 4 L. This is the buffer solution.
8. Immerse the evidentiary item in the oil red O working solution, cover, and agitate for 5–90 min. (Weak prints will take longer to appear.)
9. Remove and let the excess solution drain off.
10. Immerse the stained item in the buffer solution for a few minutes.
11. Rinse in tap water (optional).
12. Hang to dry in a fume hood or heat the item at 50°C.

Physical Developer[5,7]

Maleic acid solution

30 g	Maleic acid
1 L	Distilled water

1. Dissolve maleic acid in distilled water in a beaker over a magnetic stirrer.
2. Pour the resulting solution into a clean, nonmetallic tray that has been rinsed with distilled water.
3. Immerse the evidentiary item in the maleic acid solution for 5 min or until bubbles no longer form on the item.

PD (physical developer) stock solutions

Redox solution

900 mL	Distilled water
30 g	Ferric nitrate
80 g	Ferrous ammonium sulfate
20 g	Citric acid

1. Mix the ferric nitrate into the distilled water in a beaker over a magnetic stirrer.
2. Add the ammonium ferrous sulfate.
3. Add the citric acid.
4. Store this stock solution away from light and heat.

Surfactant solution

1 L	Distilled water
4 g	N-dodecylamine acetate
4 mL	Tween® 20 detergent solution (surfactant)

5. While stirring the distilled water, add the n-dodecylamine acetate in a beaker over a magnetic stirrer.
6. Add Tween® 20 detergent solution and mix thoroughly.

Silver nitrate solution

50 mL	Distilled water
10 g	Silver nitrate

7. While stirring the distilled water, add the silver nitrate in a beaker over a magnetic stirrer.
8. Stir until completely dissolved.
9. Store this stock solution away from light and heat.

PD working solution

10. While stirring the redox solution in a large beaker over a magnetic stirrer, add 40 mL of the surfactant solution.
11. Stir for 2 min.
12. Add the silver nitrate solution.
13. Stir for 2 min.
14. Pour the resulting solution into a clean, nonmetallic tray that has been rinsed with distilled water.
15. Following the maleic acid wash, immerse in the PD working solution and agitate until dark gray friction ridges are observed.
16. Rinse the item with tap water.
17. Optional: Immerse in a solution of 1:1 bleach to water for 2–3 min to decrease background staining.
18. Hang to dry in a fume hood.

Powder Suspension

Black fingerprint powder
Liquinox™ or PhotoFlo™ detergent
Distilled water

1. Mix equal amounts of detergent and distilled water.
2. Add black fingerprint powder until the solution is the consistency of paint.
3. Paint the solution onto the adhesive substrate using a camel hairbrush.
4. Let the solution sit on the surface for 30–60 s.

5. Rinse the item under running tap water.
6. Hang to dry in a fume hood.

Rhodamine 6G

Working solution

0.005–0.05 g	Rhodamine 6G
1 L	Methanol or distilled water

1. Dissolve rhodamine 6G in methanol or water in a beaker over a magnetic stirrer.
2. Dip or spray the superglue-processed evidentiary item.
3. If using a higher concentration, gently rinse the item with methanol or water depending on the carrier solvent used.
4. Hang to dry in a fume hood.
5. Observe the fluorescence under blue-green/green illumination (490–550 nm) using orange/red goggles.

Sudan Black (Solvent Black 3)[5]

Working solution

15 g	Sudan black
1 L	Ethanol
500 mL	Distilled water

1. Dissolve Sudan black in ethanol in a beaker over a magnetic stirrer until dissolved.
2. Add distilled water and mix until combined.
3. Soak the evidentiary item in the working solution for approximately 2 min.
4. Rinse gently under running tap water.
5. Hang to dry in a fume hood.

References

1. Bleay, S. et al. 2012. Home Office Police Scientific Development Branch. *Fingerprint Source Book*. Luton, England: White Crescent Press, Ltd.
2. Royal Canadian Mounted Police. 2003. Fingerprint development techniques. http://www.rcmp-grc.gc.ca/fsis-ssji/firs-srij/recipe-recette-eng.htm (accessed January 15, 2014).
3. Champod, C. et al. 2004. *Fingerprints and Other Ridge Skin Impressions*. Boca Raton, FL: Taylor & Francis.
4. Didierjean, C., Debart, M., and Crispino, F. 1998. New formulation of DFO in HFE7100. *Fingerprint Whorld* 24(94): 163–167.
5. Ramotowski, R. 2012. Amino acid reagents. In Ramotowski, R. (ed.), *Advances in Fingerprint Technology*, 3rd edn. Boca Raton, FL: Taylor & Francis.

6. Gaskell, C., Bleay, S.S., and Ramadani, J. 2013. Natural Yellow 3: A novel fluorescent reagent for use on grease-contaminated, nonporous surfaces. *J. Forensic Identif.* 63(3): 274–285.

7. Yamashita, B. and French, M. 2011. Latent print development. In the Scientific Working Group on Friction Ridge Analysis, Study and Technology (SWGFAST) et al., *The Fingerprint Sourcebook*, U.S. Department of Justice, Office of Justice Programs. Washington, DC: National Institute of Justice.

Appendix C Expert Witness Testimony of Sebastian F. Latona, FBI Latent Fingerprint Examiner

Warren Commission Hearings
April 2, 1964
Part IV, pp. 1–81 (redacted)

[Swearing in]

The Chairman.

The Commission will be in order.

Mr. Latona, the purpose of today's hearing is to take your testimony and that of Arthur Mandella. Mr. Mandella is a fingerprint expert from the New York City Police Department. We are asking both of you to give technical information to the Commission.

Will you raise your right hand and be sworn?

Do you solemnly swear that the testimony you are about to give will be the truth, the whole truth, and nothing but the truth, so help you God?

Mr. Latona.

I do.

The Chairman.

You may be seated. Mr. Eisenberg will conduct the examination.

[Qualifying Questions]

Mr. Eisenberg.

Mr. Latona, could you state your full name and give us your position?

Mr. Latona.

My full name is Sebastian Francis Latona. I am the supervisor of the latent fingerprint section of the identification division of the Federal Bureau of Investigation.

Mr. Eisenberg.

What is your education, Mr. Latona?

Mr. Latona.

I attended Columbia University School of Law, where I received degrees of LL.B. LL.M., M.P.L.

Mr. Eisenberg.

And could you briefly outline your qualifications as a fingerprint expert?

Mr. Latona.

Well, I have been with the Federal Bureau of Investigation for a little more than 32 years. I started in the identification division as a student fingerprint classifier, and since that time I have worked myself up into where I am now supervisor of the latent fingerprint section.

Mr. Eisenberg.

Could you approximate the number of fingerprint examinations you have made?

Mr. Latona.

Frankly, no. There have been so many in that time that I would not be able to give even a good guess.

Mr. Eisenberg.

Would the figure run in the thousands or hundreds?

Mr. Latona.

So far as comparisons are concerned, in the millions.

Mr. Eisenberg.

Have you testified in court?

Mr. Latona.

I have testified in Federal courts, State courts, commissioners' hearings, military courts, and at deportation proceedings.

Mr. Eisenberg.

Mr. Chief Justice, I ask that this witness be accepted as an expert.

The Chairman.

The witness is qualified.

[History and Background of the Science]

Mr. Eisenberg.

Mr. Latona, could you briefly outline for us the theory of fingerprint identification?

Mr. Latona.

The principle of fingerprint identification is based on the fact primarily that the ridge formations that appear on the hands and on the soles of the feet actually are created approximately 2–3 months before birth, on the unborn child, and they remain constant in the same position in which they are formed until the person is dead and the body is consumed by decomposition.

Secondly, the fact that no two people, or no two fingers of the same person, have the same arrangement of these ridge formations, either on the fingers, the palms, or the soles and toes of the feet. Plus the fact that during the lifetime of a person this ridge formation does not change, it remains constant—from the time it is formed until actual destruction, either caused by voluntary or involuntary means, or upon the death of the body and decomposition.

Mr. Eisenberg.

Mr. Latona, do you have any personal experience indicating the uniqueness of fingerprints?

Mr. Latona.

Yes; I do. My experience is based primarily upon the work which I have actually done in connection with my work with the FBI. I have had the experience of working on one case in particular in which millions of comparisons were actually and literally made with a small portion of a fingerprint which was left on a piece of evidence in connection with this particular case, which was a kidnapping case.

This fragmentary latent print which we developed consisted of approximately seven to eight points. Most fingerprints will have in them an average roughly of from 85 to about 125.

This fragmentary latent print was compared with literally millions of single impressions for the purpose of trying to effect an identification. And we were unable, over a lengthy period while we were making these millions of comparisons, not able to identify these few fragmentary points.

The important thing is simply this; that on the basis of that fragmentary print, it was not possible to determine even the type of pattern that the impression was. Accordingly, we had to compare it with all types of fingerprint patterns, of which there are really four basic types—the arch, tented arch, loop, and whorl. And we are still making comparisons in that case, and we have not been able to identify these few points.

Now, that means simply this—that the theory that we are going on an assumption that people do not have the same fingerprints—and we find it not necessary to compare, say for example, a loop pattern with a whorl pattern, and as there is a possibility that, it is contended by some of these so-called authorities, that maybe the points that you find in a loop may be found in the same arrangement in a whorl—is not true. I think that that case, a practical case we have actually worked on, disproves that theory so strongly in my mind that I am convinced that no two people can possibly have the same fingerprints.

Mr. Eisenberg.

Are palmprints as unique as fingerprints?

Mr. Latona.

Yes.

The Chairman.

Approximately how many fingerprints do you have these days?

Mr. Latona.

At the present time, we have the fingerprints of more than 77 million people.

[Evidence in the Case: Developing the Fingerprints]

Mr. Eisenberg.

Now, Mr. Latona, I hand to you an object which I will describe for the record as being apparently a brown, homemade-type of paper bag, and which I will also describe for the record as having been found on the sixth floor of the Texas School Book Depository Building near the window, the easternmost window, on the south face of that floor.

I ask you whether you are familiar with this paper bag?

Mr. Latona.

Yes, I am. This is a piece of brown wrapping paper that we have referred to as a brown paper bag, which was referred to me for purposes of processing for latent prints.

Mr. Eisenberg.

And you examined that for latent prints?

Mr. Latona.

Yes; I did.

Mr. Eisenberg.

Mr. Chairman, may I have this admitted into evidence as Commission Exhibit 626?

The Chairman.

It may be admitted.

Mr. Eisenberg.

Mr. Latona, do your notes show when you received this paper bag?

Mr. Latona.

I received this paper bag on the morning of November 23, 1963.

Mr. Eisenberg.

And when did you conduct your examination?

Mr. Latona.

I conducted my examination on that same day.

Mr. Eisenberg.

Now, Mr. Latona, how did you proceed to conduct your examination for fingerprints on this object?

Mr. Latona.

….This was subjected to what is known as the iodine-fuming method, which simply means flowing iodine fumes, which are developed by what is known as an iodine-fuming gun—it is a very simple affair, in which there are a couple of tubes attached to each other, having in one of them iodine crystals. And by simply blowing through one end, you get iodine fumes.

The iodine fumes are brought in as close contact to the surface as possible And if there are any prints which contain certain fatty material or protein material, the iodine fumes simply discolor it to a sort of brownish color. And of course such prints as are developed are photographed for record purposes.

That was done in this case here, but no latent prints were developed.

The next step then was to try an additional method, by chemicals. This was subsequently processed by a 3% solution of silver nitrate. The processing with silver nitrate resulted in developing two latent prints. One is what we call a latent palmprint, and the other is what we call a latent fingerprint.

Mr. Eisenberg.

Can you briefly explain the action of the silver nitrate?

Mr. Latona.

Silver nitrate solution in itself is colorless, and it reacts with the sodium chloride, which is ordinary salt which is found in the perspiration or sweat which is exuded by the sweat pores.

This material covers the fingers. When it touches a surface such as an absorbent material, like paper, it leaves an outline on the paper.

When this salt material, which is left by the fingers on the paper, is immersed in the silver nitrate solution, there is a combining, an immediate combining of—the elements themselves will break down, and they recombine into silver chloride and sodium nitrate. We know that silver is sensitive to light. So that material, after it has been treated with the silver nitrate solution, is placed under a strong light. We utilize a carbon arc lamp, which has considerable ultraviolet light in it. And it will immediately start to discolor the specimen. Wherever there is any salt material, it will discolor it, much more so than the rest of the object, and show exactly where the latent prints have been developed. It is simply a reaction of the silver nitrate with the sodium chloride.

That is all it is.

Mr. Eisenberg.

Do you frequently find that the silver nitrate develops a print in a paper object which the iodine fuming cannot develop?

Mr. Latona.

Yes; I would say that is true, considerably so. We have more success with silver nitrate than we do with the iodine fumes.

The reason we use both is because of the fact that this material which is exuded by the fingers may fall into one of two main types—protein material and salt material. The iodine fumes will develop protein material. Silver nitrate will develop the salt material.

The reason we use both is because we do not know what was in the subject's fingers or hands or feet. Accordingly, to insure complete coverage, we use both methods. And we use them in that sequence. The iodine first, then the silver nitrate. The iodine is used first because the iodine simply causes a temporary physical change. It will discolor, and then the fumes, upon being left in the open air, will disappear, and then the color will dissolve. Silver nitrate, on the other hand, causes a chemical change and it will permanently affect the change. So if we were to use the silver nitrate process first, then we could not use the iodine fumes. On occasion we have developed fingerprints and palmprints with iodine fumes which failed to develop with the silver nitrate and vice versa.

Mr. Eisenberg.

Now, Mr. Latona, looking at that bag I see that almost all of it is an extremely dark brown color, except that there are patches of a lighter brown, a manila-paper brown. Could you explain why there are these two colors on the bag?

Mr. Latona.

Yes. The dark portions of the paper bag are where the silver nitrate has taken effect. And the light portions of the bag are where we did not process the bag at that time, because additional examinations were to be made, and we did not wish the object to lose its identity as to what it may have been used for. Certain chemical tests were to be made after we finished with it. And we felt that the small section that was left in itself would not interfere with the general overall examination of the bag itself.

Mr. Eisenberg.

That is, the small section of light brown corresponds to the color which the bag had when you received it?

Mr. Latona.

That is the natural color of the wrapper at the time we received it.

Mr. Eisenberg.

And the remaining color is caused by the silver nitrate process?

Mr. Latona.

That is correct.

Mr. Eisenberg.

Does paper normally turn this dark brown color when treated by silver nitrate?

Mr. Latona.

Yes; it does. It will get darker, too, as time goes on and it is affected by light.

Mr. Eisenberg.

Returning to the prints themselves, you stated I believe that you found a palmprint and a fingerprint on this paper bag?

Mr. Latona.

That is correct.

Mr. Eisenberg.

Did you find any other prints?

Mr. Latona.

No; no other prints that we term of value in the sense that I felt that they could be identified or that a conclusion could be reached that they were not identical with the fingerprints or palmprints of some other person.

Mr. Eisenberg.

Did you attempt to identify the palmprint and fingerprint?

Mr. Latona.

The ones that I developed; yes.

Mr. Eisenberg.

Were you able to identify these prints?

Mr. Latona.

I—the ones I developed, I did identify.

Mr. Eisenberg.

Whose prints did you find them to be?

Mr. Latona.

They were identified as a fingerprint and a palmprint of Lee Harvey Oswald.

Mr. Latona.

I do.

Mr. Eisenberg.

Mr. Latona, you have handled me three cards, one of which appears to be a standard fingerprint card, and the other two of which appear to be prints of the palms of an individual. All these cards are marked "Lee Harvey Oswald."

Are these the cards which you received from your Dallas office which you just described as being the prints of Lee Harvey Oswald?

Mr. Latona.

They are.

Mr. Eisenberg.

Mr. Latona, do you know how the known samples we have Just marked 627, 628, and 629 were obtained?

Mr. Latona.

How they were obtained?

Mr. Eisenberg.

Yes. Can you tell the process used in obtaining them?

Mr. Latona.

You mean in recording the impressions?

Mr. Eisenberg.

Yes, sir.

Mr. Latona.

Fingerprints are recorded by the use of a printer's ink, heavy black ink, which is first placed on a smooth surface, such as glass or metal, and it is rolled out in a smooth, even film. Then the subject's fingers are brought in contact with the plate by a rolling process, rolling the finger from one complete side to the other complete side, in order to coat the finger with an even film of this heavy ink. Then the finger. is brought in contact with a standard fingerprint card and the finger again is rolled from one complete side to the opposite side in order to record in complete detail all of the ridge formation which occurs on the tip of the finger, or the first joint, which is under the nail.

Mr. Eisenberg.

Now, I believe you said you also found a fingerprint of Lee Harvey Oswald on this paper bag, 626.

Mr. Latona.

Yes; I did.

Mr. Eisenberg.

Can you tell us what finger and what portion of the finger of Lee Harvey Oswald you identified that print as being?

Mr. Latona.

The fingerprint which was developed on the paper bag was identified as the right—as the left index fingerprint of Lee Harvey Oswald. I also have a slight enlargement of it, if you care to see it.

Mr. Eisenberg.

You are showing us a true photograph of the actual fingerprint?

Mr. Latona.

As it appeared on the bag, slightly enlarged.

Mr. Eisenberg.

Now, what portion of the left index finger was that, Mr. Latona?

Mr. Latona.

That is the area which is to the left, or rather to the right of the index finger.

Mr. Eisenberg.

On which joint?

Mr. Latona.

On the first joint, which is under the nail.

Mr. Eisenberg.

Is that known as the distal phalanx?

Mr. Latona.

That's right.

Mr. Eisenberg.

So it is the right side of the distal phalanx of the left index finger?

Mr. Latona.

That is correct. Now, that would be looking at an impression made by the finger. If you were to look at the finger, you would raise the finger up and it would be on the opposite side, which would he on the left side of the distal phalanx.

Mr. Eisenberg.

Mr. Latona, could you show us where on the paper bag, Exhibit 626, this left index finger was developed by you?

Mr. Latona.

The left index fingerprint was developed in the area which is indicated by this small red arrow.

[Evidence in the Case: Fingerprint Comparison]

Mr. Eisenberg.

Mr. Latona, could you show us that chart and discuss with us some of the similar characteristics which you found in the inked and latent print which led you to the conclusion that they were identical?

Mr. Latona.

Yes. I have here what are referred to as two charted enlargements. One of the enlargements, which is marked "Inked Left Index Fingerprint. Lee Harvey Oswald" is approximately a 10-time enlargement of the fingerprint which appears on Exhibit 633A. The other enlargement, which is marked "Latent Fingerprint on Brown Homemade Paper Container," is approximately a 10-time enlargement of the latent fingerprint which was developed on the brown wrapping paper indicated by the red arrow, "B."

Mr. Eisenberg.

And that also corresponds to the photograph you gave us, which is now Exhibit 633?

Mr. Latona.

Now, in making a comparison of prints to determine whether or not they were made by the same finger, an examination is made first of all of the latent print.

An examination is made to see if there are in the latent print any points or characteristics which are unique to the person making the determination. In other words, in looking at the latent print, for example, this point, which is marked "1," is a ridge. The black lines are what we term ridges. They were made by the ridge formations on the fingers. That is, when the finger came in contact with the brown paper bag, it left an outline in these black lines on the brown paper bag.

Now, in looking at the latent print in the enlargement you notice there is one black line that appears to go upward and stop at the point which has been indicated as point No. 1.

Now, looking further we find this point that has been indicated as No. 3. And No. 3 is located— —

Mr. Dulles.

Why do you skip 2?

Mr. Latona.

I am going to come to that.

Mr. Dulles.

I see.

Mr. Latona.

I am going to tie these three in. Point No. 3 is above and to the left one ridge removed from—one black line—there is No. 3. Now looking further, we can look over to the right, or rather to the left, and we notice that one ridge removed from No. 3 are two ridges that come together and give you a point which has been indicated as No. 2.

Mr. Eisenberg.

Is that what you might call a bifurcation?

Mr. Latona.

That is referred to, generally speaking, as a bifurcation.

Mr. Eisenberg.

That is No. 2?

Mr. Latona.

And No. 1 is what is referred to as a ridge end. Now, keeping those three points in mind, and the relationship they have to each other, if this print here, the inked print, were made by the same finger which left the print on the brown paper bag, we should be able to find those three points in the same approximate area, having the same relationship to each other.

Now, at this point we have not made a determination of any kind as to whether they are or are not identical. Examining the inked fingerprint, bearing in mind the general formation of this print that we see here, the latent print, we would examine the inked print and that would direct us to this approximate area here. And looking, we find sure enough there is point No. 1—or rather there is a point which appears to be the same as point No. 1 here. Bearing in mind how we located points Nos. 2 and 3, we would then check the inked print further and say to ourselves, "If this print were the same, there should be a point No. 2 in exactly the same relationship to No. 1 as there was in this latent print." We look over here one, two, three, four—there is point No. 2.

Mr. Eisenberg.

That point, or that count that you are making, is of ridges between the first and second point?

Mr. Latona.

Between the points, that's right. Then we have over here one, two, three, four. And bearing in mind again how point No. 3 bears a relationship to point No. 2, we should find point No. 3 in the same relative position in the inked print that it occurs in the latent print. Counting over again—one we find a point which could be considered No. 3.

Now, at this time we have coordinated three points. We have tied three points together. On that basis, by themselves, we would not give a definite determination. Accordingly, we would pursue a further examination to determine whether there are other characteristics which occur.

Mr. Dulles.

How many times is that magnified?

Mr. Latona.

This is magnified approximately 10 times.

Mr. Latona.

Then we would pick up point No. 5. We notice point No. 5 is again one of those bifurcations which occurs above and slightly to the left of point No. 3. We also notice that it envelops point No. 1—as we go down further, slightly to the right of point No. 5, we notice that bifurcation envelops point No. 1. we would look around for such a characteristic in the latent print.

If the same finger made those two prints, we have to find point 5. And looking over here we find such a formation, we look at it, and sure enough it envelops point No. 1—exactly the same relationship to each other appears in the latent print, and in the inked print. It has the same relationship to point No. 3 that occurs in the latent print as occurs in the inked print. Then we would pick up point No. 4—one, two, three, four.

Mr. Eisenberg.

Again you are counting ridges?

Mr. Latona.

Counting ridges again, from point No. 5 one, two, three, four. There is a so-called ridge end, which occurs above, above and almost slightly to the left of point No. 5, point No. 5 enveloping No. 1. Point No. 5.

Mr. Dulles.

Is 5 a ridge-end?

Mr. Latona.

Five is what we term a Joining, forking, or bifurcation. These two come together at point 5. Over here, together at point 5.

Mr. Dulles.

Is that where the two ridges come together there and encase it?

Mr. Latona.

Yes, sir. From point No. 5 we pick up point No. 7, which is another one of those so-called bifurcations. One, two, three, four.

Mr. Eisenberg.

Again a ridge count?

Mr. Latona.

Ridge counting from 5 to 6.,That is in the latent print. We must find the same situation in the inked print. Counting from point No. 5 the ridges which intervene, one, two, three, and then we count four, the point itself. There is the bifurcation right here.

Mr. Eisenberg.

Mr. Latona, in making these ridge counts, do you also pay attention to the so-called, let's say, geographical relation, the spacial relation of the two points?

Mr. Latona.

Very definitely. Now, it does not always follow that the so-called geographical position will coincide exactly the same. That would be caused because of variations in the pressure used when the print was made. For example, when you make a print on a fingerprint card: when the inked print was made, the print was made for the specific purpose of recording all of the ridge details. When the print was left on the paper bag, it was an incidental impression. The person was not trying to leave a print In fact, he probably did not even know he left one. So the pressure which is left, or the position of the finger when it made the print, will be a little different. Accordingly the geographical area of the points themselves will not always coincide. But they will be in the general position the same.

Mr. Eisenberg.

Mr. Latona, without going into detail, there are some apparent dissimilarities on the two sides of that chart. Can you explain why there should be apparent dissimilarities?

Mr. Latona.

The dissimilarities as such are caused by the type of material on which the print was left, because of the pressure, because of the amount of material which is on the finger when it left the print. They would not always be exactly the same. Here again there appears a material difference in the sense there is a difference in coloration. This is because of the fact that the contrast in the latent print is not as sharp as it is in the inked impression, which is a definite black on white, whereas here we have more or less a brown on a lighter brown.

Mr. Eisenberg.

Now, Mr. Latona, when you find an apparent dissimilarity between an inked and a latent print, how do you know that it is caused by absorption of the surface upon which the latent print is placed, or by failure of the finger to exude material, rather than by the fact that you have a different fingerprint?

Mr. Latona.

That is simply by sheer experience.

Mr. Eisenberg.

Would you say, therefore, that the identification of a fingerprint is a task which calls for an expert interpretation, as opposed to a simple point-by-point laying-out which a layman could do?

Mr. Latona.

Very definitely so; yes.

......

Mr. Dulles.

These, I understand, are the particular distinguishing points, the points that you would look for to determine whether the latent print— —

Mr. Latona.

Not so much the looking for the points, as to finding points having a relationship to each other. It is the relation that is the important thing, not the point itself. In other words, all of us would have to a certain extent these points.

Mr. Dulles.

They have to be in the same relation to each other.

Mr. Latona.

That is correct. For example, on the illustration I have here— —

Mr. Eisenberg.

This is an illustration on the blackboard.

Mr. Latona.

The mere fact that this is an ending ridge and bifurcation and another ending ridge and a dot in themselves mean nothing. This is a type of pattern which is referred to as a loop, which is very common. These comprise approximately 65% of pattern types. It has four ridge counts, for example. You can find hundreds of thousands and millions of four-count loops. But you would not find but one loop having an arrangement of these characteristics in the relation that they have. For example, the enclosure is related to this ending ridge. This ending ridge is related by one ridge removed from the dot. This bifurcation is next to the so-called core which is formed by a red, the ending ridge.

The points themselves are common. The most common type of points are the ending ridge and the bifurcation. Those are the two points we have covered so far.

Mr. Eisenberg.

Mr. Latona, I see that you have marked nine characteristics on your chart. Are these all the characteristics which you were able to find— —

Mr. Latona.

On this particular chart; yes. They were the only ones that bore actually, there is still one more characteristic—there could have been 10.

Mr. Eisenberg.

Now, is there any minimum number of points that has to be found in order to make an identification, in your opinion?

Mr. Latona.

No; in my opinion, there are no number of points which are a requirement. Now, there is a general belief among lots of fingerprint people that a certain number of points are required. It is my opinion that this is an erroneous assumption that they have taken, because of the fact that here in the United States a person that qualifies in court as an expert has the right merely to voice an opinion as to whether two prints were made by the same finger or not made. There are no requirements, there is no standard by which a person can say that a certain number of points are required—primarily because of the fact that there is such a wide variance in the experience of men who qualify as fingerprint experts.

Mr. Eisenberg.

Mr. Latona, you said that not all experts are in agreement on this subject. Is there any substantial body of expert opinion that holds to a minimum number of points, let's say, 12?

Mr. Latona.

In the United States, to my knowledge, I know of no group or body that subscribe to a particular number. Now, quite frequently some of these departments will maintain a standard for themselves, by virtue of the fact that they will say, "Before we will make an identification, we must find a minimum of 12 points of similarity."

I am quite certain that the reason for that is simply to avoid the possibility of making an erroneous identification. Now, why they have picked 12—I believe that that 12-point business originated because of a certain article which was written by a French fingerprint examiner by the name of Edmond Locard back in 1917, I think—there was a publication to the effect that in his opinion where there were 12 points of similarity, there was no chance of making an erroneous identification. If there were less than 12, he voiced the conclusion that the chances would increase as to finding duplicate prints.

Now, today we in the FBI do not subscribe to that theory at all. We simply say this: We have confidence in our experts to the extent that regardless of the number of points, if the expert who has been assigned to the case for purposes of making the examination gives an opinion, we will not question the number of points. We have testified—I personally have testified in court to as few as seven points of similarity.

Mr. Dulles.

But you would not on two, would you?

Mr. Latona.

No, sir; because I know that two points, even though they would not be duplicate points, could be arranged in such a fashion that it might possibly give me the impression that here are two points which appear to be the same even though they are not.

Mr. Dulles.

But it is somewhere between two and seven—somewhere in that range?

Mr. Latona.

That is right. Where that is, I do not know. And I would not say whether I would testify to six, would I testify to five, would I refuse to testify to four.

Mr. Dulles.

You say you would—or would you?

Mr. Latona.

I don't know. That's a question I could not answer. I would have to see each case individually before I could render a conclusion.

Now, going outside of the United States, we have been approached—I mean the FBI—have been approached by other foreign experts in an attempt to set a worldwide standard of 16 characteristics, a minimum of 16, as opposed to 12, which is generally referred to by people in this country here. Now of course we would not subscribe to that at all. And I think— —

Mr. Dulles.

That would be 16 on the fingerprint of the same finger?

Mr. Latona.

That's right.

Mr. Dulles.

Obviously, if you have two fingers that would alter the number—if you had three on one and two on the other, would you consider that five?

Mr. Latona.

We would.

Now, whether the foreign experts would not, I don't know. In other words, if we were to go along with this European theory of 16 points, we would not testify to this being an identification. That is really what it would amount to. Yet to me, in my mind, there is no question that these prints here— —

Mr. Eisenberg.

Which is what exhibit?

Mr. Latona.

The enlargements in Exhibit 634 are simply reproductions of the left index fingerprint of Lee Harvey Oswald.

Representative Ford.

There is no doubt in your mind about that?

Mr. Latona.

Absolutely none at all….

Mr. Latona.

This exhibit or this item is a lift of a latent palmprint which was evidently developed with black powder.

Mr. Eisenberg.

And when did you receive this item?

Mr. Latona.

I received this item November 29, 1963.

Mr. Eisenberg.

Mr. Latona, could you describe to us what a lift is?

Mr. Latona.

A lift is merely a piece of adhesive material which is used for purposes of removing a print that has been previously developed on an object, onto the adhesive material. Then the adhesive material is placed on a hacking, in this case which happens to be the card. The adhesive material utilized here is similar to scotch tape. There are different types of lifting material. Some of them are known as opaque lifters, which are made of rubber, like a black rubber and white rubber, which has an adhesive material affixed to it, and this material is simply laid on a print which has been previously developed on an object and the full print is merely removed from the object.

Mr. Eisenberg.

When you say "the print" is removed, actually the powder— —

Mr. Latona.

The powder that adhered to the original latent print is picked off of the object.

Mr. Eisenberg.

So that the impression actually is removed?

Mr. Latona.

That is right.

Representative Ford.

Is that a recognized technique?

Mr. Latona.

Yes; it is.

Representative Ford.

In the fingerprinting business?

Mr. Latona.

It is very common, one of the most common methods of recording latent prints.

Mr. Eisenberg.

Who did you get this exhibit, this lift from?

Mr. Latona.

This lift was referred to us by the FBI Dallas office.

Mr. Eisenberg.

And were you told anything about its origin?

Mr. Latona.

We were advised that this print had been developed by the Dallas Police Department, and, as the lift itself indicates, from the underside of the gun barrel near the end of the foregrip.

Mr. Eisenberg.

Now, may I say for the record that at a subsequent point we will have the testimony of the police officer of the Dallas police who developed this print, and made the lift; and I believe that the print was taken from underneath the portion of the barrel which is covered by the stock. Now, did you attempt to identify this print which shows on the lift Exhibit 637?

Mr. Latona.

Yes; I did.

Mr. Eisenberg.

Did you succeed in making identification?

Mr. Latona.

On the basis of my comparison, I did effect an identification.

Mr. Eisenberg.

And whose print was that, Mr. Latona?

Mr. Latona.

The palmprint which appears on the lift was identified by me as the right palmprint of Lee Harvey Oswald….

Mr. Dulles.

I have no further questions. Thank you very much indeed, Mr. Latona. You have been very helpful. I have learned a great deal myself.

Mr. Latona.

Thank you very much.

Index